Welcome to Vietnam

Vietnam is a country of breathtaking natural beauty with a unique heritage. Blessed with a stupendous coastline and towering mountains, historic sites and one of the world's best cuisines, the nation is a sensory overload.

Self-confident and fast-developing, Vietnam is a country going places. Economic progress is booming in the country's metropolises, where the pace of change is intoxicating. Here ancient, labyrinthine trading quarters of still-thriving craft industries are juxtaposed with grand colonial mansions from the French era, all overseen from the sky bars of 21st-century glass-and-steel high-rises.

Away from the urban centres, you'll find unforgettable experiences everywhere. There's the sublime: gazing over a surreal seascape of limestone islands from the deck of a traditional junk in Halong Bay. The inspirational: exploring the world's most spectacular cave systems in Phong Nha-Ke Bang National Park. The comical: watching a moped loaded with honking pigs weave a wobbly route along a country lane. And the contemplative: witnessing a solitary grave in a cemetery of thousands of war victims.

Take time to savour Vietnam's incredibly subtle, flavoursome national cuisine on a street-food tour or attend a cooking class. Scoot around the rural back roads that fringe the historic old trading port of Hoi An or hike the evergreen hills of Sapa. And for horizontal 'me' time, you'll find outstanding spas – from marble temples of treatments, lotions and potions, to simple, inexpensive family-run massage salons.

...you'll find unforgettable experiences everywhere.

Ship sailing on Halong Bay (p66)
LENA SERDITOVA/SHUTTERSTOCK ©

MYANMAR

SAPA
p80

Lao Cai

Cao Bang

VIETNAM

Ou

Yen Bai

Lang

Thai
Ngu

HANOI
p35 ✪

Hai

Nin
Bin

Mekong

LAOS

Ca

Thar
Hoa

Vinh

Ha

VIENTIANE ✪

PHONG NHA-KE BANG
NATIONAL PARK
p92

THAILAND

Mekong

✪ **BANGKOK**

Siem
Reap

CAMBODI

*Andaman
Sea*

*Gulf of
Thailand*

PHNOM
PENH ✪

Mekong

Chau Doc

Long
Xuyen

Vir

Lo

Can T

PHU QUOC
p237

Rach Gia

So
Tr

MEKONG DELTA
p223

Ca Mau

Bac L

Street vendor, Hoi An (p123)
MATT MUNRO/LONELY PLANET ©

Plan Your Trip
Vietnam's Top 12

FRANK VERLINDEN/500PX ©

Hoi An

Ancient trading port and culinary mecca

Vietnam's most cosmopolitan town, this beautiful ancient port is bursting with gourmet restaurants, hip bars and cafes, quirky boutiques and expert tailors. Immerse yourself in history in the warren-like lanes of the Old Town, and tour the temples and pagodas. Dine like an emperor on a peasant's budget. Then hit glorious An Bang Beach, wander along the riverside and bike the back roads. Yes, Hoi An (p123) has it all. Above: Boats at port; Right: Lanterns, Old Town (p126)

lonely planet

VIETNAM
TOP SIGHTS, AUTHENTIC EXPERIENCES

THIS EDITION WRITTEN AND RESEARCHED BY
Iain Stewart,
Bre

Contents

Nanning

CHINA

MACAU

HONG KONG

Son

ven

Hong Gai

phong

HALONG BAY
p66

h
h
h

Gulf of
Tonkin

HAINAN

inh

Dong Hoi

Dong Ha

HUE
p102

Danang

HOI AN
p123

Quang
Ngai

SOUTH
CHINA
SEA

Kon Tum

Ba

Quy Nhon

Tuy Hoa

Buon Ma
Thuot

Nha
Trang

DALAT
p157

Phan
Rang

ay Ninh

Bien Hoa

Phan
Thiet

MUI NE
p147

h
ng
ho

HO CHI MINH CITY
p173

c
ng
eu

CON DAO
ISLANDS
p213

N   0   400 km
     0   200 miles

Ho Chi Minh City

Vietnam at its liveliest buzzing best

Increasingly international but still unmistakably Vietnamese, the former Saigon's visceral energy will delight big-city devotees. HCMC (p173) doesn't inspire neutrality: you'll either be drawn into its thrilling vortex, or you'll find the whole experience overwhelming. Dive in and be rewarded with a wealth of history, delicious food and a vibrant nightlife scene. The heat is always on in Saigon; loosen your collar and enjoy. Top: Motorbike traffic; Above, Incense burner, Jade Emperor Pagoda (p194)

Halong Bay

Thousands of amazing limestone islands

Halong Bay's (p66) stunning combination of karst limestone peaks and sheltered, shimmering seas is one of Vietnam's top tourist draws, but with more than 2000 islands, there's plenty of superb scenery to go around. Definitely book an overnight cruise and make time for your own special moments on this World Heritage wonder – rise early for an ethereal misty dawn, or pilot a kayak into grottoes and lagoons.

3

Phong Nha-Ke Bang National Park

Caves on a simply staggering scale

With jagged hills shrouded in verdant rainforest, and mountain rivers coursing through impressive ravines, above ground the Phong Nha-Ke Bang region (p92) contains one of Vietnam's most spectacular national parks. Head underground for even more delights. A fortunate few can experience Hang Son Doong, the world's largest cave, but more accessible are the ziplining and kayaking thrills of Hang Toi (Dark Cave), and the ethereal beauty of aptly named Paradise Cave (pictured).

Hue

A majestic, fascinating former imperial capital

The capital of the nation for 150 years in the 19th and early 20th centuries, Hue (p102) is perhaps the easiest Vietnamese city to love and spend time in. Its situation on the banks of the Perfume River is sublime, its complex cuisine justifiably famous, and its streets are relatively traffic free. And that's without the majesty of the Hue Citadel to explore. On the city's fringes are some of Vietnam's most impressive pagodas and royal tombs, many in wonderful natural settings. Right: Thanh Toan Bridge, Hue

XITA/SHUTTERSTOCK ©

Hanoi

Captivating capital steeped in history and culture

Ancient but dynamic, the nation's capital hurtles towards modernity, cautiously embracing visitors. Sample Hanoi's (p35) heady mix of history and ambition by wandering the streets of the Old Quarter (pictured), sipping drip-coffee and slurping on a hearty bowl of *bun rieu cua*. When you're done, check out the crumbling decadence of the French Quarter then zip up to cosmopolitan Tay Ho for finer dining and the low-down on Hanoi's burgeoning art scene.

6

Phu Quoc Island
Paradise island of tropical beaches

Lapped by azure waters and edged with the kind of white-sand beaches that make sunseekers sink to their weak knees, Phu Quoc (p237) – way down in the south of Vietnam – is ideal for slipping into low gear, reaching for a seaside cocktail and toasting a blood-orange sun as it dips into the sea. And if you want to notch it up a tad, grab a motorbike and hit the red-dirt roads: the island's the size of Singapore.

7

Mui Ne

Cosmopolitan beach and water-sport resort

Perhaps the water-sport epicentre of Vietnam, the relaxed, prosperous beach resort of Mui Ne (p147) is a kitesurfing capital with world-class wind and conditions, and excellent schools for professional training. For those who prefer dry land, sand-boarding and golf are popular alternatives. The resort itself has more than 20km of palm-fringed beachfront that stretches invitingly along the shores of the South China Sea. From guesthouses to boutique resorts, boho bars to fine-value spas, Mui Ne has a broad appeal.

KHANG DUONG/500PX ©

TELSEK/SHUTTERSTOCK ©

ZHUKOV OLEG/SHUTTERSTOCK ©

Dalat

An atmospheric old French-colonial hill station

Dalat (p157) is the queen of the southwest highlands and has been popular with international tourists since the days of the French colonialists. Grand Gallic villas are dotted amid pine groves and the whole town is centred on a pretty lake, with numerous nearby waterfalls adding to its natural appeal. Dalat is also fast becoming one of Vietnam's key adventure-sport hubs, with abseiling, canyoning, mountain biking, hiking and rafting all on offer.

Far left: Fog over Dalat; Left: Datanla falls, near Dalat

R.M. NUNES/SHUTTERSTOCK ©

Sapa

Hiking hot spot in the far north

Undulating rice terraces cascade down to valleys inhabited by Hmong, Red Dzao and Giay villages. Up above, the sinuous ridges of the Hoang Lien Mountains touch the sky. Brushed with every shade of green in the palette, the countryside surrounding Sapa (p80) is a showcase of northern Vietnam's most superb rural vistas. This is prime territory for digging out your walking boots and hitting the trails. Top: Rice terraces; Above left: Mountain path; Above right: Hmong woman

10

KUANHUONGNO/SHUTTERSTOCK ©

Mekong Delta

Tradition-rich riverine region in the deep south

A watery world of reed-fringed canals and impossibly broad rivers, the Mekong Delta (p223) is an overwhelmingly green, fecund expanse. One of the world's greatest delta regions, it's nurtured by rich sediment carried by the mighty Mekong River and yields enough rice to feed all Vietnam (with a healthy surplus). Those longing for a taste of local life will find authentic southern charm around the region's compact cities. Above: Tra Su indigo forest, near Chau Doc

OLDCATPHOTO/GETTY IMAGES ©

Con Dao Islands

Divine beaches and a sombre history

The furious energy of the cities can be intoxicating, but when you need an urban detox, these idyllic tropical islands make the perfect escape. Once hell on earth for a generation of political prisoners, Con Dao (p213) is now a heavenly destination of remote beaches, pristine dive sites and diverse nature. It's a wonderful place to explore by bike in search of that dream beach, while the main settlement of Con Son is one of Vietnam's most charming towns. Above: Bai Dram Trau (p216)

Plan Your Trip
Need to Know

When to Go

- Warm to hot summers, mild winters
- Tropical climate, wet & dry seasons

Sapa
GO Mar–May & Sep–Nov

Hanoi
GO Mar–May & Sep–Nov

Danang
GO Mar–Sep

Ho Chi Minh City
GO Nov–Feb

High Season (Jul & Aug)

o Prices increase by up to 50% by the coast; book hotels well in advance.

o All Vietnam, except the far north, is hot and humid, with the summer monsoon bringing downpours.

Shoulder (Dec–Mar)

o During the Tet festival the whole country is on the move and prices rise.

o North of Nha Trang can get cool weather. Expect cold conditions in the very far north.

o In the south, clear skies and sunshine are the norm.

Low Season (Apr–Jun, Sep–Nov)

o Perhaps the best time to tour the whole nation.

o Typhoons can lash the central and northern coastline until November.

Currency
Dong (d)

Language
Vietnamese

Visas
Complicated and fast-changing: some nationalities need a visa in advance for all visits, some don't (for 15-day stays).

Money
ATMs can be found throughout the country, even in small towns, though charges for withdrawals can be quite steep. In general cash is king in Vietnam, though credit and debit cards can be used in many hotels.

Mobile Phones
To avoid roaming charges, local SIM cards can be used in most European, Asian and Australian (and many North American) phones.

Time
Vietnam is seven hours ahead of GMT/UTC.

Daily Costs

Budget: Less than US$40

- Glass of *bia hoi*: from US$0.50
- One hour on a local bus: US$1–1.50
- Cheap hotel: US$10–15, dorms less
- Local meal of noodles: US$1.50–2.50

Midrange: US$40–100

- Comfortable double room: US$25–50
- Meal in a smart restaurant: from US$8
- One-hour massage: US$6–25
- Ten-minute taxi ride: US$4

Top End: More than US$100

- Luxury hotel room: from US$80
- Gourmet restaurant: from US$20
- Internal flight: US$30–110

Useful Websites

- **Vietnam Coracle** (http://vietnam coracle.com) Excellent independent travel advice from a long-term resident.
- **Lonely Planet** (www.lonelyplanet.com/vietnam) Destination information, hotel bookings, traveller forum and more.
- **The Word** (www.wordhcmc.com) Based in HCMC, this magazine has comprehensive coverage and excellent features.
- **Vietnam Online** (www.vietnamonline.com) Good all-rounder.
- **Rusty Compass** (www.rustycompass.com) Useful online travel guide.

Opening Hours

Hours vary little throughout the year.

Banks 8am to 3pm weekdays, to 11.30am Saturday

Offices and museums 8am to 5pm; museums closed Monday

Restaurants 11.30am to 9pm

Shops 8am to 6pm

Temples and pagodas 5am to 9pm

Arriving in Vietnam

Tan Son Nhat International Airport, Ho Chi Minh City (p284)

Taxi Taxis to central districts (around 190,000d) take about 30 minutes.

Bus The air-conditioned Route 152 bus (6000d, every 15 minutes, 6am to 6pm, around 40 minutes, see http://busmap.vn for route).

Noi Bai International Airport, Hanoi (p284)

Taxi Taxis to the centre cost 400,000d and take around 50 minutes.

Bus Jetstar shuttles (35,000d) and Vietnam Airlines minibuses (50,000d) run hourly. The Route 17 public bus to Long Bien bus station is 5000d.

Getting Around

Buses are the main mode of transport for locals in Vietnam, but travellers tend to prefer planes, trains and automobiles.

Train Reasonably priced and comfortable enough in air-conditioned carriages (and sleepers). But note there are no real express trains.

Plane Cheap if you book ahead and the network is pretty comprehensive. However, cancellations are not unknown.

Car Very useful for travelling at your own pace or for visiting regions with minimal public transport. Cars always come with a driver.

Bus On the main highways services are very frequent, although it's not a particularly relaxing way to travel. In the sticks things deteriorate rapidly. Open-tour buses are very inexpensive and worth considering.

For more on getting around, see p284

Plan Your Trip
Hot Spots For...

Vietnamese Cuisine

JOANNATKACZUK/SHUTTERSTOCK ©

Vietnamese cooking is a fascinating draw for travellers, the national cuisine combining Chinese and French influences.

Beaches

JIMMY TRAN/SHUTTERSTOCK ©

Vietnam is a beach lover's dream, its near-endless coastline dotted with surf-washed shorelines, tiny coves and hidden bays.

Historic Sites

DINOSMICHAIL/SHUTTERSTOCK ©

Fully loaded with historic interest, Vietnam has excellent war museums, a coastline dotted with Cham temples, grandiose tombs and pagodas, and French colonial architecture.

Outdoor Action

XUANHUONGHO/SHUTTERSTOCK ©

Vietnam has tremendous outdoor appeal. Water sports include world-class kitesurfing, kayaking, surfing and scuba diving, while inland there's amazing caving, hiking and cycling.

Hoi An (p123) Boasts an array of stupendous restaurants where you can try unique regional specialities, then take a cooking course.

Central Vietnam specialties For creative cooking head to Nu Eatery. (p144)

Hanoi (p35) The capital is the place to get stuck into street food, which is diverse and delicious and available everywhere.

Gastronomic Tour Check out Hanoi Street Food Tours. (p57)

Hue (p102) Ancient city that's famous for its complex, often highly refined imperial cuisine tradition and unique snacks.

Top Tip Try the delicious royal rice cakes in Hang Me Me. (p119)

Phu Quoc (p237) This tropical island has picture-perfect white-sand beaches and sheltered bays ringed by rocky headlands.

Sao Beach A dazzling crescent of snow-white sand. (p242)

Mui Ne (p147) A broad, sandy shoreline, with towering sand dunes nearby and empty beaches up the coast.

Top Tip Post-beach, explore pretty oasis-like Fairy Spring. (p152)

An Bang (p144) Ride a bicycle from Hoi An to glorious An Bang, where you're rewarded with a wonderful expanse of golden sand.

Oceanside Table For delectable seafood and fine wines head to Soul Kitchen. (p144)

Ho Chi Minh City (p173) Boasts an excellent collection of museums, as well as Chinese temples and spectacular structures dating from the French era.

War Remants Museum Highly poignant, and dedicated to the horrors of war. (p183)

My Son (p136) A very worthwhile day trip from Hoi An, this hilltop site is the nation's most impressive Cham site.

My Son Museum Provides great context and explanations. (p139)

Perfume River (p114) Hue's beautiful river is lined with spectacular monuments including an astonishing collection of emperors' tombs.

Tomb of Tu Duc Colossal mausoleum dedicated to a 19th-century ruler. (p114)

Phong Nha-Ke Bang National Park (p92) Hike through pristine mountain and valley trails, or take a river cruise, to some of the world's largest caves.

Hang Toi 'Dark Cave' is relatively accessible and tours here include ziplining. (p98)

Con Dao Islands (p213) Way south of the mainland these idyllic islands, once an offshore prison, include Vietnam's best snorkelling and diving on healthy coral reefs.

Dive Tours Dive! Dive! Dive! is an experienced, conservation-aware operator. (p220)

Sapa (p80) This French hill station is a base for trekking trails and offers stupendous vistas. Explore ethnic minority villages or consider an assault on Fansipan.

Hiking Guides Profits from Sapa O'Chau help Hmong communities. (p86)

Plan Your Trip
Local Life

MIHTIANDER/GETTY IMAGES ©

Activities

Vietnam can be a culture shock for many travellers and taking a tour can really help you understand the nation better.

You'll find a terrific array of tour operators in Vietnam, offering everything from street-food tours to vintage scooter day trips and (of course) cruises of Halong Bay. There's superb hiking, particularly in the north of the country, where the weather is cooler. Adventure sports include kayaking, rock climbing, kitesurfing, diving and snorkelling, sailing and surfing. Always stick with reputable, well-established companies as regulations are not strict and accidents do occur.

Shopping

There's a great selection of handicrafts to choose from in all the main tourist centres, including great lacquerware, wood carving, mother-of-pearl inlay, ceramics and textiles. Head to Hoi An for made-to-measure clothes such as suits and dresses. There's

also a great deal of fakery: sunglasses, designer labels, football kits and even dodgy Lonely Planet guides. Communist propaganda art posters are very popular, and you'll find tempting art and photographic galleries. Avoid purchasing any animal products such as snake wine as many items have been sourced unethically or even illegally.

Entertainment

There's a small live-music scene in Ho Chi Minh City and Hanoi with rock and hip-hop artists. Elsewhere look out for traditional dance performances and do try to take in a water-puppet show, which are highly rewarding.

Eating

Showcasing fresh and vibrant flavours, excellent street food and elegant restaurants in restored colonial architecture, Vietnam is packed with superb opportunities for eating and drinking. Cookery classes, mar-

UTA GLEISER/EYEEM/GETTY IMAGES ©

ket visits and walking tours make it easy to discover the country's culinary heritage.

Generally the more local the place is, the tastier the food; a place that bustles with Vietnamese is always a good sign. In towns popular with tourists, restaurants with English-language menus often tone down dishes for Western tastes. Seafood is nearly always live in Vietnam, just select what you want from the tanks. Beware that dog, cat and all manner of other 'delicacies' are eaten in Vietnam though they are virtually always consumed in specialist restaurants well off the tourist trail.

Drinking & Nightlife

Cafes serving Vietnamese-style coffee are found in towns and villages across the country. Bars are also wildly popular; look out for *bia hoi* (fresh beer) joints, which are incredibly cheap. Note that anything advertising karaoke is likely to be a front for prostitution. The cities all have club scenes featuring local DJs – expect a

★ Best for Beaches

Phu Quoc Island (p237)

Con Dao Islands (p213)

Mui Ne (p147)

An Bang Beach, Hoi An (p144)

mixture of pounding electronic beats and Vietnamese pop (which is not always easy on Western ears). However, as the government regulates nightlife carefully, most places open around 10am and close early (usually 2am).

From left: Kayaking Halong Bay (p72); Street-food seller, Hoi An (p143)

Plan Your Trip
Month by Month

January
🎋 Dalat Flower Festival
Held early in the month, this is always a wonderful occasion, with huge elaborate displays. It's become an international event, with music and fashion shows and a wine festival.

February
🎋 Tet (Tet Nguyen Dan)
The Big One! Falling in late January or early February, Vietnamese Lunar New Year is like Christmas, New Year and birthdays all rolled into one. Travel is difficult at this time, as transport is booked up and many businesses close.

🎋 Quang Trung
Wrestling competitions, lion dances and human chess take place in Hanoi on the fifth day of the first lunar month at Dong Da Mound, site of the uprising against the Chinese led by Emperor Quang Trung (Nguyen Hué) in 1788.

March
🏃 Saigon Cyclo Challenge
On your marks...get pedalling! Ho Chi Minh City's fastest rickshaw drivers battle it out in their three-wheeled chariots to raise funds for charity. Takes place in mid-March every year.

April
🎋 Holiday of the Dead (Thanh Minh)
It's time to honour the ancestors with a visit to graves of deceased relatives to tidy up and sweep tombstones. Offerings of flowers, food and paper are presented. It's held on the first three days of the third moon.

🎋 Hue Festival (Biennial)
Vietnam's biggest cultural event (www.huefestival.com) is held every two years, with events next held in 2018. Most of

the art, theatre, music, circus and dance performances are held inside Hue's Citadel.

🎆 Danang Firework Festival

Danang's riverside explodes with sound, light and colour during this spectacular event, which features competing pyrotechnic teams from the USA, China, Europe and Vietnam. Held in the last week of the month.

May

🎆 Buddha's Birth, Enlightenment & Death (Phong Sinh)

A big celebration at Buddhist temples with lively street processions and lanterns used to decorate pagodas. Complexes including Chua Bai Dinh near Ninh Binh and HCMC's Jade Emperor Pagoda (p194) host lavish celebrations. Fifteenth day of the fourth lunar month.

★ Best Festivals

Tet, January–February

Hue Festival, April (Biennial)

Danang Firework Festival, April

Buddha's Birth, Enlightenment & Death, May

Wandering Souls Day, August

June

🎆 Nha Trang Sea Festival

Falls at the end of May and the beginning of June and includes a street festival, photography exhibitions, embroidery displays and kite-flying competitions.

From left: Phong Sinh celebrations, Hanoi; Dance performance during Tet, Ho Chi Minh City

August

🎎 Wandering Souls Day (Trung Nguyen)

Second in the pecking order to Tet is this ancient Vietnamese tradition. Huge spreads of food are left out for lost spirits who, it's believed, wander the earth on this day. Held on the 15th day of the seventh moon.

🎎 Children's (or Mid-Autumn) Festival, Hoi An

This is a big event in Hoi An and Hanoi, when citizens celebrate the full moon, eat mooncakes and beat drums. The lion, unicorn and dragon dance processions are enacted, and children are fully involved in the celebrations.

September

🎎 Vietnam National Day

Big parades and events are held across Vietnam on 2 September. Celebrated with a rally and fireworks at Ba Dinh Square, Hanoi (in front of Ho Chi Minh's Mausoleum), and there are also boat races on Hoan Kiem Lake.

October

✕ Mid-Autumn Festival (Trung Thu)

A fine time for foodies, with mooncakes of sticky rice filled with lotus seeds, water-melon seeds, peanuts, the yolks of duck eggs, raisins and other treats. It's celebrated across the nation on the 15th day of the eighth moon and can fall in September or October.

🎎 Cham New Year (Kate)

This is celebrated at Po Klong Garai Cham Towers in Thap Cham on the seventh month of the Cham calendar. The festival commemorates ancestors, Cham national heroes and deities, such as the farmers' goddess Po Ino Nagar.

🎎 Khmer Oc Bom Boc Festival

The Mekong Delta's Khmer community celebrates on the 15th day of the 10th moon of the lunar calendar (late October or November) with colourful boat races at Ba Dong Beach in Tra Vinh province and on the Soc Trang River.

December

🎎 Christmas Day (Giang Sinh)

Not a national holiday, but is celebrated throughout Vietnam, particularly by the sizeable Catholic population. It's a special time to be in places such as Phat Diem and HCMC, where thousands attend midnight Mass.

Plan Your Trip
Get Inspired

Read

The Quiet American (Graham Greene; 1955) Classic novel set in the 1950s as the French empire is collapsing.

The Sorrow of War (Bao Ninh; 1990) The North Vietnamese perspective, retold in novel form via flashbacks.

The Sympathizer (Viet Thanh Nguyen; 2015) Superb Pulitzer Prize–winning novel of an immigrant tale and double life.

Vietnam: Rising Dragon (Bill Hayton; 2010) A candid, highly insightful assessment of the nation.

Catfish & Mandala (Andrew X Pham; 1999) Beautifully written and thought-provoking biographical tale of a Vietnamese-American who returns to his homeland.

Watch

Apocalypse Now (1979) The American War depicted as an epic 'heart of darkness' adventure.

The Deer Hunter (1978) Examines the emotional breakdown suffered by small-town US servicemen.

Platoon (1986) Based on the first-hand experiences of director Oliver Stone, it follows idealistic volunteer Charlie Sheen to 'Nam.

Cyclo (Xich Lo; 1995) Visually stunning masterpiece that cuts to the core of HCMC's underworld.

The Quiet American (2002) Atmospherically set in Saigon during the French colonial period, with rebellion in the air.

Listen

Give Peace a Chance (Plastic Ono Band) John Lennon classic adopted by the anti-war movement.

19 (Paul Hardcastle) Electro classic featuring a sample that (claimed) the average age of serving US soldiers in Vietnam was just 19.

Bring 'em Home (Pete Seeger) Penned by a folk-music legend who opposed American involvement in the American War.

Vietnam (Jimmy Cliff) Jamaican reggae musician's very catchy protest song.

Doi (Suboi) Saigon-born, Suboi is Vietnam's 'Queen of Hip Hop' and rapped to Obama on his visit in 2016.

Above: Hoan Kiem Lake (p38), Hanoi

AMADEUSTX/SHUTTERSTOCK ©

Plan Your Trip
Five-Day Itineraries

Northern Adventure

Take in the delights of the capital and explore a Unesco World Heritage site.

1 Hanoi (p35) Experience the evocative Old Quarter, architecture and museums before a street food feast. 🚌 4 hrs to Halong City

2 Halong Bay (p66) Cruise this unique seascape, with more than 2000 limestone outcrops dotting the ocean. ⚓ 1 hr to Cat Ba Island

3 Cat Ba Island (p74) Enjoy the relaxed ambience of Cat Ba Town, dine on fresh seafood and visit beaches.

Southern Charm

This adventure includes a taste of life in one of Asia's most exciting cities, the chance to spot primates and a visit to a relaxed hill town.

2 Cat Tien National Park (p168) Home to gibbons and bountiful birdlife, this is one of Vietnam's premier national parks.
🚌 4 hrs to Dalat

3 Dalat (p157) The graceful hill station of Dalat has a number of quirky sights, and is a base for adventure sports.

1 Ho Chi Minh City (p173) Revel in this cauldron of commerce by hitting the markets and indulging in the cuisine.
🚌 4 hrs to Cat Tien National Park

FROM LEFT: FEATHERCOLLECTOR/SHUTTERSTOCK ©, XUANHUONGHO/SHUTTERSTOCK ©

Plan Your Trip
10-Day Itinerary

Caves, Coastline & Culture

Central Vietnam contains some stupendous cave systems and two of the nation's most enjoyable small cities, both famed for their historic sites and regional specialities.

3 Phong Nha-Ke Bang National Park (p92) This truly remarkable national park is the world's greatest caving region.

2 Hue (p102) The old imperial capital of Hue has a unique walled citadel and a roster of impressive tombs and pagodas. 🚌 5 hrs to Phong Na-Ke Bang National Park

1 Hoi An (p123) Enjoy the town's unique ambience, tour temples, pagodas and museums, then hit the beach. 🚌 3 hrs to Hue

Plan Your Trip
Two-Week Itinerary

North to South

Making the most of Vietnam's spectacular coastline, this route hugs the shore and is bookended by the country's two greatest cities. You'll have ample time to indulge at the beaches and hit the cultural sights.

1 Hanoi (p35) Experience the Old Quarter's atmosphere and street life, and tuck into the terrific street food. 🚌 4 hrs to Halong City

2 Halong Bay (p66) Gaze over a horizon-filling expanse of seemingly innumerable craggy islands. ✈ 1 hr to Hue

3 Hue (p102) Enjoy the relaxed ambience of this grand city, explore the riverside streets and tour the temples. 🚌 🚌 3 hrs to Hoi An

4 Hoi An (p123) Search for souvenirs, hit An Bang beach, take in the Cham ruins and enjoy the cosmopolitan vibe. 🚌 ✈ 4 hrs to Mui Ne

6 Ho Chi Minh City (p173) Eat some of the globe's best cuisine and take a day trip to the Cu Chi Tunnels.

5 Mui Ne (p147) Rest up by the beach in this tropical idyll, or get stuck into some adrenaline sports. 🚌 6 hrs to Ho Chi Minh City

Plan Your Trip
Family Travel

Vietnam for Kids

Travelling with children is very rewarding in Vietnam. Kids will often find that they're the centre of attention and that almost everybody wants to play with them. However, this can sometimes be overwhelming, particularly for blonde-haired, blue-eyed babies and toddlers.

Big cities have plenty to keep kids interested, though in most smaller towns and rural areas boredom may set in from time to time. There are some great beaches, but pay close attention to any playtime in the sea, as there are some riptides along the main coastline. Some popular beaches have warning flags and lifeguards, but at quieter beaches parents should test the current first. Seas around Phu Quoc Island are usually more sheltered.

Eating & Drinking

Kids generally enjoy local cuisine, which is rarely too spicy. Spring rolls, noodles and rice dishes usually go down very well. Comfort food from home (pizzas, pasta, burgers and ice cream) is an option in most places too. The range of fruit is simply staggering, and it can be fun (and educational) to explore a market picking out exotica such as dragon fruit, rambutans and fresh coconuts. Bottled water is available everywhere.

Getting Around

Travelling around Vietnam takes a lot of organisation, even more so for a family. Avoid long bus journeys along busy highways whenever possible as they can get tedious for kids. If you're planning to see a lot of the country, internal flights are inexpensive. Definitely consider a train journey as kids love the adventure of rail travel: four- and six-bed berths can be booked (so you're all in the same compartment). Many travel agencies can organise a minibus for trips between destinations; reckon on US$100 for a full day's travel.

In cities your biggest worry is likely to be walking across the road safely; traffic does not stop for pedestrians so you'll have to

ANNA LEVAN/SHUTTERSTOCK ©

get used to negotiating your way through a flow of moving cars and motorbikes. Taxis are very affordable.

Discounts for kids are available. Vietnam Airlines charges 75% of the adult fare for children aged from 2 to 12 and 10% of the adult fare for babies. On trains, children under five travel free, and those between five and 10 years get a 50% reduction.

Packing

Pack plenty of high-factor sunscreen before you go as it's not that widely available in Vietnam (and costs more than in many Western countries). Antibacterial hand gel is a great idea.

Babies & Infants

Baby supplies are available in the major cities, but dry up quickly in the countryside. You'll find cots in most midrange and top-end hotels, but not elsewhere. There are no safety seats in rented cars or taxis, but some restaurants can find a high chair.

★ Best for Kids

Cruising Halong Bay by boat (p70)

Phong Nha Ke-Bang National Park (p92)

Vintage Vespa tour (p134)

Water puppet shows (p64 and p210)

Cooking courses (p132)

Breastfeeding in public is quite common in Vietnam, but there are few facilities for changing nappies (diapers) other than using toilets and bathrooms. For kids who are too young to handle chopsticks, most restaurants also have cutlery.

The main worry throughout Vietnam is keeping an eye on what strange things infants are putting into their mouths. Their natural curiosity can be a lot more costly in a country where dysentery, typhoid and hepatitis are commonplace.

From left: Tour boat, Halong Bay (p70); Water-puppet show (p210), Ho Chi Minh City

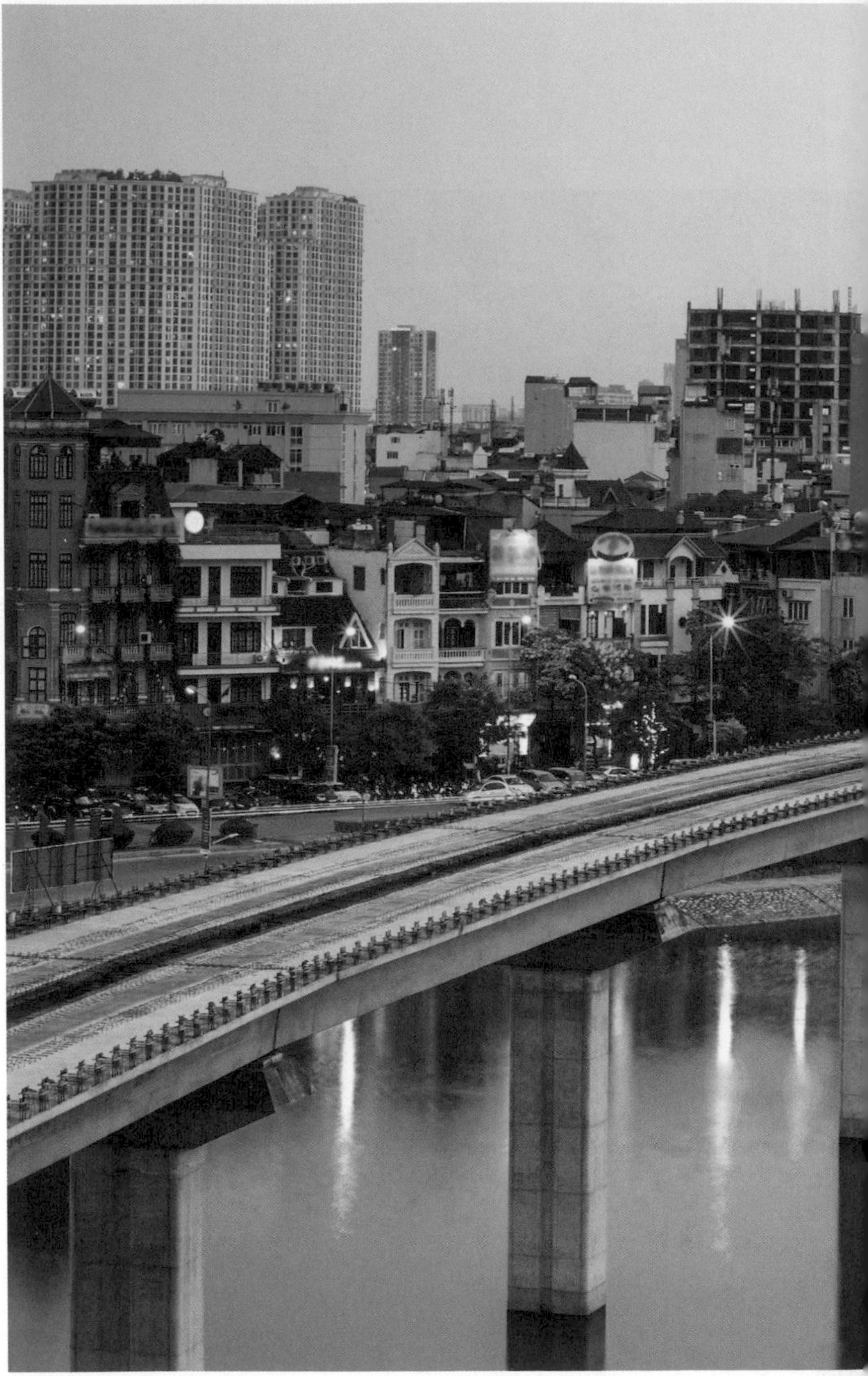

Ho Tay
(West
Lake)

Tr
Ba
La

Ho Chi Minh
Mausoleum
Complex

HO CHI MINH'S MAUSOLEUM

West of the Old Quarter
Visit Ho Chi Minh's
expansive mausoleum
complex, as well as the
Temple of Literature and
the Imperial Citadel of
Thang Long.

Giang
Vo Lake

Hanoi S
(Train Stat

Tran Quy Cap Sta
(Train Statio

Fren
This
towr
colle
crun
villas

Dong
Da Lake

Old Quarter
This labyrinth of streets is Asia at its raw, pulsating best.

Long Bien

OLD QUARTER

Song Hong
(Red River)

HOAN KIEM LAKE

Around Hoan Kiem Lake
Temples, gardens and a peaceful lake lie at the centre of this area close to the Old Quarter.

tion
A)

ion
B)

Quarter
egant part of
s blessed with a
ion of fine, though
ling, colonial

Thien Quang Lake

Thong Nhat Park (Lenin Park)

Bay Mau Lake

Hanoi (p54)
Old Quarter & Hoan Kiem Lake (p59)

In this Chapter

Hanoi at a Glance...

Vietnam's graceful capital races to make up for time lost to the ravages of war. Its streets surge with scooters vying for right of way amid the din of constantly blaring horns, and all around layers of history reveal periods of French and Chinese occupation.

The Old Quarter is where defiant real-deal farmers hawk their wares, while city folk breakfast on noodles and oldies practise t'ai chi at dawn on the shores of Hoan Kiem Lake. Dine on the wild and wonderful at every corner, sample market wares, uncover an evolving arts scene, then sleep soundly in a little luxury for very little cost.

Hanoi in One Day

Rise early for a morning walk around misty **Hoan Kiem Lake** (p40). Visit the **Ho Chi Minh Mausoleum Complex** (p48) before taking a look at the **Fine Arts Museum of Vietnam** (p50). Lunch at **La Badiane** (p62) then continue to the peaceful **Temple of Literature** (p52). Immerse yourself in the chaos of the **Old Quarter** (p42), before eating at **Nha Hang Koto Van Mieu** (p61).

Hanoi in Two Days

Head into the suburbs to the excellent **Vietnam Museum of Ethnology** (p50). Lunch at **Chim Sao** (p62) before exploring the **Museum of Vietnamese Revolution** (p51) and the adjacent **National Museum of Vietnamese History** (p41). After dinner at **Cha Ca Thang Long** (p58) or **Old Hanoi** (p62), head for drinks at the **Summit Lounge** (p64).

Imperial Citadel of Thang Long (p53)

Arriving in Hanoi

Noi Bai International Airport
(p284) About 35km north of the city,
connected by airport shuttle buses,
or a taxi is US$20. The journey time is
around 45 minutes.

Bus Hanoi has four main bus stations.
Taxis are readily available.

Train From southern destinations, trains
arrive at **Hanoi train station** (p64).
All northbound trains arrive from **Tran
Quy Cap Station** (p64).

Where to Stay

Most visitors to Hanoi find themselves
staying in the Old Quarter, the most
atmospheric, but chaotic and noisy, part
of the city. Consider the quieter, nearby
French Quarter for a more relaxing (and
central) base. There are also luxury
hotels in the northern suburbs, close to
Ho Tay (Tay lake).

For more information on the best
neighbourhoods to stay in, see p65.

Huc Bridge over Hoan Kiem Lake

Hoan Kiem Lake

This small lake is the perfect place to begin exploring old Hanoi and get your bearings. It even has its own temple (and its waters harboured several turtles until recently).

Great For...

Ngoc Son Temple   Martyrs' Monument

St Joseph Cathedral   Hoan Kiem Lake

Đ Trần Quang Khải

National Museum of Vietnamese History

ⓘ Need to Know

The lakeside roads are pedestrianised on Sundays.

★ **Top Tip**
Don't miss the stuffed turtles inside the Ngoc Son Temple.

Hoan Kiem Lake

According to a 15th-century legend, Emperor Ly Thai To was sent a magical sword from heaven, which he used to drive the Chinese from Vietnam. After the war a giant golden turtle grabbed the sword and disappeared into the depths of this lake to restore the sword to its divine owners, inspiring the name Ho Hoan Kiem (Lake of the Restored Sword).

Every morning at around 6am local residents practise traditional t'ai chi on the shore.

Ngoc Son Temple

Meaning 'Temple of the Jade Mountain', Hanoi's most visited **temple** (Den Ngoc Son; Map p59; Hoan Kiem Lake; adult/student 20,000/10,000d; ☺7.30am-5.30pm) sits on a small island in the northern part of the lake, connected to the lakeshore by an elegant scarlet bridge, constructed in classical Vietnamese style.

The temple is dedicated to General Tran Hung Dao (who defeated the Mongols in the 13th century), La To (patron saint of physicians) and the scholar Van Xuong.

St Joseph Cathedral

Hanoi's neo-Gothic **St Joseph Cathedral** (Map p59; Nha To Lon Ha Noi; P Nha Tho; 8am-noon & 2-6pm) was inaugurated in 1886, and boasts a soaring facade that faces a little plaza.

Thap Rua tower on Hoan Kiem Lake

Its most noteworthy features are its twin bell towers, elaborate altar and fine stained-glass windows. Entrance via the main gate is only permitted during Mass: times are listed on a sign on the gates to the left of the cathedral.

At other times, enter via the Diocese of Hanoi compound, a block away at 40 P Nha Chung. When you reach the side door to the cathedral, to your right, ring the small bell high up on the right-hand side of the door.

☑ **Don't Miss**

The tiny **Thap Rua tower** (on an islet at the southern end of the lake), is topped with a red star on special occasions and is an emblem of Hanoi.

HANOI PHOTOGRAPHY/SHUTTERSTOCK ©

National Museum of Vietnamese History

Built between 1925 and 1932, the architecturally impressive **National Museum of Vietnamese History** (Bao Tang Lich Su Quoc Gia; Map p54; ☑04-3824 2433; http://baotanglichsu.vn; 1 P Trang Tien; adult/student 40,000/15,000d; ☺8am-noon & 1.30-5pm, closed 1st Mon of the month) was formerly home to the École Française d'Extrême Orient. Its architect, Ernest Hébrard, was among the first in Vietnam to incorporate a blend of Chinese and French design elements.

Exhibit highlights include bronzes from the Dong Son culture (3rd century BC to 3rd century AD), Hindu statuary from the Khmer and Champa kingdoms, jewellery from imperial Vietnam, and displays relating to the French occupation and the Communist Party.

Martyrs' Monument

This photogenic monument depicting a woman with a sword and two men holding guns and a torch was erected as a memorial to those who died fighting for Vietnam's independence.

✕ **Take a Break**

On the west side of the lake, Mon Hue (p58) serves delicious central Vietnamese food.

Old Quarter

Hanoi's historic centre boasts over 1000 years of trade, commerce and activity. Exploring the maze of backstreets is fascinating, though the traffic and pollution are punishing.

Great For...

ℹ Need to Know

It's very easy to get lost (day or night) – carry your hotel's business card.

★ **Top Tip**
Definitely try the street food – the Old Quarter has loads of good options.

You're likely to find negotiating the narrow streets of the Old Quarter an intimidating experience, at first. Waves of motorbikes compete with cars and pedestrians pushing their way through the maze of countless copy-cat cheap hotels, shopfronts of knock-off wares and hawkers with their sizzling baskets, beneath an ever-present honking of horns and the heady aromas of exhaust fumes, street food and sweat.

Watch where you tread on the sticky pavements, employ a strategy and determination when crossing the street, and remember to look up when you can: glimpses of the old and the very old indeed peek out occasionally from behind garish, modern facades. You'll gain your confidence soon enough, and when you do, there's no better way to spend time here than to wander, soaking up the sights, sounds and smells.

Hanoi Ceramic Road

Bach Ma Temple

In the heart of the Old Quarter, the small **Bach Ma Temple** (Den Bach Ma; Map p59;cnr P Hang Buom & P Hang Giay; ⊙8-11am & 2-5pm Tue-Sun) FREE is said to be the oldest temple in the city, though much of the current structure dates from the 18th century and a shrine to Confucius was added in 1839.

It was originally built by Emperor Ly Thai To in the 11th century to honour a white horse that guided him to this site, where he chose to construct his city walls.

Pass through the wonderful old wooden doors of the pagoda to see a statue of the legendary white horse, as well as a beautiful red-lacquered funeral palanquin.

Memorial House

One of the Old Quarter's best-restored properties, this traditional **merchants' house** (Ngoi Nha; Map p59; 87 P Ma May; 5000d; ⊘9am-noon & 1-5pm) is sparsely but beautifully decorated, with rooms set around two courtyards and filled with fine furniture. Note the high steps between rooms, a traditional design incorporated to stop the flow of bad energy around the property.

There are crafts and trinkets for sale here, including silver jewellery, basketwork and Vietnamese tea sets, and there's usually a calligrapher or other craftsperson at work too.

☑ **Don't Miss**

The quarter's tunnel (or tube) houses, so called because of their narrow frontages and long rooms.

Dong Xuan Market

The largest covered **market** (Cho Dong Xuan; Map p54; cnr P Hang Khoai & P Dong Xuan; ⊘6am-7pm) in Hanoi was originally built by the French in 1889 and almost completely destroyed by fire in 1994.

Almost everything you can think of, from fresh (and live) produce to cheap clothing, souvenirs, consumer goods and traditional arts and crafts, can be found inside.

Hanoi Ceramic Road

Spanning almost 4km along the Song Hong dyke, from its terminus at the Long Bien Bridge, this ceramic mosaic **mural project** (Con Duong Gom Su; Map p54) was commenced in 2007 and completed in 2010 for Hanoi's 1000th-birthday celebrations.

Made from ceramics produced at nearby Bat Trang, the colourful mural depicts different periods in Vietnam's history and is the combined work of many local and international artists.

It retains its Guinness World Record for being the largest ceramic mosaic on the planet.

SEREE TANSRISAWAT/SHUTTERSTOCK ©

✕ **Take a Break**

Le Pub (p64) is a great spot to recharge your sightseeing batteries.

Walking Tour: The Old Quarter

This amble around the Old Quarter and the fringes of Hoan Kiem Lake is the ideal way to get to grips with inner city Hanoi. You'll encounter crafts-people carving, street vendors selling and there's plenty to tempt your wallet en route.

Start Ngoc Son Temple
Distance 3km
Duration Minimum two hours

5 Continue via the city gateway to **Dong Xuan Market** (p45), which has hundreds of stalls.

6 Wind your way south via **P Thuoc Bac**, passing herb merchants, tin-box makers and silk shops.

OLD QUARTER

Take a Break... There's a cluster of good cafes around St Joseph Cathedral.

7 Graceful, neo-Gothic **St Joseph Cathedral** (p40) is one of Hanoi's most famous landmarks.

FINISH
7

HOAN KIEM DISTRICT

DONG DA DISTRICT

Hanoi Station (Train Station A)

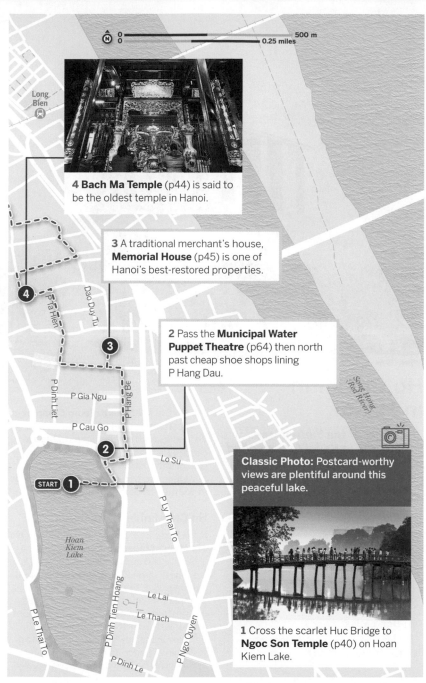

0 ———— 500 m
0 ———— 0.25 miles

4 Bach Ma Temple (p44) is said to be the oldest temple in Hanoi.

3 A traditional merchant's house, **Memorial House** (p45) is one of Hanoi's best-restored properties.

2 Pass the **Municipal Water Puppet Theatre** (p64) then north past cheap shoe shops lining P Hang Dau.

Classic Photo: Postcard-worthy views are plentiful around this peaceful lake.

1 Cross the scarlet Huc Bridge to **Ngoc Son Temple** (p40) on Hoan Kiem Lake.

Long Bien

Song Hong (Red River)

Dao Duy Tu

P Ta Hien

P Dinh Liet

P Gia Ngu

P Cau Go

P Hang Be

Lo Su

START

Hoan Kiem Lake

P Ly Thai To

P Dinh Tien Hoang

Le Lai

Le Thach

P Ngo Quyen

P Le Thai To

P Dinh Le

Ho Chi Minh's Mausoleum

AQSH.VN/SHUTTERSTOCK ©

Ho Chi Minh in Hanoi

The father of the Vietnamese nation lived in Hanoi for extended periods, and it's possible to visit his modest home and grandiose mausoleum.

Great For...

☑ **Don't Miss**

The fascinating historic photographs inside the Ho Chi Minh Museum.

The **Ho Chi Minh Mausoleum Complex** is an important place of pilgrimage for many Vietnamese. A traffic-free area of botanical gardens, monuments, memorials and pagodas, it's usually crowded with groups of Vietnamese who come from far and wide to pay their respects to 'Uncle Ho'.

Ho Chi Minh's Mausoleum

In the tradition of Lenin, Stalin and Mao, **Ho Chi Minh's Mausoleum** (Lang Chu Tich Ho Chi Minh; ⊘8-11am Tue-Thu, Sat & Sun Dec-Sep, last entry 10.15am) FREE is a monumental marble edifice. Contrary to his desire for a simple cremation, the mausoleum was constructed from materials gathered from all over Vietnam between 1973 and 1975. Set deep in the bowels of the building in a glass sarcophagus is the frail, pale body of Ho Chi Minh. The mausoleum is usually

Statue of Ho Chi Minh, Ho Chi Minh Museum

Ho Chi Minh's
**Ho Chi Minh's
Stilt House**

Ho Chi Minh
Mausoleum
Complex

**Ho Chi Minh's
Mausoleum**

P Ngoc Ha

**Ho Chi Minh
Museum**

ℹ Need to Know

Map p54; ☎04-3845 5128; www.bqllang.gov.
vn; entrance cnr P Ngoc Ha & P Doi Can

✕ Take a Break

Check out Bar Betta (p63) for coffee
or a cocktail.

★ Top Tip

It's a short walk from the mausoleum
complex to the Ho Tay lake.

(⊙8-11.30am daily & 2-4pm Tue-Thu, Sat & Sun)
where Ho lived intermittently from 1958
to 1969 is set in a well-tended garden
adjacent to a carp-filled pond and has been
preserved just as Ho left it. From here, you
look out onto Hanoi's most opulent building, the beautiful, beaux-arts Presidential
Palace (p53), constructed in 1906 for
the Governor General of Indochina.

Ho Chi Minh Museum

The huge concrete Soviet-style **Ho Chi
Minh Museum** (Bao Tang Ho Chi Minh; ☎04-
3845 5435; www.baotanghochiminh.vn; 25,000d;
⊙8-11.30am daily & 2-4pm Tue-Thu, Sat & Sun)
is a triumphalist monument dedicated to
the life of the founder of modern Vietnam
and to the onward march of revolutionary socialism. Mementos of Ho's life are
showcased, and there are some fascinating photos and dusty official documents
relating to the overthrow of the French and
the rise of communism. Photography is
forbidden and you may be asked to check
your bag at reception.

closed from 4 September to 4 November
while his embalmed body goes to Russia
for maintenance.

Dress modestly: wearing shorts, tank
tops or hats is not permitted. You may be
requested to store day packs, cameras and
phones before you enter. Talking, putting
your hand in your pocket and photography
are strictly prohibited. The queue usually
snakes for several hundred metres to the
mausoleum entrance and inside, filing
past Ho's body at a slow but steady pace.
If you're lucky, you'll catch the changing
of the guard outside – the pomp and
ceremony displayed here rivals the British
equivalent at Buckingham Palace.

Ho Chi Minh's Stilt House

This humble, traditional **stilt house**
(Nha San Bac Ho & Phu Chu Tich Tai; 25,000d;

Exhibit, Hoa Lo Prison Museum

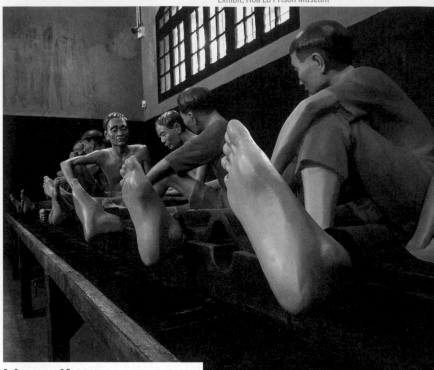

Hanoi's Museums

Hanoi, as the country's capital, has a fine selection of museums dealing with everything from fine art to revolutionary history, tribal culture to Vietnamese women.

Great For

☑ Don't Miss

The flight suit of Senator John McCain (a Republican nominee for the US presidency) who was jailed in Hoa Lo Prison.

Vietnam Museum of Ethnology

This fabulous **museum** (☎04-3756 2193; www.vme.org.vn; Đ Nguyen Van Huyen; adult/concession 40,000/15,000d, guide 100,000d; ⊙8.30am-5.30pm Tue-Sun) relating to Vietnam's ethnic minorities features well-presented tribal art, artefacts and everyday objects gathered from across the nation, and examples of traditional village houses. Displays are well labelled in Vietnamese, French and English. If you're into anthropology, it's well worth the 200,000d each-way taxi to the Cau Giay district, 7km from the city centre, where the museum is located.

Fine Arts Museum of Vietnam

This excellent **museum** (Bao Tang My Thuat Viet Nam; Map p54; ☎04-3733 2131; www.vnfam. vn; 66 P Nguyen Thai Hoc; adult/concession 30,000/15,000d; ⊙8.30am-5pm) is housed

Water puppet, Vietnam Museum of Ethnology

GREG ELMS/GETTY IMAGES ©

Fine Arts Museum of Vietnam

Hanoi Station (Train Station A)

Hoa Lo Prison Museum

Hoan Kiem Lake

Museum of Vietnamese Revolution

Tran Quy Cap Station (Train Station B)

Vietnamese Women's Museum

ℹ️ Need to Know
Some museums close for a lunch break.

✖️ Take a Break
Minh Thuy's (p60) is very easy on the wallet and big on flavours.

⭐ Top Tip
Other important museums include the National Museum of Vietnamese History (p41) and the Ho Chi Minh Museum (p49).

in two buildings that were once the French Ministry of Information. Treasures abound, including ancient Champa stone carvings and some astonishing effigies of Guan Yin, the thousand-eyed, thousand-armed goddess of compassion. Look out for the collection of contemporary art and folk-naive paintings. Guided tours are available for 150,000d.

Hoa Lo Prison Museum
This thought-provoking site is all that remains of the former **Hoa Lo Prison** (Map p54; 🕿04-3824 6358; cnr P Hoa Lo & P Hai Ba Trung; adult/child 30,000d/free; 🕙8am-5pm), ironically nicknamed the 'Hanoi Hilton' by US POWs during the American War. Most exhibits relate to the prison's use up to the mid-1950s, focusing on the Vietnamese struggle for independence from France.

A gruesome relic is the ominous French guillotine, used to behead Vietnamese revolutionaries. There are also displays focusing on the American pilots who were incarcerated at Hoa Lo during the American War.

Vietnamese Women's Museum
This excellent, modern **museum** (Map p54; 🕿04-3825 9936; www.baotangphunu.org.vn; 36 P Ly Thuong Kiet; 30,000d; 🕙8am-5pm) showcases women's role in Vietnamese society and culture. Labelled in English and French, it's the memories of the wartime contribution by individual heroic women that are most poignant. There is a stunning collection of propaganda posters, as well as costumes, tribal basketware and fabric motifs from Vietnam's ethnic minority groups.

Museum of Vietnamese Revolution
This **museum** (Bao Tang Cach Mang Viet Nam; Map p54; 🕿04-3825 4151; 216 Đ Tran Quang Khai; adult/student 40,000/20,000d; 🕙8am-noon & 1.30-5pm, closed 1st Mon of the month), housing over 40,000 exhibits, enthusiastically presents the histories of conflict and revolution in Vietnam.

◎ SIGHTS

Temple of Literature
Confucian Temple

(Van Mieu Quoc Tu Giam; Map p54; ☑04-3845 2917; P Quoc Tu Giam; adult/student 30,000/15,000d; ⊗8am-5pm) Founded in 1070 by Emperor Ly Thanh Tong, the Temple of Literature is dedicated to Confucius (Khong Tu). Inside you'll find a pond known as the 'Well of Heavenly Clarity', a low-slung pagoda, and statues of Confucius and his disciples. A rare example of well-preserved traditional Vietnamese architecture, the complex honours Vietnam's finest scholars and men of literary accomplishment. It is the site of Vietnam's first university, established here in 1076, when entrance was only granted to those of noble birth.

After 1442, a more egalitarian approach was adopted and gifted students from all over the nation headed to Hanoi to study the principles of Confucianism, literature and poetry. In 1484 Emperor Ly Thanh Tong ordered that stelae be erected to record the names, places of birth and achievements of exceptional scholars: 82 of 116 stelae remain standing. Paths lead from the imposing tiered gateway on P Quoc Tu Giam through formal gardens to the Khue Van pavilion, constructed in 1802.

Hai Ba Trung Temple
Buddhist Temple

(Map p54; P Tho Lao) Two kilometres south of Hoan Kiem Lake, this temple was founded in 1142. A statue shows the two Trung sisters (from the 1st century AD) kneeling with their arms raised in the air. Some say the statue shows the sisters, who had been proclaimed the queens of the Vietnamese, about to dive into a river. They are said to have drowned themselves rather than surrender in the wake of their defeat at the hands of the Chinese.

Lotte Tower Observation Deck
Viewpoint

(☑04-3333 6016; www.lottecenter.com.vn/eng/observation/visit_information.asp; 54 P Lieu Giai, Ba Dinh; adult/student day 230,000/170,000d, night 130,000/110,000d; ⊗9am-10pm) The city's best views can be found on the 65th floor of the landmark Lotte building, opened in 2014, in the western corner of Hanoi's Ba Dinh district. From this uninter-

From left: Temple of Literature; Hai Ba Trung Temple; Traditional Hanoi dish *bun cha* (p61); Tran Quoc Pagoda

rupted vantage point, high above Hanoi's hustle and bustle, one can consider the size of the Old Quarter relative to the sheer scale of Hanoi's voracious growth. The tower also houses a hotel, all manner of restaurants, a rooftop bar and a department store on its lower floors.

Lotte Tower is around 20 minutes by taxi from the Old Quarter.

Tay Ho Pagoda   Buddhist Temple
(Phu Tay Ho; Đ Thai Mai) Jutting into Ho Tay, beautiful Tay Ho Pagoda is perhaps the most popular place of worship in Hanoi. Throngs of people come here on the first and 15th day of each lunar month in the hope of receiving good fortune from the Mother Goddess, to whom the temple is dedicated.

Imperial Citadel of Thang Long   Historic Site
(Hoang Thanh Thang Long; Map p54; www. hoangthanhthanglong.vn; 19c P Hoang Dieu; 30,000d; ⊗8-11.30am daily & 2-4pm Tue-Thu, Sat & Sun) Added to Unesco's World Heritage list in 2010 and reopened in 2012, Hanoi's Imperial Citadel was the hub of Vietnamese

military power for over 1000 years. Ongoing archaeological digs of ancient palaces, grandiose pavilions and imperial gates are complemented by fascinating military command bunkers from the American War – with maps and 1960s communications equipment – used by the legendary Vietnamese General Vo Nguyen Giap.

The leafy grounds are also an easy-going and quiet antidote to Hanoi's bustle.

Tran Quoc Pagoda   Buddhist Temple
(Chua Tran Quoc; Map p54; P Thanh Nien) One of the oldest pagodas in Vietnam, Tran Quoc Pagoda is on the eastern shore of Ho Tay, just off Đ Thanh Nien, which divides this lake from Truc Bach Lake. A stela here, dating from 1639, tells the history of this site. The pagoda was rebuilt in the 15th century and again in 1842.

Presidential Palace   Historic Building
(Map p54) This restored colonial building was constructed in 1906 as the Palace of the Governor General of Indochina. It is now used for official receptions and isn't open to the public. Visitors may wander the grounds if you stick to the paths.

Hanoi

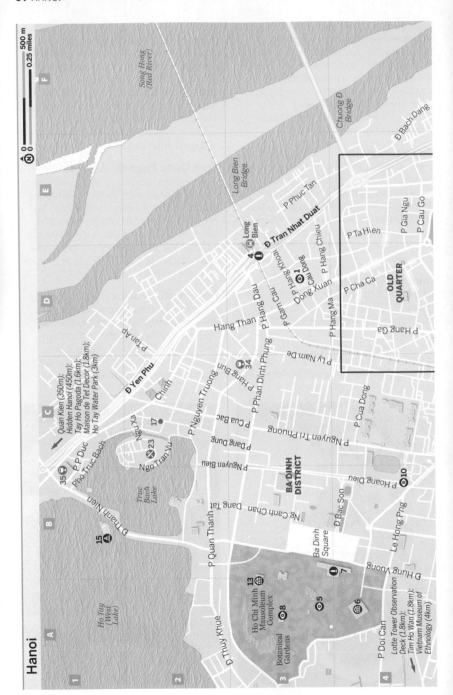

Ho Tay
(West Lake)

Quan Kien (350m);
Hidden Hanoi (450m);
Tay Ho Pagoda (1.6km);
Maison de Tet Decor (1.8km);
Ho Tay Water Park (3km)

Đ Thanh Nien

Truc
Bach Lake

P P Duc

Pho Truc Bach

Ngu Xa

Ngo Tran Vu

Đ Yen Phu

P Tan Ap

P Tran Vu

Hang Than

P Hang Than

P Phan Dinh Phung

P Nguyen Truong To

P Hang Bun

P Dang Dung

P Cua Bac

P Nguyen Bieu

P Quan Thanh

Đ Quan Thanh

Chinh

BA DINH
DISTRICT

Ho Chi Minh
Mausoleum
Complex

Botanical
Gardens

Ba Dinh
Square

Đ Bac Son

Nẻ Canh Chan

Đ Dang Tat

Đ Doi Can

Đ Thuy Khue

Lotte Tower Observation
Deck (1.8km);
Tim Ho Wan (1.8km);
Vietnam Museum of
Ethnology (4km)

Đ Hung Vuong

Le Hong Png

P Hoang Dieu

P Cua Dong

P Nguyen Tri Phuong

P Ly Nam De

P Hang Ma

Đ Phung Hung

Hang Ga

P Cha Ca

OLD
QUARTER

P Ta Hien

P Gia Ngu

P Cau Go

P Hang Chieu

P Phuc Tan

Đ Tran Nhat Duat

P Hang Khoai

P Hang Dong

Dong Xuan

P Gam Cau

P Hang Dau

Long
Bien

Long Bien
Bridge

Song Hong
(Red River)

Chuong Đ
Bridge

Đ Bach Dang

15

35

23

17

34

4

1

1

7

13

8

5

6

10

500 m
0.25 miles

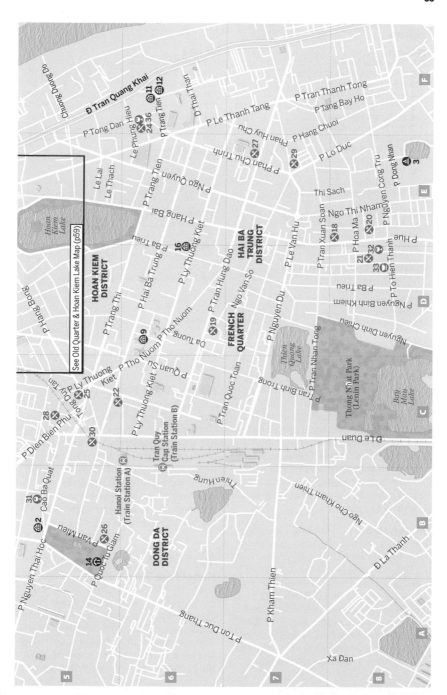

See Old Quarter & Hoan Kiem Lake Map (p59)

HOAN KIEM
DISTRICT

HAI BA
TRUNG
DISTRICT

FRENCH
QUARTER

DONG DA
DISTRICT

Hoan
Kiem
Lake

Hanoi Station
(Train Station A)

Tran Quy
Cap Station
(Train Station B)

Thien
Quang
Lake

Thong Nhat Park
(Lenin Park)

Bay
Mau
Lake

Hanoi

🏃 ACTIVITIES

Hanoi Cooking Centre — Cooking
(Map p54; 📞04-3715 0088; www.hanoicooking centre.com; 44 P Chau Long; per class from 1,330,000d) Excellent interactive classes, including market visits and a special Kids' Club – handy if your children are aspiring chefs. The Hanoi Cooking Centre also runs a highly recommended walking tour exploring Hanoi's street-food scene, and cookery classes conclude with a shared lunch in its elegant restaurant.

Hidden Hanoi — Cooking, Language
(📞0912-254 045; www.hiddenhanoi.com.vn; 147 P Nghi Tam, Tay Ho; per class with/without market tour US$55/45; ⏰11am-2pm Mon-Sat) Offers cooking classes from its kitchen near the eastern side of Ho Tay (West Lake). Options include seafood and village-food menus. Walking tours (per person US$20 to US$25) exploring the Old Quarter and Hanoi street food are available. Hidden Hanoi also offers a language-study program (per person from $US200), including two field trips.

Ho Tay Water Park — Swimming
(Cong Vien Ho Tay; 📞04-3718 4222; www.congvienhotay.vn; under 130cm/over 130cm 80,000/150,000d; ⏰9am-9pm Wed-Mon Apr-Nov) If you're desperate for a swim, this water park 5km north of the Old Quarter on the northern edge of Ho Tay has pools, slides and a lazy river. It gets extremely busy here on hot summer afternoons and might not satisfy everyone's standards for safety and hygiene.

🎫 TOURS

Hanoi Free Tour Guides — Walking
(0974 596 895; http://hanoifreetourguides.com) There's no better way to experience the real Hanoi than with this not-for-profit social organisation run by a team of over 400 volunteer staff and guides comprising students and ex-students, speaking a multitude of languages. A variety of suggested

tours are available, or work with your guide to tailor your own itinerary. Book online.

Vietnam Awesome Travel Walking
(Map p59; ☑04-3990 1733; www.vietnamawe-sometravel.com; 19b P Hang Be; tours from US$15) Offers a wide range of good-value walking tours, including the popular Food on Foot (US$25) street-food walking tours around the Old Quarter. A wide range of day trips and longer guided tours are available. See the website for details.

Hanoi Street Food Tours Walking
(☑0904 517 074; www.streetfoodtourshanoi. blogspot.com.au; tours from US$75) There's a local company running tours under the same name, but we continue to recommend this pricier, private option, run by Tu and Mark, a couple of passionate Hanoi foodies. Tours can be customised to different interests.

Sophie's Art Tour Cultural
(☑0168 796 2575; www.sophiesarttour.com; tours from $55) These fascinating tours are based on the lives of artists who studied, fought, witnessed and documented major changes in 20th- and 21st-century Vietnam, and will be appreciated not only by art lovers but by those who want to gain a deeper understanding of the complexities of Vietnam's unique history and culture.

🔒 SHOPPING

Bookworm Books
(Map p54; www.bookwormhanoi.com; 44 P Chau Long; ⊙9am-7pm) Stocks over 10,000 new and used English-language books. There's plenty of fiction and it's good on South Asian history and politics.

Hanoi Moment Arts & Crafts
(Map p59; ☑04-3926 3630; www.hanoimoment. vn; 101 P Hang Gai; ⊙8am-9pm) An oasis of classier Vietnamese souvenirs, including lacquerware and jewellery, amid the T-shirt overkill of nearby stores. Bamboo, stone and porcelain are also used to great effect.

Art in Hanoi

Modern Vietnamese artists are highly technically trained – many could copy a photographic portrait by hand with remarkable detail and accuracy, in a short space of time. Prior to the Communist Party takeover, Vietnam had over 900 years of artistic heritage, which to this day provides many young Vietnamese with an exceptional creative skill set. That said, the Communist Party still curbs freedom of expression, forcing some artists and artisans to work underground. However, with an influx of tourism and interest from the West in recent years, Hanoi's art scene in particular is gaining attention from the outside world. Ever so slowly, talented Vietnamese artists are getting the chance to expand their horizons and broaden their skills.

For visitors interested in art, this means a burgeoning art scene begging for appreciation. Keen shoppers can pick up an original work on canvas by a local artist from as little as US$40 in any one of the Old Quarter's many private galleries – **Mai Gallery** (p58) is a good start. Kick back and check out the vibe at **Tadioto** (p63), **Manzi Art Space** (p63), **Bar Betta** (p63), or all three: you'll lock in with like-minded arty folk in no time at all. For the low-down on the scene, visit the informative local art blog, www.andofotherthings. com. Better still, take one of **Sophie's Art Tours**.

Dragon detail, Hanoi Ceramic Road (p45)
SEREE TANSRISAWAT/SHUTTERSTOCK ©

Tan My Design   Clothing
(Map p59; 📞04-3938 1154; www.tanmydesign.
com; 61 P Hang Gai; ⊗8am-8pm) Stylish
clothing, jewellery and accessories, with
the added bonus of a funky cafe for a break
from shopping. The homewares and bed
linen are definitely worth a look.

Metiseko   Fashion & Accessories
(Map p59; 📞04-3935 2645; www.metiseko.com;
71 P Hang Gai; ⊗8am-9pm) Lots of stylish,
organic and ecofriendly spins on clothing,
homewares and accessories. Cotton and
silk are used in Metiseko's chic collections.

Things of Substance   Clothing
(Map p59; 📞04-3828 6965; 5 P Nha Tho; ⊗9am-
6pm) Tailored fashions and some off-the-
rack items at moderate prices. The staff are
professional and speak decent English.

Mai Gallery   Art
(Map p59; 📞04-3828 5854; www.maigallery-vi-
etnam.com; 113 P Hang Bong; ⊗9am-7pm) Run
by resident artist Mai, this is a good place
to learn more about Vietnamese art before
making a purchase.

Mekong+   Arts & Crafts
(Map p59; 📞04-3926 4831; http://mekong-plus.
com; 13 P Hang Bac; ⊗8am-8pm) Beautiful
quilts handcrafted by rural women working
in a not-for-profit community development
program.

Dong Xuan Market   Market
(Map p54; Dong Xuan; ⊗6am-7pm) A large, non-
touristy market in the Old Quarter of Hanoi,
900m north of Hoan Kiem Lake. There are
hundreds of stalls here, and it's a fascinating place to explore if you want to catch
a flavour of Hanoian street life. The area
around it also has loads of bustling shops.

Night Market   Market
(Map p59; P Hang Giay; ⊗7pm-midnight Fri-Sun)
This market runs north to south through
the Old Quarter, from P Hang Giay to P
Hang Dao. Content-wise it's something of
a spillover for the area's shops, but at least
the streets are closed to traffic. Watch out
for pickpockets.

EATING

Hanoi is an international city, and whatever
your budget (or tastes), it's available here.
If you've just flown in, get stuck into the
local cuisine, which is wonderfully tasty, fra-
grantly spiced and inexpensive. And don't
miss the essential experience of dining on
Hanoi's street food.

🚫 Old Quarter

New Day   Vietnamese $
(Map p59; 📞04-3828 0315; http://newday
restaurant.com; 72 P Ma May; meals 50,000-
100,000d; ⊗8am-late) Clean and tidy New
Day attracts locals, expats and travellers
with its broad menu. The eager staff always
find space for new diners, so look forward
to sharing a table with some like-minded
fans of Vietnamese food.

Mon Hue   Vietnamese $
(Map p59; 📞0986 981 369; 37 P Ly Quoc Su;
meals 40,000-80,000d; ⊗10am-10pm; 📶)
While this simple, somewhat grubby little
restaurant is by no means a member of the
famous Ho Chi Minh–based chain whose
name it has appropriated, it does have
genuinely friendly staff, good food in the
style of Hue (adopted by a Hanoian family
to local tastes) and a picture menu to ease
you in to the almost-street-food experience.

Highway 4   Vietnamese $$
(Map p59; 📞04-3926 0639; www.highway4.com;
3 P Hang Tre; meals 120,000-275,000d; ⊗noon-
late) This is the original location of a restaurant family famed for adapting Vietnamese
cuisine for Western palates, although with
increasing popularity it becomes harder to
please everybody. There are now four other
branches in Hanoi: check the website for
locations. Come for small plates to share,
cold beer and funky decor.

Cha Ca Thang Long Vietnamese $$
(Map p59; 📞04-3824 5115; www.chacathanglong.
com; 19-31 P Duong Thanh; cha ca fish meal
180,000d; ⊗10am-3pm & 5-10pm) Bring along
your DIY cooking skills and grill your own
succulent fish with a little shrimp paste and

Old Quarter & Hoan Kiem Lake

◉ N 0 | 200 m
0 | 0.1 miles

Old Quarter & Hoan Kiem Lake

plenty of herbs. *Cha ca* is an iconic Hanoi dish heavy on turmeric and dill, and while another nearby more-famous *cha ca* eatery gets all the tour-bus traffic, the food here is actually better.

Green Tangerine   Fusion $$

(Map p59; 04-3825 1286; www.greentangerine hanoi.com; 48 P Hang Be; meals US$12-20; noon-late) Experience the mood and flavour of 1950s Indochine at this elegant restaurant located in a beautifully restored French-colonial house with a cobbled courtyard. The fusion French-Vietnamese cuisine is not always entirely successful, but it's still worth popping in for coffee or a drink. Two-course lunches (218,000d) are good value.

Around Hoan Kiem Lake

Minh Thuy's   Vietnamese $

(Map p59; 04-3200 7893; 2a P Duong Thanh; meals 45,000-155,000d; 11am-10pm) *MasterChef Vietnam* contestant Minh Thuy's eponymous restaurant is tucked away in backpacker central and worth

your attention. It's cheap, clean and serves mouthwatering Vietnamese food with some very original European twists. Highly recommended.

La Place   Cafe $

(Map p59; 04-3928 5859; www.laplaceha-noi.com; 4 P Au Trieu; meals from 70,000d; 7.30am-10.30pm;) This stylish, popular little cafe adjacent to St Joseph Cathedral has walls covered in propaganda art and an East–West menu. Plenty of wine by the glass is on offer and the coffee has a real kick. Good for breakfast also.

Hanoi Social Club   Cafe $$

(Map p59; 04-3938 2117; www.facebook.com/ TheHanoiSocialClub; 6 Hoi Vu; meals 95,000-175,000d; 8am-11pm) On three funky levels with retro furniture, the Hanoi Social Club is the city's most cosmopolitan cafe and an artist hub. Dishes include potato fritters with chorizo for breakfast, and pasta, burgers and wraps for lunch or dinner. Vegetarian options feature a tasty mango curry, and the quiet laneway location is a good spot for an end-of-day coffee, beer or wine.

Diners at Highway 4 (p58)

GREG ELMS/GETTY IMAGES ©

Madame Hien   Vietnamese $$$
(Map p59; 04-3938 1588; www.facebook.
com/madamehienrestaurant; 15 Chan Cam; set
menus from 365,000d, meals 95,000-350,000d;
⊙11am-10pm) Housed in a restored
19th-century villa, Madame Hien is a tribute
to French chef Didier Corlu's Vietnamese
grandmother. Look forward to elegant ver-
sions of traditional Hanoi street food, with
the '36 Streets' fixed menu (535,000d) an
easy-going place to kick off your culinary
knowledge of the city.

 West of Old Quarter

Ray Quan   Vietnamese $
(Map p54; 0913 578 588; 8a Nguyen Khuyen;
dishes from 30,000-120,000d) Popular with
expats in the know, this quirky spot directly
on the train tracks won't be for everyone,
but those who like it, really do. A wide range
of delicious Vietnamese cuisine is cooked
to order by the eccentric owner-chef who
ferments her own rice wine: it's strong and
delicious.

Net Hue   Vietnamese $
(Map p54; 04-3938 1795; http://nethue.
com.vn; cnr P Hang Bong & P Cam Chi; snacks
& meals from 35,000d; ⊙11am-9pm) One of a
small chain, Net Hue is well priced for such
comfortable surroundings. Head to the top
floor for the nicest ambience and enjoy
Hue-style dishes like *banh nam* (steamed
rice pancake with minced shrimp).

Nha Hang Koto Van Mieu   Cafe $$
(Map p54; 04-3747 0338; www.koto.com.au; 59
P Van Mieu; meals 120,000-160,000d; ⊙7.30am-
10pm, closed dinner Mon) Stunning four-storey
modernist cafe-bar-restaurant overlooking
the Temple of Literature, where the interior
design has been taken very seriously, from
the stylish seating to the fresh flowers by
the till. Daily specials are chalked up on
a blackboard, and the short menu has
everything from excellent Vietnamese food
to yummy pita wraps and beer-battered
fish and chips.

    KOTO is a not-for-profit project providing
career training and guidance to disadvantaged children and teens.

Hanoi Street Food

Deciphering Hanoi's street-food scene
can be bewildering, but it's worth persevering and diving in. Note that opening
hours may change and prices vary.
Expect to pay 25,000d to 70,000d.

Bun Rieu Cua (Map p59; 40 P Hang Tre;
⊙7-10.30am) Get to this incredibly popular spot early, as its sole dish of *bun rieu
cua* (noodle soup with beef in a spicy
crab broth) is only served for a couple of
hours from 7am. A Hanoi classic.

Bun Cha Nem Cua Be Dac Kim (Map
p59; 67 P Duong Thanh; ⊙11am-7pm) Visiting Hanoi and not eating *bun cha* (barbecued pork with rice vermicelli) with
a side of *nem cua be* (sea-crab spring
rolls) should be a capital offence.

Banh Mi Pho Hue (Map p54; 118 P Hue;
⊙8am-9pm) *Banh mi* (sandwich) vendors abound in Hanoi, although the phe-
nomenon is less popular than in Ho Chi
Minh City. This place is usually packed
with locals – always a good sign.

Pho Thin (Map p54; 13 P Lo Duc; ⊙5am-
9pm) Negotiate your way to the rear of
this narrow, rustic establishment and
sit down to some excellent *pho bo* (beef
noodle soup). A classic Hanoi experience that hasn't changed in decades.

Banh Cuon (Map p59; 14 P Hang Ga;
⊙8am-3pm) No need to order here; just
squeeze in and a plate of gossamer-light
banh cuon (steamed rice crepes filled
with minced pork, mushrooms and
shrimp) will be placed in front of you.

Banh cuon

Staying Safe

First the good news: Hanoi is generally a safe city to explore, and serious crimes against tourists are extremely rare, but it's pertinent to exercise some caution. While it's generally safe to walk around the streets of the Old Quarter at night, it's best to avoid the darker lanes after around 10pm and sensible for solo female travellers to take a metered taxi with a reputable company when travelling across the city at night. Watch out for pickpockets around market areas and unwanted baggage 'helpers' in crowded transport terminals – particularly when boarding night trains.

Traffic and pollution are other irritants. The city's traffic is so dense and unrelenting that simply crossing the street can be a real headache. Pollution levels are punishing: Hanoi actually had the unenviable record of having the worst (measured) air quality in the world for a few days in March 2016.

Police officer directing traffic

Old Hanoi   Vietnamese $$$
(☑04-3747 8337; www.oldhanoi.com; 4 Ton That Thiep; meals 90,000-179,000d; ⏱11am-2pm & 5-10pm) This sophisticated eatery in a restored French-colonial villa with a pleasant casual courtyard outside and starched white tablecloths inside was once host to celebrity chef Gordon Ramsay. Serving traditional Hanoian and Vietnamese specialities with aplomb, you'll enjoy the selection and find the best value for money if you dine in a group.

🟢 French Quarter

Moto-san Uber Noodle   Noodles $
(Map p54; ☑04-6680 9124; 4 P Ly Dao Thanh; meals 45,000-70,000d) Brainchild of Hanoi artist, journalist and designer Nguyen Qui Duc (of Tadioto bar fame), this wonderful noodle stall seats eight eager eaters. The menu is simple: miso, *shōyu* (soy) or *shio* (salty) ramen, and spicy *banh my thit ko* (stewed pork) sandwiches with killer hot sauce (optional) *à la* central Vietnam. Sake and beer are, of course, readily available.

Chim Sao   Vietnamese $$
(Map p54; ☑04-3976 0633; www.chimsao.com; 63-65 Ngo Hue; meals 45,000-120,000d; ⏱11am-11pm; 🌱) Sit at tables downstairs or grab a more traditional spot on the floor upstairs and discover excellent Vietnamese food, with some dishes inspired by the ethnic minorities of Vietnam's north. Definite standouts are the hearty and robust sausages, zingy and fresh salads, and duck with starfruit. Even simple dishes are outstanding. Try to come with a group so you can explore the menu fully.

Izakaya Yancha   Japanese $$
(Map p54; ☑04-3974 8437; 121 P Trieu Viet Vuong; meals 120,000-250,000d; ⏱11am-11pm) Surrounded by local cafes on 'Coffee Street', Izakaya Yancha serves *izakaya* – Japanese tapas – in a buzzy and friendly atmosphere. Secure a spot near the open kitchen and work your way through lots of Osaka-style goodies, including excellent tuna sashimi and miso with udon noodles.

Chay Nang Tam   Vegetarian $$
(Map p54; ☑04-3942 4140; 79a P Tran Hung Dao; items from 100,000d; ⏱11am-8pm; 🌱) Dishes of vegetables that look like meat, reflecting an ancient Buddhist tradition designed to make carnivore guests feel at home.

La Badiane   International $$$
(Map p54; ☑04-3942 4509; www.labadiane-hanoi.com; 10 Nam Ngu; meals from 280,000d; ⏱11.30am-9.45pm) This stylish bistro is set in a restored whitewashed French villa arrayed around a breezy central courtyard.

French cuisine underpins the menu – La Badiane translates as 'star anise' – but Asian and Mediterranean flavours also feature. Menu highlights include sea bass tagliatelle with smoked paprika, and prawn bisque with wasabi tomato bruschetta. Three-course lunches from 375,000d are excellent value.

⊗ Other Areas

Tim Ho Wan   Dim Sum $

(☑04-3333 1725; 36th fl, Lotte Tower, 54 P Lieu Giai, Ba Dinh; dim sum 69,000-95,000d) Do yourself a favour and reserve a window table at the Hanoi branch of this legendary Hong Kong dim sum chain, high above the city on the 36th floor of the Lotte Tower. Bring a friend or six and an empty stomach, and we guarantee you won't regret it.

Maison de Tet Decor   Cafe $$

(☑0966 611 383; http://tet-lifestyle-collection. com; 156 Tua Hoa, Nghi Tam, Tay Ho; meals from 180,000d; ☺7am-10pm) Sumptuous, healthy and organic (wherever possible) wholefoods are presented with aplomb in this, one of Hanoi's loveliest settings, an expansive, airy villa overlooking lake Ho Tay.

Quan Kien   Vietnamese $$

(☑0983 430 136; www.quankien.com; 143 P Nhgi Tam; meals 80,000-130,000d; ☺11am-11pm) An interesting spot for cuisine from the Hmong, Muong and Thai ethnic minorities – try the grilled chicken with wild pepper – traditional Vietnamese *ruou* (wine) made from apricots or apples, and more challenging snacks like grilled ants' eggs and crickets. If insects aren't your thing, it's still a fun night sitting at the low tables eating excellent Vietnamese dishes.

Mâu Dich 37   Vietnamese $$

(Map p54; ☑04-3715 4336; 37 Nam Trang, Truc Bach; snacks 35,000-55,000d, meals 90,000-180,000d; ☺10am-10pm) Styled after a government-run food shop from the impoverished period after 1976, Mâu Dich 37 is a unique exercise in nostalgia. Waiters are dressed as state workers, and diners queue to 'purchase' coupons that can be exchanged for food. The menu focuses on robust northern flavours, and features a few challenging dishes like braised frog and snails with ginger leaves.

🍸 DRINKING & NIGHTLIFE

Tadioto   Bar

(Map p54; ☑04-6680 9124; www.tadioto.com; 24b P Tong Dan; ☺7am-midnight) Nguyen Qui Duc's unofficial clubhouse for the underground arts scene's latest incarnation is this dark and quirky colonial bar in the French Quarter. Obligatory red accents (seat covers, wrought-iron grill on the doors), reworkings of art deco furniture and plenty of recycled ironwork feature heavily. The highlight of the cool cocktail list is the sweet mojito.

Nola   Bar

(Map p59; 89 P Ma May; ☺9am-midnight) Retro furniture is mixed and matched in this bohemian labyrinth tucked away from Ma May's tourist bustle. Pop in for a coffee and banana bread, or return after dark for one of Hanoi's best little bars.

Bar Betta   Bar

(Map p54; ☑0165 897 9073; www.facebook.com/ barbetta34; 34 Cao Ba Quat; ☺9am-midnight) Retro decor and a jazz-age vibe combine with good cocktails, coffee and cool music in this breezy French-colonial villa. Two-for-one beers are available from 3pm to 7pm, and the rooftop terrace (from 8pm) is essential on a sultry Hanoi night.

Manzi Art Space   Bar

(Map p54; ☑04-3716 3397; www.facebook.com/ manzihanoi; 14 Phan Huy Ich; ☺cafe 9am-midnight, shop 10am-6pm) Part cool art gallery, part chic cafe and bar, Manzi is worth seeking out north of the Old Quarter. A restored French villa hosts diverse exhibitions of painting, sculpture and photography, and the compact courtyard garden is perfect for a coffee or glass of wine. There's also a small shop selling works by contemporary Vietnamese artists.

Summit Lounge   Bar

(Map p54; 20th fl, Sofitel Plaza, 1 Ð Thanh Nien; ☺4.30pm-late) Enjoy fabulous views from this 20th-floor lounge bar. Order a (pricey) cocktail or beer, grab a spot on the outside deck, and take in Truc Bach Lake and the city beyond.

Le Pub   Pub

(Map p59; ☎04-3926 2104; 25 P Hang Be; ☺7am-late) Le Pub is a great place to hook up with others, as there's always a good mix of travellers and Hanoi expats. There's a cosy, tavern-like interior (with big screens for sports fans), a street-facing terrace and a rear courtyard. Bar snacks are served, the service is slick and the music usually includes tunes you can sing along to.

GC Pub   Gay & Lesbian

(Map p59; ☎04-3825 0499; 7 P Ngo Bao Khanh; ☺noon-midnight) Hanoi's long-standing, only established gay bar, and unofficial LGBT HQ, might seem small and vanilla midweek, but it gets pumped on weekend nights. The reasonably priced drinks and chatty bar staff make it popular with a mixed local crowd and easy for gay visitors to drop by, especially those fond of playing pool.

✪ ENTERTAINMENT

Municipal Water
Puppet Theatre   Theatre

(Map p59; ☎04-3824 9494; www.thanglongwater puppet.org; 57b P Dinh Tien Hoang; adult/child 100,000/60,000d; ☺4 afternoon performances daily, also 9.30am Sun) Water-puppetry shows are a real treat for children. Multilingual programs allow the audience to read up on each vignette as it's performed. Although there are multiple performances daily, book well ahead, especially from October to April.

Hanoi Rock City   Live Music

(www.hanoirockcity.com; 27/52 To Ngoc Van, Tay Ho) Hanoi Rock City is tucked away down a residential lane about 7km north of the city near Tay Ho, but it's a journey well worth taking for an eclectic mix, including reggae, Hanoi punk and regular electronica nights. A few international acts swing by, so check the website or www.newhanoian.xemzi. com for listings.

Vietnam National
Tuong Theatre   Opera

(Map p59; ☎04-837 0046; www.vietnamtuong theatre.com; 51 P Duong Thanh; 100,000d; ☺6.30pm Thu-Sun) *Hat tuong* is a uniquely Vietnamese variation of Chinese opera that enjoyed its greatest popularity under the Nguyen dynasty in the 19th century. Until 2007, performances at this theatre were by invitation only. Now they are open to locals and visitors, and a night watching *hat tuong* is an interesting traditional alternative to Hanoi's wildly popular water puppets.

❶ GETTING THERE & AWAY

Hanoi's **Noi Bai International Airport** (☎04-3827 1513; www.hanoiairportonline.com) is about 35km north of the city.

The main **Hanoi train station** (Ga Hang Co; Train Station A; ☎04-3825 3949; 120 Ð Le Duan; ☺ticket office 7.30am-12.30pm & 1.30-7.30pm) on P Tran Hung Dao serves southern destinations while **Tran Quy Cap Station** (Train Station B; ☎04-3825 2628; P Tran Quy Cap; ☺ticket office 4-6am & 4-10pm) serves Lao Cai (for Sapa).

GETTING AROUND

Hanoi Taxi (☎04-3853 5353) and **Mai Linh** (☎04-3822 2666) are reliable taxis. Cyclo drivers are available but usually ask for more than taxis.

Where to Stay

Hanoi is one city where paying a little extra can make a big difference: splurge if you can. Always check whether tax and service are included in the rate, and if it is cheaper to pay in dong or dollars and in cash.

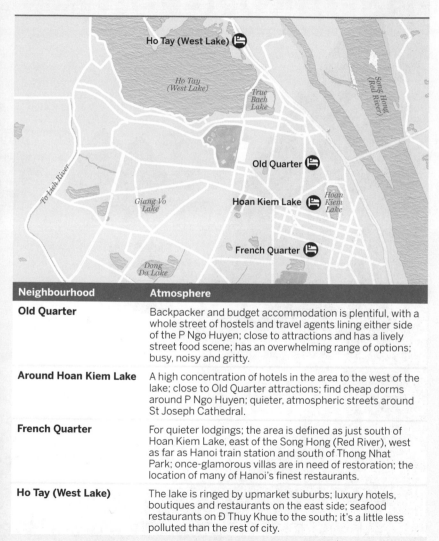

Neighbourhood	Atmosphere
Old Quarter	Backpacker and budget accommodation is plentiful, with a whole street of hostels and travel agents lining either side of the P Ngo Huyen; close to attractions and has a lively street food scene; has an overwhelming range of options; busy, noisy and gritty.
Around Hoan Kiem Lake	A high concentration of hotels in the area to the west of the lake; close to Old Quarter attractions; find cheap dorms around P Ngo Huyen; quieter, atmospheric streets around St Joseph Cathedral.
French Quarter	For quieter lodgings; the area is defined as just south of Hoan Kiem Lake, east of the Song Hong (Red River), west as far as Hanoi train station and south of Thong Nhat Park; once-glamorous villas are in need of restoration; the location of many of Hanoi's finest restaurants.
Ho Tay (West Lake)	The lake is ringed by upmarket suburbs; luxury hotels, boutiques and restaurants on the east side; seafood restaurants on Đ Thuy Khue to the south; it's a little less polluted than the rest of city.

HALONG BAY

Halong Bay at a Glance...

Majestic and mysterious, inspiring and imperious, Halong Bay's 3000 or more incredible islands rise from the emerald waters of the Gulf of Tonkin. A Unesco World Heritage site, this mystical seascape of limestone islets is a vision of breathtaking beauty. The islands are dotted with wind- and wave-eroded grottoes, many now illuminated with technicolour lighting effects.

Halong Bay attracts visitors year-round with peak season between late May and early August. January to March is often cool and drizzly, and the ensuing fog can make visibility low, but adds eerie atmosphere.

Halong Bay in Two Days

Rather than attempt to tour Halong independently, it's far easier to book a tour from Hanoi. Prepare yourself for a long road trip: Halong City is over three hours away by bus. Once you're aboard your boat it's time to kick back and simply revel in the outstanding **karst island scenery**, tour a **floating village** and pause for some kayaking and swimming.

Halong Bay in Four Days

Extend your stay with a couple of days in lovely Cat Ba Island. Tour the **Cannon Fort** (p75) and **Hospital Cave** (p74) on the first morning and spend the afternoon on pretty **Cat Co Cove** (p74), then enjoy a seafood feast at **Vien Duong** (p78). The next day sign up for a boat tour of gorgeous **Lan Ha Bay** (p75), perhaps factoring in some rock climbing or kayaking.

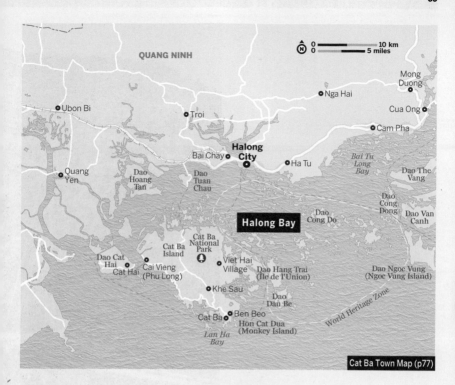

QUANG NINH

0 — 10 km
0 — 5 miles

Mong Duong
Nga Hai
Cua Ong
Ubon Bi
Troi
Cam Pha
Halong City
Bai Chay
Ha Tu
Bai Tu Long Bay
Dao The Vang
Quang Yen
Dao Hoang Tan
Dao Tuan Chau
Dao Cong Dong
Dao Van Canh
Halong Bay
Dao Cong Do
Cat Ba National Park
Cat Ba Island
Dao Cat Hai
Cat Hai
Cai Vieng (Phu Long)
Viet Hai Village
Dao Hang Trai (Ile de l'Union)
Dao Ngoc Vung (Ngoc Vung Island)
Khe Sau
Dao Dan Be
World Heritage Zone
Cat Ba
Ben Beo
Hon Cat Dua (Monkey Island)
Lan Ha Bay

Cat Ba Town Map (p77)

Arriving in Halong Bay

It's possible to join a tour in Halong City but most people travel from Hanoi on a prearranged tour.

Halong City is 160km from Hanoi; it takes over three hours by private vehicle.

Where to Stay

Aboard a boat in Halong Bay! Preferably on a traditional wooden junk if you have the resources.

Otherwise both Halong City and Cat Ba Town have a good selection of hotels.

Dramatic rock formations, Halong Bay

Cruising Halong Bay

The most popular way to experience Halong Bay's karst scenery is on a cruise. For many travellers this is an utterly memorable part of their trip to Vietnam.

Great For...

ⓘ Need to Know

Tropical storms can occur between July and October and sailing trips can be cancelled.

★ **Top Tip**
Never contemplate a rushed day trip of Halong Bay; it's definitely worth at least one overnight stay.

Caves

Halong Bay's islands are peppered with caves, many now illuminated with colourful lighting effects. Sadly, litter and trinket-touting vendors are also part of the experience.

Which of the caves you'll visit depends on certain factors including the weather and the number of other boats in the vicinity.

Islands & Islets

Cat Ba Island is the most developed of Halong Bay's islands, with Cat Ba Town the launching pad for the beautiful Lan Ha Bay region. Some Halong Bay cruise operators include Cat Ba and Lan Ha Bay on their itineraries.

Kayaking

A kayak among the karsts is an option on most Halong Bay tours. Count on about an hour's paddling, often including negotiating your way through karst grottoes and around lagoons, or to a floating village in the bay.

If you're really keen on kayaking, contact **Handspan Adventure Travel** (Map p59; ☎04-3926 2828; www.handspan.com; 78 P Ma May; ☺9am-8pm) in Hanoi or Blue Swimmer (p76) on Cat Ba Island, both of which run professionally organised trips and have qualified guides. Trips are operated in less-touristed Lan Ha Bay.

Choosing the Right Tour

Tours sold out of Hanoi start from a rock-bottom US$60 per person for a dodgy

Aerial view of floating villages and karst islands, Halong Bay

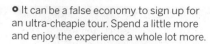

day trip, and can rise to around US$220 for two nights. For around US$110 to US$130, you should get a worthwhile overnight cruise.

At the other end of the scale, cruising the karsts aboard a luxury Chinese-style junk is hard to beat. But be aware that paying top dollar doesn't necessarily compute into heading away from the crowds.

Most cruise-tours include return transport from Hanoi, Halong Bay entrance fees, and meals. A decent overnight tour usually includes kayaking. Drinks are extra.

This is one destination where it definitely pays to do your homework beforehand. Here are some suggestions to help make Halong Bay memorable for the right, rather than wrong, reasons:

○ It can be a false economy to sign up for an ultra-cheapie tour. Spend a little more and enjoy the experience a whole lot more.

○ At the very least, check basic on-board safety standards. Life jackets should be provided. If kayaking is included, make sure it's guided. Currents close to the karst formations are surprisingly strong. Accidents can occur when visitors are left to paddle off themselves.

○ Realise that most Halong Bay cruises follow a strict itinerary, with stops at caves often at the same time as other boats. On an overnight trip there's simply not the time to stray far from Halong City.

○ Make sure you know what you're paying for to avoid disappointment later. Many cruises (including luxury options) are marketed as 'two-day' trips but are actually overnight tours, some involving less than 24 hours on board.

○ Ascertain in advance what the tour company's refund policy is if the cruise is cancelled due to bad weather.

Cruise Operators

Cat Ba Ventures (p77) Overnight tours set out from Cat Ba Island and concentrate on the Lan Ha Bay area.

Handspan Adventure Travel (www.handspan. com; overnight cruise d from US$354) Operates the only true sailing ship on the bay; meander peacefully through the karsts without the constant hum of a diesel engine.

Indochina Sails (☑04-3984 2362; www. indochinasails.com; overnight tour d cabin from US$478) Cruise Halong on a traditional junk with great viewing decks and cabins kitted out to a three-star standard.

Vega Travel (☑04-3926 2092; www.vegatravel. vn; 24a P Hang Bac, Hanoi, cnr P Ma May; overnight tour s/d cabin from US$130/240; ☺8am-8pm) Good-value overnight tours of Halong Bay, with comfortable cabins. Two-night tours also explore Lan Ha Bay and Cat Ba Island, including kayaking, cycling and hiking.

Beach resort, Cat Ba Island

ROMAS_PHOTO/SHUTTERSTOCK ©

Exploring Cat Ba Island

Rugged, craggy and jungle-clad Cat Ba is the largest island in Halong Bay. For climbers, kayakers and hikers, it's the launching pad for a swag of sweat-inducing activities.

Great For...

☑ Don't Miss

Hospital Cave is one of the most fascinating war sites in Vietnam.

Hospital Cave

This **cave** (📞031-368 8215; admission 15,000d; ⏰7am-4.30pm) served both as a secret, bombproof hospital during the American War and as a safe house for VC leaders. Built between 1963 and 1965 (with assistance from China), this incredibly well-constructed three-storey feat of engineering was in constant use until 1975. The cave is about 10km north of Cat Ba Town on the road to the Cat Ba National Park entrance.

A guide (most know a little English) will show you around the 17 rooms, point out the old operating theatre and take you to the huge natural cavern that was used as a cinema (and even had a small swimming pool).

Cat Co Cove

A 10-minute walk southeast from Cat Ba Town, the three Cat Co Cove beaches boast

❶ Need to Know

Cat Ba Town is quite tricky to reach, as getting there involves travelling by boat and road.

✕ Take a Break

Check out the friendly Flightless Bird Café (p79) for a relaxed drink.

★ Top Tip

Other beaches on Cat Ba Island include Cai Vieng, Hong Xoai Be and Hong Xoai Lon.

the nearest sand to town, although rubbish in the water can be problematic some days. **Cat Co 3** is the closest, with a blink-and-you-miss-it sliver of sand. From there a walking trail, cut into the cliff and with gorgeous sea views, winds its way to **Cat Co 1** dominated by a rather ugly resort, then on to the pretty white-sand swath of **Cat Co 2**.

Lan Ha Bay

Lying south and east of Cat Ba Town, the 300 or so karst islands and limestone outcrops of Lan Ha are just as beautiful as those of Halong Bay and have the additional attraction of numerous white-sand beaches.

Due to being a fair way from Halong City, not so many tourist boats venture here, meaning Lan Ha Bay has a more isolated appeal. Sailing and kayak trips here are best organised in Cat Ba Town.

Cannon Fort

For one of the best views in Vietnam – no, we're not kidding – head to **Cannon Fort** (admission 40,000d; ⏱sunrise-sunset), where there are astounding panoramas of Cat Ba Island's jungle-clad hills rolling down to colourful tangles of fishing boats in the harbour and out to the karst-punctuated sea beyond.

Well-labelled paths guide visitors past underground tunnels, and two well-preserved gun emplacements (one 'manned' by life-size Viet Minh mannequins), out to two viewpoints overlooking the island. There's even a cafe (with more great views) and a tiny museum.

The tunnels and gun emplacements here were first installed by the Japanese in WWII, but were also utilised by the French and Vietnamese during subsequent conflicts.

The entrance gate is a steep 10-minute walk from Cat Ba Town and from the gate it's another stiff 20-minute walk to the fort, or take a *xe om* (motorbike taxi) from Cat Ba Town (15,000d).

Halong City

Development has not been kind to Halong City (Bai Chay). Despite enjoying a stunning position on the cusp of Halong Bay, this is a gritty town with pockets of bland high-rise hotel development dotting the shoreline.

EATING

Linh Dan Restaurant   Vietnamese $
(📞033-384 6025; 104 Đ Bai Chay; meals US$3-5; ⏰11am-9pm) Linh Dan has a novella-length menu conjuring up pretty much every stir-fried variation on pork, chicken, seafood and vegetables.

Tuan Huong   Vietnamese $
(📞033-384 4651; 1 Đ Vuon Dao; meals from 80,000d; ⏰10am-10pm) A simple place with a small menu (in English and French) that specialises in fresh seafood. You can also pick your fish or crab from the tanks outside, but make sure you check the price (worked out by weight) first.

❶ GETTING THERE & AWAY

All buses leave from **Bai Chay bus station** (off Hwy 18), 6km south of central Bai Chay. Note that many buses to Halong City will be marked 'Bai Chay' rather than 'Halong City'.

Halong City is quite spread out; **Mai Linh** (📞033-382 2226) is a reliable taxi option.

Cat Ba Island

The best sights are out of town.

◉ SIGHTS

Cat Ba National Park   National Park
(📞031-216 350; admission 30,000d; ⏰sunrise-sunset) Cat Ba's beautiful national park is home to 32 types of mammal, including most of the world's 65 remaining golden-headed langur, the world's most endangered primate. There are some good hiking trails here, including a hardcore 18km route up to a mountain summit.

To reach the **park headquarters** at Trung Trang, hop on the green QH public bus from the docks at Cat Ba Town, hire a *xe om* (around 80,000d one way) or rent a motorbike for the day.

Cat Ba Island Market   Market
(⏰7am-7pm) The market at the northern end of Cat Ba Town's harbour is a great local affair with twitching crabs, jumbo shrimps and pyramids of fresh fruit.

Ho Chi Minh Monument   Monument
(off Đ Nui Ngoc) This monument stands up on imaginatively named Mountain No 1, the hillock opposite the pier in Cat Ba Town.

ACTIVITIES

Cat Ba is a superb base for adventure sports – on the island, and in, on and over the water.

Asia Outdoors   Climbing
(📞031-368 8450; www.asiaoutdoors.com. vn; Noble House, Đ 1-4, Cat Ba Town; half-/full-day climbing US$67/86; ⏰8am-7.30pm) The pioneers of climbing in Vietnam, Asia Outdoors is a one-stop shop for adventurous travellers. Climbing is their real expertise, with fully licensed and certified instructors leading trips, but it also offers climbing and kayaking packages with an overnight on their boat (US$132). It has also launched stand-up paddle-boarding (SUP) trips (US$37).

Blue Swimmer   Adventure
(📞0915-063 737, 031-368 8237; www.blue swimmersailing.com; Ben Beo Harbour; overnight sailing trip per person from US$182; ⏰8am-6pm) This environmentally conscious outfit was established by Vinh, one of the founders of respected tour operator Handspan Adventure Travel. Superb sailing and kayaking trips, trekking and mountain-biking excursions (some with overnight homestay accommodation) are offered. Check it out at Ben Beo Harbour or at its booking office in Cat Ba Town at the Green Bamboo Forest restaurant (p78).

Cat Ba Town

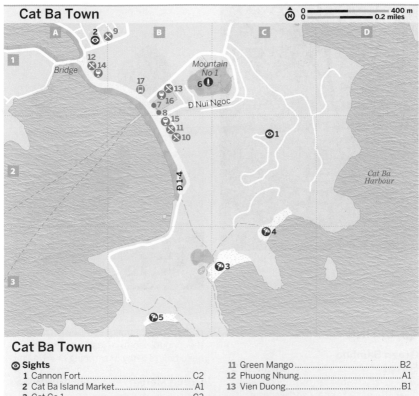

N | 0 _____ 400 m
0 _____ 0.2 miles

Cat Ba Town

Cat Ba Ventures   Boating
(☎0912-467 016, 031-388 8755; www.
catbaventures.com; 223 Đ 1-4, Cat Ba Town;
overnight boat tour per person from US$130;
⊙8am-7pm) Locally owned and operated
company offering boat trips around Lan
Ha and Halong Bays, one-day kayaking
trips (US$30) and guided hikes in Cat

Ba National Park. Excellent service from
Mr Tung is reinforced by multiple reader
recommendations.

These guys are a font of knowledge
on everything Cat Ba and a great source
of information on onward transport
options.

From left: Jungle path, Cat Ba Island (p74); Guide sitting on a carved ship's figurehead, Halong Bay; Rock formations in Thien Cung Cave, Halong Bay

🍴 EATING

Green Bamboo Forest
Vietnamese $

(Đ 1-4, Cat Ba Town; meals 50,000-150,000d; ⊙7am-11pm; 🛜) Friendly and well-run waterfront eatery that also acts as a booking office for Blue Swimmer (p76). There's some good seafood on offer and myriad rice and noodle dishes. The quieter location is also a bonus.

Buddha Belly
Vegetarian $

(Đ 1-4, Cat Ba Town; meals 30,000-80,000d; ⊙10am-9pm; 🍃) Right next to Cat Ba market, this bamboo-clad place serves up lots of vegetable and tofu goodness, and doesn't use any dairy or eggs (or much seasoning) so is a top choice for vegans as well. Its 30,000d daily-changing set menu is excellent value.

Phuong Nhung
Vietnamese $

(184 Đ 1-4, Cat Ba Town; meals 45,000d; ⊙7-10am) Bustling breakfast spot that's a popular place for a hearty bowl of *pho bo* (beef noodle soup) – just the thing you need before a day of climbing or kayaking.

Green Mango
International $$

(📞031-388 7151; www.greenmango.vn; Đ 1-4, Cat Ba Town; meals 110,000-220,000d; ⊙8am-10pm; 🛜) With a menu traipsing from steaks to seafood, and over to Italy for pasta and pizza (with a small selection of Asian dishes as well), Green Mango is a great dinner choice, with friendly staff. It's also a chilled-out spot for a glass of wine or cocktail.

Vien Duong
Vietnamese $$

(12 Đ Nui Ngoc, Cat Ba Town; meals from 120,000d; ⊙11am-11pm) One of the most popular of the seafood spots lining Đ Nui Ngoc, and often heaving with Vietnamese tourists diving into local crab, squid and steaming seafood hotpots.

Definitely not the place to come if you're looking for a quiet night.

TAKASHI IMAGES/SHUTTERSTOCK ©

🍷 DRINKING & NIGHTLIFE

Rose Bar   Bar
(15 Đ Nui Ngoc, Cat Ba Town; ⊗noon-3am; 🛜)
With cheap (US$2) cocktails, loads of
happy-hour specials and *shisha* (water
pipes), Rose Bar ticks all the boxes for
backpacker fun a long way from home.
It often stays open after midnight in the
busy season.

Oasis Bar   Bar
(Đ 1-4, Cat Ba Town; ⊗noon-11pm; 🛜) A free-
use pool table, smiley staff and a location
slap in the centre of the seafront strip make
Oasis a popular spot to plonk yourself
down for a beer or two. The menu is pretty
decent if you're feeling peckish.

Flightless Bird Café   Bar
(📞031-388 8517; Đ 1-4, Cat Ba Town; ⊗noon-
11pm; 🛜) Discover your inner Kiwi at this

friendly bar decorated with New Zealand
memorabilia. For those that need to always
multitask, you can also get your nails
painted while you drink, with well-priced
massage and manicure services on offer.

ℹ️ GETTING THERE & AWAY

Departing from Hanoi's Luong Yen bus station,
Hoang Long (📞031-268 8008; Đ 1-4, Cat Ba
Town; ticket 250,000d) operates an efficient
bus-boat-bus combo to Cat Ba Town.

ℹ️ GETTING AROUND

Bicycle and motorbike rentals are available from
most Cat Ba hotels (both around US$5 per day).
If you're heading out to the beaches or national
park, pay the parking fee for security.

SAPA

Sapa at a Glance...

Established as a hill station by the French in 1922, Sapa today is the prime tourism centre in the northwest. Sapa is orientated to make the most of the spectacular views overlooking a plunging valley, with mountains towering above on all sides. Views of this epic scenery are often subdued by thick mist rolling across the peaks, but even when it's cloudy, local hill-tribe people fill the town with colour.

This is northern Vietnam's premier trekking base. The town of Sapa is undergoing a construction boom, but once you've stepped out into the lush fields you'll understand the region's real charm.

Sapa in One Day

Do some research first and choose an agency to sign up for a day hike. Enjoy a full day exploring minority villages and revelling in the views before returning to Sapa to a local-style meal at one of the **barbecue restaurants** (p90), and for those with the stamina, drinks at the **Mountain Bar & Pub** (p91).

Sapa in Two Days

Sign up for a morning cooking course with **Hill Station Signature Restaurant** (p88), then enjoy a walk around town taking in **Sapa Market** (p88) and **Sapa Museum** (p88). Dine at **Nature View** (p90).

Sapa Map (p89)

Arriving in Sapa

The gateway to Sapa is Lao Cai, 38km away via a well-maintained highway. There's a good train service between Hanoi and Lao Cai too. There's no airport nearby.

Where to Stay

You'll find hotels dotted around town. Many of the best places are on the outskirts.

Hmong woman in traditional dress

Hiking Around Sapa

Once you've left the confines of town, you find the surrounding countryside of cascading rice terraces, muddy trails and tiny hill-tribe villages a world apart.

Great For...

ⓘ **Need to Know**

Most hill-tribe villages have admission fees from 20,000d to 40,000d.

★ **Top Tip**
By choosing a Hmong-managed trekking agency you are directly supporting minority people.

You won't step too far out of your hotel in Sapa before being accosted by guides offering to lead you on hikes.

For longer treks with overnight stays in villages, it's important to hook up with someone who knows the terrain and culture and speaks the language. We recommend using minority guides, as this offers them a means of making a living. Note it's illegal to stay overnight in villages that are not officially recognised as homestays. Ignoring this could cause significant problems for your hosts and yourself.

Guided Tours

Many visitors arrive on tour packages prearranged in Hanoi but there are a couple of standout local operators in town that are well worth looking into.

As well as hiking tours, many companies offer more culturally focused trips such as community-based tours to the nearby Hmong village of **Sin Chai**, with an overnight in the village to learn about textiles or music. Other popular communities to visit include the Giay village of **Ta Van** and the Hmong village of **Matra**.

Excellent local company **Sapa O'Chau** (☎020-377 1166; www.sapaochau.com; 8 Đ Thac Bac; ⊙6.30am-6.30pm) ✍ offers day walks, longer homestay treks, Bac Ha market trips and Fanispan hikes. It also runs culturally immersive tours that focus on handicrafts and farmstays. Profits provide training to Hmong children in a learning centre.

Run by a group of savvy and knowledgeable Hmong women, **Sapa Sisters** (☎0203-773 388; www.sapasisters.com; Sapa Graceful Hotel, 9 Đ Phan Si; ⊙8am-5pm) offers fully

Children riding water buffalo

customised private day hikes and longer village homestay treks. Excellent English is spoken, and some French, Spanish and Japanese.

Hikes

Cat Cat

The nearest village within walking distance is **Cat Cat** (40,000d), 3km south of Sapa. It's a steep and beautiful hike down, and there are plenty of *xe om* (motorbike taxis) for the return uphill journey.

Sa Seng & Hang Da

For spectacular valley views (if the mist and cloud gods relent), there's a beautiful hike along a high ridge east of Sapa through the Black Hmong settlements of Sa Seng and Hang Da down to the Ta Van River, where you can get transport back to Sapa.

DANIEL WILLIAM/SHUTTERSTOCK ©

Ta Phin

A very popular hike from Sapa is to **Ta Phin village** (admission 20,000d), home to Red Dzao and about 10km from Sapa. Most people take a *xe om* to a starting point about 8km from Sapa, and then make a 14km loop through the area, passing through Black Hmong and Red Dzao villages.

Fansipan

Surrounding Sapa are the **Hoang Lien Mountains**, dubbed the Tonkinese Alps by the French. These mountains include the often cloud-obscured Fansipan (3143m), Vietnam's highest peak. Fansipan is accessible year-round to sensibly equipped trekkers in good shape, but don't under-estimate the challenge. It is very wet, and can be perilously slippery and generally cold.

The summit of Fansipan is 19km by foot from Sapa. The terrain is rough and adverse weather is frequent. The round trip usually takes three days; some experienced hikers do it in two days, but you'll need to be fit. After walking through hill-tribe villages on the first morning, it's just forest, mountain vistas and occasional wildlife, including monkeys, mountain goats and birds.

Weather-wise the best time to visit is from mid-October to mid-December, and in March, when wild flowers are in bloom. Don't attempt an ascent if Sapa's weather is poor, as limited visibility on Fansipan can be treacherous.

Fansipan's wild, lonesome beauty has been somewhat shattered with the opening of a 6282m-long cable car, taking people across the Muong Hoa Valley and up to the summit in 15 minutes.

◎ SIGHTS

Sapa Museum
Museum

(103 P Cau May; ⊙7.30-11.30am & 1.30-5pm)
FREE Excellent showcase of the history and ethnology of the Sapa area, including the colonial times of the French. Dusty exhibitions demonstrate the differences between the various ethnic minority people of the area, so it's definitely worth a quick visit when you first arrive in town, even if some descriptions are too faded to read. Behind Sapa Tourism.

Sapa Market
Market

(Đ Ngu Chi Son; ⊙6am-2pm) Unfortunately turfed out of central Sapa, and now in a purpose-built modern building near the bus station, Sapa Market is still a hive of colourful activity outside with fresh produce, a butcher's section not for the squeamish and hill-tribe people from surrounding villages heading here most days to sell handicrafts. Saturday is the busiest day.

Tram Ton Pass
Viewpoint

The road between Sapa and Lai Chau crosses the Tram Ton Pass on the northern side of Fansipan, 15km from Sapa. At 1900m this is Vietnam's highest mountain pass, and acts as a dividing line between two weather fronts. The lookout points here have fantastic views. Most people also stop at 100m-high **Thac Bac** (Silver Waterfall), 12km from Sapa.

On the Sapa side, it's often cold and foggy, but drop a few hundred metres onto the Lai Chau side, and it can be sunny and warm. Surprisingly, Sapa is the coldest place in Vietnam, but Lai Chau can be one of the warmest.

❸ ACTIVITIES

Indigo Cat
Crafts

(☏0982-403 647; www.facebook.com/indigo-catsapa; 46 Đ Phan Si; class 100,000-200,000d; ⊙9am-7pm) Craft shop Indigo Cat runs afternoon workshops where you can learn traditional Hmong weaving and embroidery skills. Workshops take place in the village of Ta Ven. Call into the lovely Sapa shop for details.

Hill Station Signature Restaurant
Cooking

(☏0203-887 112; 37 Đ Phan Si; per person US$29; ⊙from 9am) Excellent three-hour cooking classes with an English-speaking Hmong chef starting with a 30-minute market tour and featuring five local dishes, including homemade tofu, smoked buffalo and Hmong-style black pudding, as well as tasting local rice wine. Book the evening before.

👍 A Hmong Future

Inherent in Sapa's burgeoning prosperity is cultural change for the hill-tribe people.

Traditionally, the Hmong have been employees of Vietnamese-owned trekking companies, restaurants and accommodation, with many Hmong children kept out of school to sell handicrafts or act as trekking guides, often walking up to 10km daily from their villages to Sapa to earn money. A new generation, though, is now focused on securing a more independent and positive future for their people.

Sapa O'Chau (p86), meaning 'thank you Sapa' in the Hmong language, is focused on providing training and opportunities to Hmong children. The organisation is run by former handicraft peddler Shu Tan, who created the Sapa O'Chau Learning Centre, a live-in school where up to 20 Hmong children can learn English and Vietnamese. The organisation also runs excellent walks and treks.

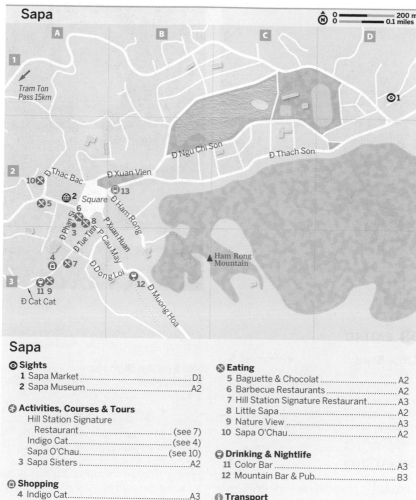

Sapa

◉ **Sights**
1 Sapa Market D1
2 Sapa Museum A2

⊕ **Activities, Courses & Tours**
Hill Station Signature
Restaurant .... (see 7)
Indigo Cat .... (see 4)
Sapa O'Chau .... (see 10)
3 Sapa Sisters A2

⬢ **Shopping**
4 Indigo Cat A3

⊗ **Eating**
5 Baguette & Chocolat A2
6 Barbecue Restaurants A2
7 Hill Station Signature Restaurant A3
8 Little Sapa A2
9 Nature View A3
10 Sapa O'Chau A2

◉ **Drinking & Nightlife**
11 Color Bar A3
12 Mountain Bar & Pub B3

ⓘ **Transport**
13 Minibuses to Lao Cai B2

⬢ SHOPPING

Indigo Cat   Arts & Crafts

(www.facebook.com/indigocatsapa; 46 Đ
Phan Si; ⊚9am-7pm) This Hmong-owned
handicrafts shop offers a wonderful
selection of interesting local crafts,
including bags, clothing, pillows and belts.

Many items have hip design touches
unique to the store and the set-price labels
can be a real relief if you have haggling
fatigue.

Co-owner Pang speaks good English and
her little kids are real charmers.

From left: Hmong woman carrying basket; Traditional Hmong embroidery; Thac Bac (Silver Waterfall; p88)

🌀 EATING

Little Sapa
Vietnamese $
(18 P Cau May; meals 50,000-80,000d; ⏰8am-10pm; 🛜✏️) One of the better-value eateries along touristy P Cau May, Little Sapa also lures in locals. Steer clear of the largely mediocre European dishes and concentrate on the Vietnamese menu.

Sapa O'Chau
Cafe $
(www.sapaochau.org; 8 Đ Thac Bac; snacks from 20,000d; ⏰6.30am-6.30pm; 🛜) 🍃 Don't miss warming up with a cup of ginger tea sweetened with Sapa mountain honey at this simple cafe attached to the Sapa O'Chau tour company. Also does good breakfasts and a few simple snacks.

Barbecue Restaurants
Vietnamese $
(Đ Phan Si; meals around 70,000-120,000d; ⏰noon-11pm) Several easygoing spots along the northern end of Đ Phan Si specialise in grilled meat and vegetables. Pull up a pew at one of the simple tables and tuck in.

Hill Station Signature Restaurant
Vietnamese $$
(www.thehillstation.com; 37 Đ Phan Si; meals 60,000-180,000d; ⏰7am-11pm; ❄️🛜✏️) A showcase of Hmong cuisine with cool Zen decor and superb views. Dishes include flash-cooked pork with lime, ash-baked trout in banana leaves, and traditional Hmong-style black pudding. Tasting sets of local rice and corn wine are also of interest to curious travelling foodies. Don't miss trying the delicate rainbow-trout ricepaper rolls; think of them as 'Sapa sushi'.

Nature View
Vietnamese $$
(51 Đ Phan Si; meals 90,000-150,000d; ⏰8am-10pm; 🛜✏️) You've got to love the photos of the owner's kids on the walls at this friendly spot with great valley views. Look forward to decent Vietnamese and European food and just maybe Sapa's best fruit smooth-

ies. Those who aren't fans of tofu should try the sizzling tofu with lemongrass and be converted. Don't worry – it's not all vegetarian food.

Baguette & Chocolat Cafe $$

(☎020-387 1766; Đ Thac Bac; cakes from 30,000d, snacks & meals 70,000-160,000d; ⊙7am-10pm; 🛜) 🍴 Head to this converted villa for a decent breakfast, baguette or slab of lemon tart. Many of the staff are students at the Hoa Sua School for disadvantaged youth and are being trained in the cooking and hospitality industry.

🍷 DRINKING & NIGHTLIFE

Mountain Bar & Pub Bar

(2 Đ Muong Hoa; ⊙noon-11pm; 🛜) Dangerously strong cocktails, cold beer and ultra-competitive games of table football

conspire to make this Sapa's go-to place for a great night out. Even if it's freezing outside, a *shisha* beside the open fire will soon perk up the chilliest of travellers. Try the warm apple wine for some highland bliss.

Color Bar Bar

(www.facebook.com/colorbar; 56 Đ Phan Si; ⊙noon-11pm; 🛜) Owned by a Hanoi artist, this atmospheric spot ticks all the boxes with reggae, table football, *shisha* and ice-cold Bia Lao Cai. A great refuelling option on the steep walk up from Cat Cat village.

ℹ️ GETTING THERE & AWAY

The gateway to Sapa is Lao Cai, 38km away. Minibuses (30,000d, 30 minutes) leave every half-hour between 6am and 6pm, from a bus stop near Sapa Church.

PHONG NHA-KE BANG
NATIONAL PARK

Phong Nha-Ke Bang National Park at a Glance...

Designated a Unesco World Heritage site, the remarkable Phong Nha-Ke Bang National Park contains the oldest karst mountains in Asia. Riddled with hundreds of cave systems – many of extraordinary scale and length – and spectacular underground rivers, Phong Nha is a speleologists' heaven on earth.

Above the ground, most of the mountainous 885 sq km of Phong Nha-Ke Bang National Park is near-pristine tropical evergreen jungle, more than 90% of which is primary forest.

Phong Nha-Ke Bang National Park in One Day

Book ahead for an early morning tour of stunning **Paradise Cave** (p98), part of a simply colossal cave system. In the afternoon head over to **Hang Toi** (p100) for more caving shenanigans, this time with the added bonus of zip-lining, kayaking, swimming and a mud bath. In the evening, chill at **Bamboo Cafe** (p100) in Son Trach.

Phong Nha-Ke Bang National Park in Two Days

Book ahead for a terrific one-day tour of **Tu Lan** (p98), run exclusively by Oxalis in Son Trach. The trip includes an early start, then some jungle trekking past karst mountains, spectacular swimming through a wonderful river cave and a barbecue lunch beside a waterfall. In the evening enjoy a relaxed meal at the snappily named **The Best Spit Roast Pork & Noodle Shop in the World (probably...)** (p100).

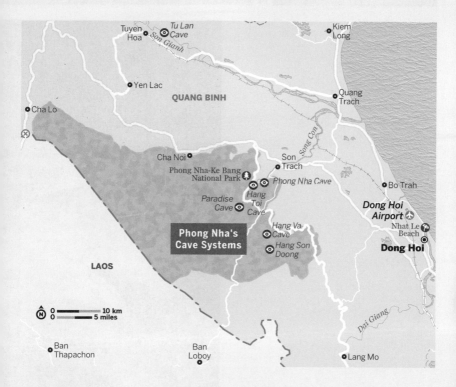

Tuyen Hoa
Tu Lan Cave
Son Gianh
Kiem Long

Yen Lac

QUANG BINH

Quang Trach

Cha Lo

Cha Noi

Son Trach

Phong Nha-Ke Bang National Park
Phong Nha Cave

Bo Trah

Song Con

Paradise Cave
Hang Toi Cave

Dong Hoi Airport

Nhat Le Beach

Phong Nha's Cave Systems

Hang Va Cave

Dong Hoi

Hang Son Doong

LAOS

N
0 ——— 10 km
0 ——— 5 miles

Dat Giang

Ban Thapachon

Ban Loboy

Lang Mo

Arriving in Phong Nha-Ke Bang National Park

The coastal town of Dong Hoi is the main gateway to both Phong Nha and Son Trach town, and has the nearest airport and train station.

Hotels organise lifts in private cars to/ from Dong Hoi (500,000d).

Where to Stay

Son Trach town has simple local hotels (all charging around 350,000d) and a few midrange options but no luxury places.

Other hotels and guesthouses are scattered in the countryside around Son Trach.

Some travellers base themselves in Dong Hoi and travel to Phong Nha on day trips.

Paradise Cave (p98)

Phong Nha's Cave Systems

Serious exploration of this extraordinary national park only began in the 1990s. Since then some astonishing cave systems have been discovered, including the world's largest cave: Hang Son Doong.

Great For...

🛈 **Need to Know**

Officially you are not allowed to hike inside the national park without a licensed tour operator.

★ **Top Tip**
Overnight caving tours for Tu Lan and
Hang Va should be booked in advance.

DUDAREV MIKHAIL/SHUTTERSTOCK ©

Tu Lan Cave

The Tu Lan cave trip begins with a country-side hike then a swim (with headlamps and life jackets) through two spectacular river caves before emerging in an idyllic valley. Then there's more hiking through dense forest to a 'beach' where rivers merge that's an ideal campsite. There's more wonderful swimming here in vast caverns. Moderate fitness levels are necessary. Tu Lan is 65km north of Son Trach and can only be visited on a guided tour.

Hang Toi

Incorporating an above-water zipline, followed by a swim into the cave, and then exploration of a pitch-black passageway of oozing mud, it's little wonder Hang Toi (Dark Cave) is the cave experience you may have already heard about from other travellers. Upon exiting the cave, a leisurely kayak paddle heads to a jetty where there are more into-the-water zipline thrills to be had.

Hang Toi can be visited independently or on the Farmstay's National Park Tour (p100).

Paradise Cave

Surrounded by forested karst peaks, this remarkable cave system extends for 31km, though most people only visit the first kilometre. The scale is breathtaking, as wooden staircases descend into a cathedral-like space with colossal stalag-mites and glimmering stalactites.

Get here early to beat the crowds, as during peak times (early afternoon), tour guides shepherd groups using megaphones. Paradise Cave is about 14km southwest of Son Trach. Electric buggies (per person one way/return

15,000/25,000d) ferry visitors from the car park to the entrance.

To explore deep inside Paradise Cave, consider booking Phong Nha Farm-stay's (p100) 7km Paradise Cave tour (2,650,000d, minimum two people), which includes a swim through an underground river and lunch under a light shaft.

Phong Nha Cave & Boat Trip

The spectacular boat trip through Phong Nha Cave is an enjoyable, though touristy, experience beginning in Son Trach village. Boats cruise along past buffalo, limestone peaks and church steeples to the cave's gaping mouth. The engine is then cut and the boats are negotiated silently through cavern after garishly illuminated cavern.

On the return leg there's the option to climb (via 330 steps) up to the mountain-

Hang Son Doong

✕ Take a Break

After a tiring day exploring the caves, relax at the very local Pub with Cold Beer (p101).

side Tien Son Cave (80,000d) to see the remains of 9th-century Cham altars.

Hang Va

Discovered in 2012, and opened to visitors in 2015, Hang Va is explored on a two-day/one-night excursion that travels firstly along an underground river in Hang Nuoc Nut.

Tours overnight in a jungle camp at the entrance to Hang Va, where the cave's highlight is a spectacular stalagmite field partly submerged in crystalline waters. Ropes and harnesses are used extensively.

Hang Son Doong

Ho Khanh, a hunter, stumbled across gargantuan Hang Son Doong (Mountain River Cave) in the early 1990s, but the sheer scale and majesty of the principal cavern (more than 5km long, 200m high and, in some places, 150m wide) was only confirmed as the world's biggest cave when British explorers returned with him in 2009.

Hang Son Doong is one of the most spectacular sights in Southeast Asia (some stalagmites are up to 80m high). The only specialist operator permitted to lead tours here is Son Trach-based Oxalis (p100).

Son Doong is no day-trip destination; it's in an extremely remote area and the only way to visit is by booking a seven-day expedition, costing US$3000 per person.

Son Trach

TOURS

Oxalis Adventure Tours Adventure
(☑091-990 0423; www.oxalis.com.vn; Son
Trach) Oxalis are unquestionably *the*
experts in caving and trekking expeditions,
and are the only outfit licensed to conduct
tours to Hang Son Doong. Staff are all
fluent English speakers, and trained by
world-renowned British cavers Howard
and Deb Limbert. All excursions, from day
trips to Tu Lan to week-long expeditions to
the world's largest cave, are meticulously
planned and employ local guides and
porters, so the wider community benefits.
You can discuss trips at their riverside
Expedition Cafe.

Prebooking Son Doong for the following
year is essential and, if possible, booking a
few months ahead for expeditions in Tu Lan
is recommended to avoid disappointment.

**Phong Nha
Farmstay Tours** Adventure
(☑052-367 5135; www.phong-nha-cave.com; Cu
Nam) The Farmstay can book cave tours –
in conjunction with Oxalis – but equally
interesting is bouncing in a US jeep or
Russian Ural motorbike and sidecar exploring the area's scenery and war history.
The Farmstay's popular National Park Tour
(per person 1,450,000d) travels by minibus
to incorporate the Ho Chi Minh Trail with
Paradise Cave and **Hang Toi** (Dark Cave; per
person 350,000d).

Jungle Boss Trekking Hiking
(☑094-374 8041; www.junglebosshomestay.com;
Phong Nha village, Son Trach; per person US$75)
Originally from the DMZ, Dzung – aka 'Jungle Boss' – has been in Phong Nha for eight
years, and is an experienced guide to the
area. He speaks excellent English and runs
an exciting one-day tour around the Ho
Chi Minh Trail and the remote Abandoned
Valley area of the national park. You'll need
moderate to high fitness levels.

**Hai's Eco
Conservation Tour** Hiking
(☑096-260 6844; www.phong-nha-bamboo-cafe.
com; per person 1,300,000d) Interesting day
tours combining hiking in the jungle – you'll
need to be relatively fit – with a visit to
Phong Nha's Wildlife Rescue and Rehabilitation Centre, which rehabilitates rescued
animals (mainly macaques from nearby
regions, but also snakes and birds). Prices
include a barbecue lunch, and there's an
opportunity to cool off at the end of the day
in a natural swimming hole. Hai is usually at
his Bamboo Cafe in the evenings.

Thang's Phong Nha Riders Tours
(www.easytigerhostel.com/thangs-phong-nha-
riders; beside Easy Tiger) A day's hire of a bike
and driver is around 400,000d; they're well
versed in the sights of Phong Nha-Ke Bang
National Park, and you'll be providing work
for enthusiastic locals with basic English.
Thang's can also arrange motorbike transfers through absolutely stunning scenery to
Hue or Khe Sanh.

EATING

Bamboo Cafe Cafe $
(www.phong-nha-bamboo-cafe.com; Son Trach;
meals 35,000-80,000d; ☺7am-10.30pm; 🛜☑)
This laid-back haven on Son Trach's main
drag has colourful decor, a cool outside
deck, and well-priced food and drink, including excellent fresh-fruit smoothies and
varied vegetarian options. It's also where
you'll usually find the friendly Hai who runs
eco conservation tours.

**The Best Spit Roast Pork
& Noodle Shop in the
World (probably...)** Vietnamese $
(Son Trach; meals 30,000-50,000d; ☺7am-4pm)
Also probably the longest name of any res-
taurant in Vietnam, serving excellent grilled
pork paired with noodles, baguettes or rice.
Get ready to smell this place well before
you see it as you're wandering Son Trach's
sleepy main street.

Mountain
Goat Restaurant   Vietnamese $$
(Son Trach; goat from 150,000d; ◷11am-9pm)
Dine on grilled and steamed *de* (goat) – try
the goat with lemongrass – at this riverside
spot in Son Trach. Other options include
spicy chicken and ice-cold beer. From the
Phong Nha Cave boat station, walk 150m
along the river, just past the church.

🍷 DRINKING & NIGHTLIFE

Pub with Cold Beer   Barbecue, Bar
(Bong Lai valley; beer 20,000d, meals from
50,000d; ◷8am–8pm) Up a dirt track in the
middle of nowhere (but well signposted),
this excellent barn-cum-bar is owned by a
local farming family and does what it says
on the tin – the beer is ice cold. Hungry?
Order roast chicken with peanut sauce
(all ingredients are farm-fresh). A kilo of
perfectly grilled chicken is 200,000d.

Jungle Bar   Bar
(Son Trach; ◷7am-midnight; 📶) The in-house
bar/cafe at Easy Tiger is the most happening place in Son Trach, with cheap beer,
pool tables, and live music four nights a

week. Add to the growing display of national flags if you're feeling patriotic. There's
loads of local information on hand, even if
you're not staying at **Easy Tiger** (📞052-367
7844; www.easytigerphongnha.com; Son Trach;
dm 160,000d; ✳@📶♨).

ℹ INFORMATION

Hai at the Bamboo Cafe is a superb source of
independent travel information, and the helpful
staff at the Phong Nha Farmstay and Easy Tiger
can assist with tours, information and transport.

ℹ GETTING THERE & AWAY

Son Trach town is 50km northwest of Dong Hoi.
Phong Nha-Ke Bang National Park abuts Son
Trach. Hotels can organise cars from Dong Hoi
(500,000d).

ℹ GETTING AROUND

Motorcycling around the national park is not recommended for inexperienced drivers – the area
is not well signposted. Bicycling is recommended
to explore Phong Nha's rural back roads; Easy
Tiger rent bikes and can supply a handy map.

Ferns inside Hang Son Doong (p99)

Palace gate, Hue Citadel (p106)

HUE

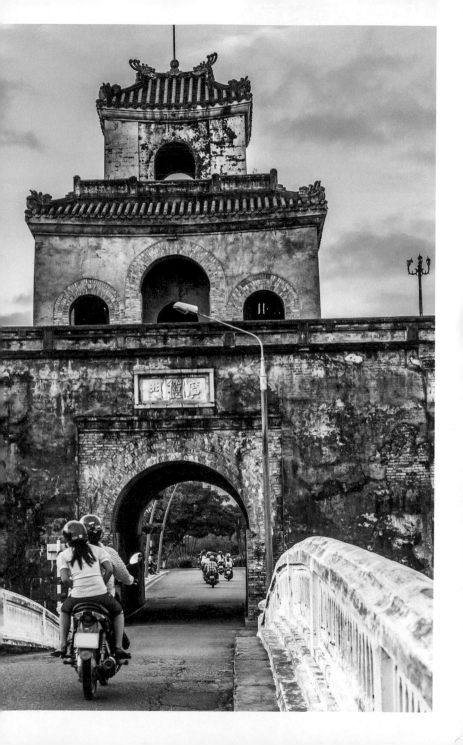

Hue at a Glance...

Pronounced 'hway', this deeply evocative capital of the Nguyen emperors still resonates with the glories of imperial Vietnam, even though many of its finest buildings were destroyed during the American War. Hue owes its charm partly to its location on the Perfume River – picturesque on a clear day, atmospheric even in less flattering weather.

Today the city blends new and old as sleek modern hotels tower over crumbling Citadel walls. A few touts are a minor hassle, but Hue remains a tranquil, conservative city, and only a few bars open late.

Hue in One Day

Head straight for the **Imperial Enclosure** (p106) taking in key temples such as **Thai To Mieu Temple Complex** (p110) and important sights like the **Halls of the Mandarins** (p109). In the late afternoon, wander the lanes off Đ Hung Vuong and enjoy a sundowner at **Sirius** (p121).

Hue in Two Days

On day two, book a Perfume River tour to the impressive emperors' tombs and pagodas. Return to town to browse boutiques such as **Spiral Foundation Healing the Wounded Heart Center** (p117) before a memorable dinner at **Les Jardins de la Carambole** (p120).

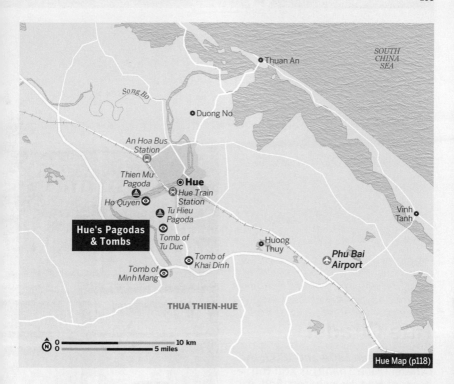

SOUTH
CHINA
SEA

Thuan An

Song Bo

Duong No

An Hoa Bus
Station

Thien Mu
Pagoda

Hue

Hue Train
Station

Ho Quyen

Tu Hieu
Pagoda

Vinh
Tanh

**Hue's Pagodas
& Tombs**

Tomb of
Tu Duc

Huong
Thuy

*Phu Bai
Airport*

Tomb of
Khai Dinh

Tomb of
Minh Mang

THUA THIEN-HUE

0   10 km
0   5 miles

Ⓝ

Hue Map (p118)

Arriving in Hue

Hue's Phu Bai Airport is 14km south of the city. Metered taxis cost about 220,000d to the centre.

The main bus station, 4km southeast of the centre, has connections south to Danang (for Hoi An). An Hoa bus station serves northern destinations.

The Hue train station is at the south-western end of Đ Le Loi.

Where to Stay

The main hotel enclave is between Đ Le Loi and Đ Vo Thi Sau, and other good options are along Đ Nguyen Cong Tru. You'll also find luxury hotels on the beach, around 7km east of the centre, and on the western fringes of town.

Hue Citadel

Built between 1804 and 1833, the Citadel (Kinh Thanh) is still the heart of Hue. Heavily fortified, it consists of 2m-thick, 10km-long walls, a moat and 10 gateways.

Great For...

🛈 Need to Know

Imperial Enclosure (adult/child 150,000/30,000d; ⊙7am-5.30pm)

★ **Top Tip**
Note that if you're planning on also visiting the royal tombs, combination tickets including the Citadel and the tombs are available.

Imperial Enclosure

The Imperial Enclosure is a citadel-within-a-citadel, housing the emperor's residence, temples and palaces and the main buildings of state within 6m-high, 2.5km-long walls. What's left is only a fraction of the original – the enclosure was badly bombed during the French and American wars, and only 20 of its 148 buildings survived. This is a fascinating site easily worth half a day, but poor signage can make navigation a bit difficult. Restoration and reconstruction is ongoing.

Expect a lot of broken masonry, rubble, cracked tiling and weeds as you work your way around. Nevertheless it's enjoyable as a leisurely stroll and some of the less-visited areas are highly atmospheric. There are little cafes and souvenir stands dotted around.

It's best to approach the sights starting from Ngo Mon Gate and moving anti-clockwise around the enclosure.

Ngo Mon Gate

The principal entrance to the Imperial Enclosure is Ngo Mon Gate, which faces the Flag Tower. The central passageway with its yellow doors was reserved for the use of the emperor, as was the bridge across the lotus pond. Others had to use the gates to either side and the paths around the pond. On top of the gate is Ngu Phung (Belvedere of the Five Phoenixes); on its upper level is a huge drum and bell.

Red lacquered doors, Hue Citadel

The emperor appeared here on important occasions, most notably for the promulgation of the lunar calendar. On 30 August 1945, the Nguyen dynasty ended here when Emperor Bao Dai abdicated to a delegation sent by Ho Chi Minh.

Thai Hoa Palace

This **palace** (Palace of Supreme Harmony; 1803) is a spacious hall with an ornate timber roof supported by 80 carved and lacquered columns. It was used for the emperor's official receptions and important ceremonies. On state occasions the emperor sat on his

> ☑ **Don't Miss**
>
> The impressive audiovisual display in the Thai Hoa Palace, which gives excellent historical context.

CESTFOU PHOTOGRAPHY/500PX ©

elevated throne, facing visitors entering via the Ngo Mon Gate. No photos are permitted, but be sure to see the audiovisual display for a comprehensive overview of the entire Citadel, its architecture and the historical context.

Halls of the Mandarins

Located immediately behind Thai Hoa Palace, on either side of a courtyard, these halls were used by mandarins as offices and to prepare for court ceremonies.

The hall on the right showcases fascinating old photographs (including boy-king Vua Duya Tan's coronation), gilded Buddha statues and assorted imperial curios. Behind the courtyard are the ruins of the Can Chanh Palace, where two wonderful long galleries, painted in gleaming scarlet lacquer, have been reconstructed.

Emperor's Reading Room

The exquisite (though crumbling) little two-storey **Emperor's Reading Room** (Royal Library; Thai Binh Lau) was the only part of the Forbidden Purple City to escape damage during the French reoccupation of Hue in 1947.

The Gaudi-esque, yin-yang roof mosaics outside are in stark contrast to the sombre, recently renovated interior, the circular hallway of which you can now walk around on the small ground level.

The exterior features poems by Emperor Khai Dinh on either side, and three Chinese characters that translate as 'Emperor's Reading Room'.

> ✕ **Take a Break**
>
> There are snack stands inside the Citadel, or for a meal head to Hong Mai (p119).

Royal Theatre

The **Royal Theatre** (Duyen Thi Duong; ☏054-351 4989; www.nhanhac.com.vn; performances 50,000d-100,000d; ⊘performances 9am, 10am, 2.30pm & 3.30pm), begun in 1826 and later home to the National Conservatory of Music, has been rebuilt on its former foundations. Cultural performances here last 45 minutes.

Southeast of here almost nothing remains of the **Thai To Mieu temple complex** (it's now a plant nursery) and former University of Arts.

Co Ha Gardens

Occupying the northeast corner of the Imperial Enclosure, these delightful **gardens** (Royal Gardens) were developed by the first four emperors of the Nguyen dynasty but fell into disrepair. They've been beautifully recreated in the last few years, and are dotted with little gazebo-style pavilions and ponds. This is one of the most peaceful spots in the entire Citadel.

The latest section to be discovered, excavated and restored was due for completion in early 2017.

Forbidden Purple City

In the very centre of the Imperial Enclosure, there's almost nothing left of the once-magnificent **Forbidden Purple City** (Tu Cam Thanh). This citadel was reserved solely for the personal use of the emperor – the only servants allowed into this compound were eunuchs who would pose no threat to the royal concubines.

The Forbidden Purple City was almost entirely destroyed in the wars, and its crumbling remains are now overgrown with weeds.

Dien Tho Residence

The stunning, partially ruined Dien Tho Residence (1804) once comprised the apartments and audience hall of the Queen Mothers of the Nguyen dynasty.

The audience hall houses an exhibition of photos illustrating its former use, and there is a display of embroidered royal garments.

To Mieu Temple Complex

Taking up the southwest corner of the Imperial Enclosure, this highly impressive walled complex has been beautifully restored.

The imposing three-tiered **Hien Lam Pavilion** sits on the south side of the complex; it dates from 1824. On the other side of a courtyard is the solemn **To Mieu Temple**, housing shrines to each of the emperors, topped by their photos. Between these two temples are **Nine Dynastic Urns** (dinh), cast between 1835 and 1836, each dedicated to one Nguyen sovereign.

Dragon detail over gateway, Hue Citadel

About 2m in height and weighing 1900kg to 2600kg each, the urns symbolise the power and stability of the Nguyen throne. The central urn, also the largest and most ornate, is dedicated to dynasty founder Gia Long.

Also in the courtyard are two dragons, trapped in what look like red phone boxes.

On the north side of the complex, a gate leads into a small walled enclosure that houses the **Hung To Mieu Temple**, a reconstruction of the 1804 original, built to honour Gia Long's parents.

Nine Holy Cannons

Located just inside the Citadel ramparts, near the gates to either side of the Flag Tower, are the Nine Holy Cannons (1804),
symbolic protectors of the palace and kingdom. Commissioned by Emperor Gia Long, they were never intended to be fired.

The four cannons near **Ngan Gate** represent the four seasons, while the five cannons next to **Quang Duc Gate** represent the five elements: metal, wood, water, fire and earth.

Each brass cannon is 5m long and weighs about 10 tonnes.

✕ Take a Break

Just outside the Dien Tho Residence, a pleasure pavilion above a lily pond has been transformed into a cafe worthy of a refreshment stop.

KONSTANTIN YOLSHIN/SHUTTERSTOCK ©

Hue's Imperial Enclosure

EXPLORING THE SITE

An incongruous combination of meticulously restored palaces and pagodas, ruins and rubble, the Imperial Enclosure is approached from the south through the outer walls of the Citadel. It's best to tackle the site as a walking tour, winding your way around the structures in an anticlockwise direction.

You'll pass directly through the monumental **Ngo Mon Gateway ❶** where the ticket office is located. This dramatic approach quickens the pulse and adds to the sense of occasion as you enter this citadel-within-a-citadel. Directly ahead is the **Thai Hoa Palace ❷** where the emperor would greet offical visitors from his elevated throne. Continuing north you'll step across a small courtyard to the twin **Halls of the Mandarins ❸**, where mandarins once had their offices and prepared for ceremonial occasions.

To the northeast is the Royal Theatre, where traditional dance performances are held several times daily. Next you'll be able to get a glimpse of the Emperor's Reading Room built by Thieu Tri and used as a place of retreat. Just east of here are the lovely Co Ha Gardens. Wander their pathways, dotted with hundreds of bonsai trees and potted plants, which have been recently restored.

Guarding the far north of the complex is the Tu Vo Phuong Pavilion, from where you can follow a moat to the Truong San residence and then loop back south via the **Dien Tho Residence ❹** and finally view the beautifully restored temple compound of To Mieu, perhaps the most rewarding part of the entire enclosure to visit, including its fabulous **Nine Dynastic Urns ❺**.

TOP TIPS

Allow half a day to explore the Citadel. Drink vendors are dotted around the site, but the best places to take a break are the delightful Co Ha Gardens, the Tu Vo Phuong Pavilion and the Dien Tho Residence (the latter two also serve food).

PETER STUCKINGS / SHUTTERSTOCK ©

Dien Tho Residence
This pretty corner of the complex, with its low structures and pond, was the residence of many Queen Mothers. The earliest structures here date from 1804.

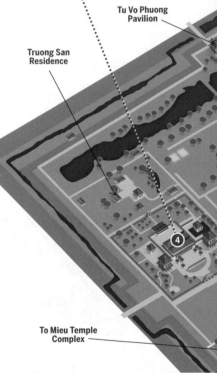

Tu Vo Phuong Pavilion

Truong San Residence

To Mieu Temple Complex

Nine Dynastic Urns
These colossal bronze urns were commissioned by Emperor Minh Mang and cast between 1835 and 1836. They're embellished with decorative elements including landscapes, rivers, flowers and animals.

LULU AND ISABELLE / SHUTTERSTOCK ©

Tu Vo Phuong Pavilion

The two-storey Tu Vo Phuong Pavilion, elevated above a moat, was once a defense bastion for the northern part of the Imperial Enclosure. It combines both European and Vietnamese architectural styles (note the elaborate roof dragons).

Halls of the Mandarins

Unesco-sponsored conservation work is ongoing in the eastern hall here to preserve the elaborate ceiling and wall murals.

MICHAEL RUNKEL / GETTY IMAGES ©

Emperor's Reading Room

Co Ha Gardens

Royal Theatre

③

②

①

⑤

Ngo Mon Gateway

A huge, grandiose structure that guards the main approach to the Imperial Enclosure, this gateway has a fortified lower level and a more architecturally elaborate upper part. It dates from 1833.

ANDERS BLOMQVIST / GETTY IMAGES ©

Thai Hoa Palace

Be sure to check out this palace's incredible ironwood columns, painted in 12 coats of brilliant scarlet and gold lacquer. The structure was saved from collapse by restoration work in the 1990s.

PETER STUCKINGS / SHUTTERSTOCK ©

Thien Mu Pagoda

RPBAIAAO/SHUTTERSTOCK ©

Hue's Pagodas & Tombs

The extravagant mausoleums of the rulers of the Nguyen dynasty (1802–1945) are spread out along the banks of the Perfume River between 2km and 16km south of the city. There are also fine pagodas and other sights.

Great For...

☑ Don't Miss

Thien Mu Pagoda has a pavilion containing a stele dating from 1715.

Thien Mu Pagoda

Built on a hill overlooking the Perfume River, 4km southwest of the Citadel, this **pagoda** is an icon of Vietnam and as potent a symbol of Hue as the Citadel. The 21m-high octagonal tower, **Thap Phuoc Duyen**, was constructed under the reign of Emperor Thieu Tri in 1844. Each of its seven storeys is dedicated to a *manushi-buddha* (a Buddha that appeared in human form). Visit in the morning before tour groups show up.

Tomb of Tu Duc

This tomb, constructed between 1864 and 1867, is the most popular and impressive of the royal mausoleums. Emperor Tu Duc designed it himself to use before and after his death. The enormous expense of the tomb and the forced labour used in its

ⓘ Need to Know

Entrance to the main sites is adult/child 100,000/20,000d per site; discounted combination tickets are also available.

✕ Take a Break

Refresh yourself with a delicious cup of Vietnamese tea at the Wounded Heart Tea Room (p121)

★ Top Tip

Many river cruises include stops at the most impressive tombs and temples.

an explosion of colourful mosaic. Khai Dinh was the penultimate emperor of Vietnam, from 1916 to 1925, and widely seen as a puppet of the French. The construction of his flamboyant tomb took 11 years. The tomb of Khai Dinh is 10km from Hue in Chau Chu village.

Ho Quyen

Wildly overgrown but evocative, **Ho Quyen** was built in 1830 for the royal pastime of watching elephants and tigers face off in combat. The tigers (and leopards) were usually relieved of their claws and teeth so that the elephants – a symbol of the emperor's power – triumphed every time. Climb up grassy ramparts and imagine the scene in the old arena – the last fight was held in 1904.

Tu Hieu Pagoda

Nestled in a pine forest, this popular **pagoda** was built in 1843 and later co-opted by eunuchs from the Citadel. Today 70 monks reside at Tu Hieu; they welcome visitors to the twin temples (one dedicated to Cong Duc, the other to Buddha). Listen to their chanting daily at 4.30am, 10am, noon, 4pm and 7pm. Tu Hieu Pagoda is about 5km from the centre of Hue, on the way to the tomb of Tu Duc.

construction spawned a coup plot that was discovered and suppressed. Tu Duc's tomb is 5km south of Hue on Van Nien Hill in Duong Xuan Thuong village.

Tomb of Minh Mang

This majestic tomb is renowned for its architecture and sublime forest setting. The tomb was planned during Minh Mang's reign (1820–40) but built by his successor, Thieu Tri. Minh Mang's tomb is in An Bang village, on the west bank of the Perfume River, 12km from Hue.

Tomb of Khai Dinh

This hillside monument is a synthesis of Vietnamese and European elements. Most of the tomb's grandiose exterior is covered in blackened concrete, creating an unexpectedly Gothic air, while the interiors resemble

◉ SIGHTS

Most of Hue's principal sights lie within the moats of its Citadel and Imperial Enclosure (p106). Other museums and pagodas are dotted around the city. The royal tombs (p114) are south of Hue. A good-value 'package tour ticket' (adult/child 360,000/70,000d) is available that includes admission to the Citadel and the tombs of Gia Long, Khai Dinh and Minh Mang (p115).

Dieu De
National Pagoda Buddhist Temple
(Quoc Tu Dieu De; 102 Đ Bach Dang) **FREE** Overlooking Dong Ba Canal, this pagoda was built under Emperor Thieu Tri's rule (1841–47) and is famous for its four low towers, one either side of the gate and two flanking the sanctuary. The pavilions on either side of the main sanctuary entrance contain the 18 La Ha, whose rank is just below that of bodhisattva, and the eight Kim Cang, protectors of Buddha. In the back row of the main dais is Thich Ca Buddha, flanked by two assistants.

Dieu De was a stronghold of Buddhist and student opposition to the South Vietnamese government and the American War, and many arrests were made here when police stormed the building in 1966.

Royal Fine Arts Museum Museum
(150 Đ Nguyen Hue; ⏰6.30am-5.30pm summer, 7am-5pm winter) **FREE** This recently renovated museum is located in the baroque-influenced An Dinh Palace, commissioned by Emperor Khai Dinh in 1918 and full of elaborate murals, floral motifs and trompe l'oeil details. Emperor Bao Dai lived here with his family after abdicating in 1945. Inside, you'll find some outstanding ceramics, paintings, furniture, silverware, porcelain and royal clothing, though information is a little lacking.

ⓕ TOURS

Many sights around Hue, including Thien Mu Pagoda and several of the royal tombs, can be reached by boat via the Perfume River.

Most hotels and travellers' cafes offer shared day tours from US$5 to US$20 per

Tomb of Tu Duc (p114)

DMITRIEVAL/SHUTTERSTOCK ©

person. Better ones start with a morning river cruise, stopping at pagodas and temples, then after lunch a minibus travels to the main tombs before returning to Hue. On the cheaper options you'll often have to hire a motorbike to get from the moorings to the tombs, or walk in tropical heat.

At the moorings on the south side of the river you can theoretically negotiate your own route. Rates for chartering a boat start at US$10 for an hour's cruise, but these boats are slow. A full day is needed for the more impressive, distant tombs. Be clear on your requirements, preferably in writing.

Cafe on Thu Wheels   Tours
(🖉054-383 2241; minhthuhue@yahoo.com; 10/2 Đ Nguyen Tri Phuong) Inexpensive cycle hire, and motorbike, minibus and car tours around Hue and the DMZ. Can also arrange transfers to Hoi An by motorbike (US$45) or car (US$55).

Hue Flavor   Food & Drink
(🖉0905-937 006; www.hueflavor.com; per person US$49) Excellent street-food tours exploring the delights of Hue cuisine. Transport is by *cyclo* and around 15 different dishes are sampled over four hours.

Tran Van Thinh   Tours
(🖉0905-731 537; tranvanthinhhue@yahoo.com) Knowledgeable motorbike guide who can arrange city tours and explorations of the royal tombs. Thinh is a long-time resident of Hue and speaks excellent English.

🔒 SHOPPING

Hue produces the finest conical hats in Vietnam. The city's speciality is 'poem hats', which, when held up to the light, reveal shadowy scenes of daily life. It's also known for its rice paper and silk paintings.

Spiral Foundation Healing the Wounded Heart Center   Arts & Crafts
(🖉054-383 3694; www.spiralfoundation.org; 23 Đ Vo Thi Sau; ⊙8am-6pm) Generating cash from trash, this shop stocks lovely

🍽 Royal Rice Cakes

These savoury Hue specialities come in different shapes and sizes, but are all made with rice flour. The most common is the crispy fried, filled crepe *banh khoai* (smaller and denser than southern Vietnam's *banh xeo* crepes). The other variations are steamed and sticky-rice-like, and are usually topped with shrimp and dipped in sweet fish sauce. Look for *banh beo*, which come in tiny dishes; banana-leaf-wrapped *banh nam*; transparent dumplings *banh loc*; and the leaf-steamed pyramids *banh it*, which can come in sweet mung-bean or savoury varieties.

Hue rice cakes
XUANHUONGHO/SHUTTERSTOCK ©

handicrafts – such as quirky bags from plastic, and picture frames from recycled beer cans – made by artists with disabilities. Profits aid heart surgery for children in need.

Blue de Hue   Antiques
(43 Đ Vo Thi Sau; ⊙7.30am-6.30pm) Well-regarded antiques store selling stonework, ceramics, lacquerware and wooden carvings.

✖ EATING

We have the famed fussy eater Emperor Tu Duc to thank for the culinary variety of Hue.

Vegetarian food has a long tradition in Hue. Stalls in Dong Ba Market serve it on the first and 15th days of the lunar month.

Hue

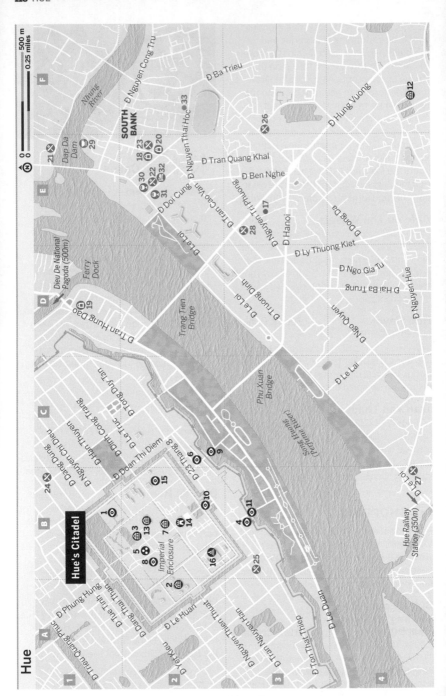

Hue's Citadel

500 m
0.25 miles

Nhung River

SOUTH BANK

Đ Nguyen Cong Tru

Đ Ba Trieu

Đ Nguyen Thai Hoc 33

26

Đ Hung Vuong

12

21
Dap Da
Dam
29
18 23
20
30
22
31 32

Đ Tran Quang Khai

Đ Ben Nghe

Đ Đoi Cung
Đ Tran Cao Van
Đ Nguyen Thai Phuong
17
28
Đ Hanoi
Đ Ly Thuong Kiet
Đ Ngo Gia Tu
Đ Hai Ba Trung
Đ Dong Da
Đ Nguyen Hue

Dieu De National
Pagoda (500m)
Ferry
Dock

19
Đ Tran Hung Dao

Trang Tien
Bridge

Đ Le Loi
Đ Truong Dinh

Đ Ngo Quyen
Đ Le Lai

Phu Xuan
Bridge

Song Huong (Perfume River)

Đ Dinh Cong Trang
Đ Le Truc
Đ Tong Duy Tan
Đ Han Thuyen
Đ Nguyen Chi Dieu

Đ Dang Dung
24
Đ Doan Thi Diem
Đ 23 Thang 8
6
15
9
10
4 11
25
16
8 5
7 14
13 3
1
2
Imperial
Enclosure

Đ Phung Hung
Đ Tue Tinh
Đ Dang Thai Than
Đ Le Kieu
Đ Nguyen Thien Han
Đ Tran Nguyen Han
Đ Le Huan
Đ Ton That Thiep
Đ Le Duan

27
Đ Le Loi
Hue Railway
Station (350m)

Hue

Hue also has great street food. Follow our recommendations or join a street-food tour with Hue Flavor.

Hang Me Me   Vietnamese $

(16 Đ Vo Thi Sau; meals from 40,000d; ⊙8am-11pm; ⋑) A top, unfussy spot to try Hue's dizzying menu of royal rice cakes. Serving portions are pretty big, so rustle up a few friends to try the different variations. Our favourite is the *banh beo*, perfect little mouthfuls topped with spring onions and dried shrimp.

Com Hen   Vietnamese $

(17 Đ Han Mac Tu; meals from 10,000d; ⊙7am-11pm) Tuck into bowls of rice *(com hen)* or noodles *(bun hen)* combining fresh herbs and tasty local clams from a nearby island in the middle of the Perfume River. Servings are fairly small, so maybe have a bowl of each.

Lien Hoa   Vegetarian $

(⊉054-381 2456; 3 Đ Le Quy Don; meals 50,000-75,000d; ⊙6.30am-9pm; ⋑) No-nonsense Viet vegetarian restaurant renowned for filling food at bargain prices. Fresh *banh beo*,

noodle dishes, crispy fried jackfruit and aubergine with ginger all deliver. The menu has very rough English translations to help you order (staff speak little or no English).

Hong Mai   Vietnamese $

(110 Đ Dinh Tien Toang; snacks from 20,000d; ⊙11am-8pm) After you've admired the Citadel, make your way to this excellent Vietnamese eatery for superior versions of two local street-food classics. The *banh khoai* (rice crepes filled with pork and shrimp) are light and crammed with bean sprouts, and the *nem lui* (minced pork grilled on lemongrass sticks) go perfectly with a chilled Huda lager.

Quan Thai Phu   Vietnamese $

(2 Đ Dien Bien Phu; meals 15,000-30,000d; ⊙9am-9pm) Our favourite spot for Hue's famous *bun thit nuong* – grilled pork with vermicelli and a forest of fresh herbs. Don't forget a dollop of the special peanut sauce.

Gecko Pub   Cafe $$

(9 Đ Pham Ngu Lao; meals 30,000-110,000d; ⊙8am-midnight; ⋑) With a laid-back vibe,

From left: *Banh beo* (p117); Bicycle loaded with vegetables; Street procession, Hue

this is our favourite of the cafes and restaurants along Pham Ngu Lao. Friendly service and Asian-chic decor combine with the best street-side tables in town, and food is a versatile mix of Western and Vietnamese favourites. Look forward to one of central Vietnam's best mojitos, too.

Ta.ke   Japanese $$
(34 Đ Tran Cao Van; meals 50,000-135,000d; ☯10.30am-10pm; ✿) An authentic Japanese restaurant with tasteful furnishings including lanterns and calligraphy, and a winsome menu with sushi, tempura and yakitori dishes. The air-conditioned interior is a calming haven away from Hue's increasingly busy streets.

Les Jardins de
la Carambole   Fusion $$
(☎054-354 8815; www.lesjardinsdelacarambole. com; 32 Đ Dang Tran Con; meals 120,000-300,000d; ☯7am-11pm; ☋) A memorable dining experience, this classy French restaurant occupies a gorgeous colonial-style building in the Citadel quarter. The menu that's majors in Gallic classics, and has a

Vietnamese set menu popular with groups. Add a lengthy wine list and informed service, and it's just the place for a romantic meal – arrive by *cyclo* and it's easy to roll back the years to Indochine times.

🍸 DRINKING & NIGHTLIFE

For an often dusty town, Hue has a very active bar, pub and club scene. Most of the action happens along Đ Pham Ngu Lao and Đ Vo Thi Sau.

Cafe Tre Nga   Cafe
(7 Đ Nguyen Cong Tru) Families, courting couples and card players all hang out at this hidden bamboo-shrouded riverside haven that's our favourite place in Hue for a *caphe sua da* (iced coffee with milk). Walk down the lane off Đ Nguyen Cong Tru past the art galleries to find the cafe.

DMZ Travel   Bar
(www.dmz.com.vn; 60 Đ Le Loi; ☯7am-1am; ☋) Ever-popular bar near the river with a free pool table, cold Huda beer, cocktails (try a watermelon mojito) and antics most nights.

Also serves Western and local food until midnight, smoothies and juices. Happy hour is 3pm to 8pm. Check out the upside-down map of the DMZ – complete with a US chopper – on the ceiling of the bar.

Wounded Heart
Tea Room   Teahouse

(www.hwhshop.com; 23 Đ Vo Thi Sau; tea 40,000d; ☉8am-6pm) Attached to a fair-trade gift shop, this little place specialises in Vietnamese tea (including jasmine, ginger and oolong), but it will also rustle up a coffee. Complimentary snacks are served with your drink.

Sirius   Bar

(www.moonlighthue.com; 20 Đ Pham Ngu Lao; ☉10am-10pm) Outdoors, on the 15th floor of the Moonlight Hotel, Sirius is the best place in town for sunset drinks. Combine barbecue snacks (beef, squid, prawns; from 55,000d) and a few beers or a cocktail, and view the arrival of dusk on the Perfume River.

❶ INFORMATION

The Sinh Tourist (☎054-384 5022; www.thesinh tourist.vn; 37 Đ Nguyen Thai Hoc; ☉6.30am-10pm) Books Open-Tour buses, and buses to Laos and many other destinations in Vietnam.

❶ GETTING THERE & AROUND

There are several daily flights to both Hanoi and Ho Chi Minh City.

For Phong Nha (around 120,000d, five hours), the Hung Thanh Open-Tour bus leaves 49 Đ Chu Van An at 4.30pm, and the Tan Nha bus leaves from the Why Not? bar on Đ Vo Thi Sau around 6.30am.

Hotels rent bicycles for around US$3 per day, motorbikes from US$5 and a car with driver from US$50. Traffic around Hue can be busy, especially on the bridges crossing the river, so take care when cycling.

HOI AN

Hoi An at a Glance...

Graceful, historic Hoi An is Vietnam's most atmospheric and delightful town. Once a major port, it features the grand architecture and beguiling riverside setting that befits its heritage, but the 21st-century curses of traffic and pollution are almost entirely absent.

The Old Town boasts an incredible legacy of tottering Japanese merchant houses, Chinese temples and ancient tea warehouses. Travel a few kilometres further – you'll find some superb bicycle, motorbike and boat trips – and some of central Vietnam's most enticingly laid-back scenery and beaches are within easy reach.

Hoi An in Two Days

Spend the entire day in the **Old Town**, taking in its remarkable sights including the emblematic **Japanese Covered Bridge** (p129), **Assembly Hall of the Fujian Chinese Congregation** (p129) and **Tan Ky House** (p130). On day two book a bicycle, scooter or motorbike tour to explore the glorious hinterland around Hoi An, hit the beach at **An Bang** then eat at **Morning Glory** (p144).

Hoi An in Four Days

Book a morning trip to the impressive nearby Cham ruins of **My Son**, then return to Hoi An for a gorgeous lunch of local specialities at **Nu Eatery** (p144). In the afternoon, take in some of the lesser-known temples and museums. On day four, sign up for a **cooking course**, then treat yourself to a spa treatment before a memorable dinner at **Bale Well** (p143).

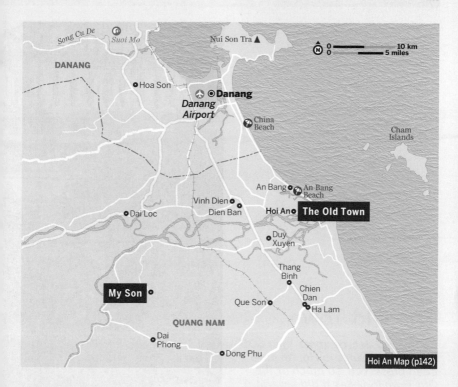

Hoi An Map (p142)

Arriving in Hoi An

Danang airport is a 45-minute drive from Hoi An; taxis charge 400,000d.
Go Travel Vietnam (p145) offers shuttle bus transfers between Hoi An and Danang (80,000d, one hour).

Very few intercity buses stop in Hoi An. Most travellers use Open-Tour buses.

The nearest train station is in Danang.

Where to Stay

Hoi An has good-value accommodation in all price categories. There are only a couple of hotels in the Old Town but many budget and midrange places are spread out to the northwest.

Many luxury hotels are a few kilometres from town by the coast but all offer shuttle-bus transfers. An Bang beach also has lots of good options.

The Old Town

By Unesco decree, more than 800 historic buildings in Hoi An have been preserved, so much of the Old Town looks as it did several centuries ago.

Great For...

Đ Phan Chu Trinh | Tran Family Chapel
Japanese Covered Bridge
Assembly Hall of the Fujian Chinese Congregation | **Quan Cong Temple**
Tan Ky House | Đ Nguyen Thai Hoc
Đ Nguyen Phuc Chu | Đ Bach Dang | *Thu Bon River*

ℹ Need to Know

An Old Town ticket (120,000d, valid 10 days) allows access to five different heritage attractions.

★ **Top Tip**
Visitors should dress modestly as some of the old houses are still private homes.

A Historic Port

From the 2nd to the 10th centuries, Hoi An was a busy seaport of the Champa kingdom. After the 15th century Hoi An – known as Faifoo to Western traders – was one of Southeast Asia's major ports. Chinese, Japanese, Dutch, Portuguese, Spanish, Indian, Filipino, Indonesian, Thai, French, British and American ships came to call, and the town's warehouses teemed with treasures: high-grade silk, fabrics, paper, porcelain, areca nuts, pepper, Chinese medicines, elephant tusks, beeswax, mother-of-pearl and lacquerware.

Japanese, Chinese & Western Influences

The Japanese ceased coming to Hoi An after 1637 (when the Japanese government forbade contact with the outside world), but the Chinese lingered. The Chinese who settled in Hoi An identified themselves according to their province of origin. Each community built its own assembly hall, known as *hoi quan* in Vietnamese, for social gatherings, meetings and celebrations.

Under French rule, Hoi An served as an administrative centre. It was virtually untouched in the American War, thanks to the cooperation of both sides. The town was declared a Unesco World Heritage site in 1999.

Surviving Architecture

The historic buildings of Hoi An not only survived the 20th century's wars, they also retained features of traditional architecture rarely seen today. As they have been for centuries, some shopfronts are shuttered

Japanese Covered Bridge

at night with horizontal planks inserted into grooves that cut into the columns that support the roof.

Some roofs are made up of thousands of brick-coloured *am* and *duong* (yin and yang) roof tiles – so called because of the way the alternating rows of concave and convex tiles fit snugly together.

A number of houses have round pieces of wood with an *am-duong* symbol in the middle surrounded by a spiral design over the doorway. These *mat cua* (door eyes) are supposed to protect the residents from harm.

Entering the Buildings
The Old Town has dozens of historic structures, of which 18 are open to visitors with an Old Town ticket.

Hoi An's historic structures are gradually being sensitively restored. Strict rules govern the colour that houses can be painted and the signs that can be used.

Japanese Covered Bridge

This beautiful little **bridge** (Cau Nhat Ban; ⏱24hr) FREE is emblematic of Hoi An. A bridge was first constructed here in the 1590s by the Japanese community to link them with the Chinese quarters. Over the centuries the ornamentation has remained relatively faithful to the original Japanese design. The French flattened out the roadway for cars, but the original arched shape was restored in 1986.

While access to the Japanese Bridge is free, you have to surrender a ticket to see a small, unimpressive temple built into the bridge's northern side. If you are challenged for simply crossing the bridge, politely explain that you are not there for the temple.

Assembly Hall of the Fujian Chinese Congregation

Originally a traditional **assembly hall** (Phuc Kien Hoi Quan; opposite 35 Đ Tran Phu; admission by Old Town ticket; ⏱7am-5.30pm) 🍃, this structure was later transformed into a temple for the worship of Thien Hau, a deity from Fujian province. The green-tiled triple gateway dates from 1975. The mural on the right-hand wall depicts Thien Hau, her way lit by lantern light as she crosses a stormy sea to rescue a foundering ship. Opposite is a mural of the heads of the six Fujian families who fled from China to Hoi An in the 17th century.

In the hall's last chamber, the central altar contains seated figures of the heads of the six Fujian families. The smaller figures below them represent their

EFIRED/SHUTTERSTOCK ©

Touring the Sites
Short guided tours of the old houses tend to be efficient, if a tad perfunctory. All four museums are small with basic displays and limited information.

successors as clan leaders. Behind the altar on the right are three fairies and smaller figures representing the 12 *ba mu* (midwives), each of whom teaches newborns a different skill necessary for the first year of life: smiling, sucking and so forth. Childless couples often come here to pray for offspring and leave fresh fruit as offerings.

Tan Ky House

Built two centuries ago by an ethnically Vietnamese family, this gem of a **house** (101 Đ Nguyen Thai Hoc; admission by Old Town ticket; ⊗8am-noon & 2-4.30pm) has been lovingly preserved through seven generations. Look out for signs of Japanese and Chinese influences on the architecture. Japanese elements include the ceiling (in the sitting area), which is supported by three progressively shorter beams, one on top of the other. Under the crab-shell ceiling are carvings of crossed sabres wrapped in silk ribbon. The sabres symbolise force, the silk represents flexibility.

The interior is brightened by a beautiful detail: Chinese poems written in inlaid mother-of-pearl hang from some of the columns that hold up the roof. The Chinese characters on these 150-year-old panels are formed entirely of birds gracefully portrayed in various positions of flight.

Tran Family Chapel

Built for worshipping family ancestors, this **chapel** (21 Đ Le Loi; admission by Old Town ticket; ⊗7.30am-noon & 2-5.30pm) dates back to 1802. It was commissioned by Tran Tu, one of the clan who ascended to the rank of mandarin and served as an ambassador to China. His picture is to the right of the chapel. The architecture of the building reflects the influence of Chinese (the 'turtle' style roof), Japanese (triple beam) and vernacular (look out for the bow-and-arrow detailing) styles.

The central door is reserved for the dead – it's opened at Tet and on 11 November, the death anniversary of the main ancestor. Traditionally, women entered from the left and men from the right, although these distinctions are no longer observed.

The wooden boxes on the altar contain the Tran ancestors' stone tablets, with chiselled Chinese characters setting out the dates of birth and death, along with some small personal effects. On the anniversary of each family member's death, their box is opened, incense is burned and food is offered.

Quan Cong Temple

Founded in 1653, this small **temple** (Chua Ong; 24 Đ Tran Phu; admission by Old Town ticket; ⊗8am-5pm) is dedicated to Quan Cong, an esteemed Chinese general who is worshipped as a symbol of loyalty, sincerity, integrity and justice. His partially gilded

Monks at Phuoc Lam Pagoda

statue, made of papier-mâché on a wooden frame, is on the central altar at the back of the sanctuary. When someone makes an offering to the portly looking Quan Cong, the caretaker solemnly strikes a bronze bowl that makes a bell-like sound.

On the left of Quan Cong is a statue of General Chau Xuong, one of his guardians, striking a tough-guy pose. On the right is the rather plump administrative mandarin Quan Binh. The life-size white horse recalls a mount ridden by Quan Cong.

Shoes should be removed when mounting the platform in front of the statue of Quan Cong.

Phuoc Lam Pagoda

This **pagoda** (Thon 2a, Cam Ha; ☺8am-5pm), founded in the mid-17th century, is associated with An Thiem, a Vietnamese prodigy

and monk from the age of eight. When he was 18, he volunteered for the army so his brothers could escape the draft; he eventually rose to the rank of general. Later he returned to the monkhood, but to atone for his sins of war he volunteered to clean the Hoi An market for 20 years, then joined this pagoda as its head monk.

Streetscapes

It's not just individual buildings that have survived in Hoi An – it's whole streetscapes, particularly around Đ Tran Phu and waterside promenade Đ Bach Dang.

The French Quarter

East of Cam Nam Bridge, there's a whole block of colonnaded houses, painted in the mustard yellow typical of French colonial buildings.

PETER STUCKINGS/SHUTTERSTOCK ©

Preparing ingredients at a Hoi An cooking school

MATT MUNRO/LONELY PLANET ©

Cooking Courses

Hoi An has become a mecca for Vietnamese cooking courses, with many restaurants offering classes. These range from a simple setup in someone's backyard to purpose-built schools.

Green Bamboo Cooking School

Directed by Van, a charming local chef and English speaker, these **courses** (📞090-581 5600; www.greenbamboo-hoian.com; 21 Đ Truong Minh Hung, Cam An; per person US$45) are more personalised than most. Groups are limited to a maximum of 10, and take place in Van's spacious kitchen. Choose what to cook from a diverse menu including vegetarian choices. It's 5km east of the centre, near Cu Dai beach, and transport from Hoi An is included.

Herbs & Spices

Excellent **classes** (📞0510-393 6868; www. herbsandspicesvn.com; 2/6 Đ Le Loi; per person US$35-59; ⏱10.30am, 4.30pm & 8pm) with three different menu options, and smaller more hands-on groups than some other cookery classes.

Great For...

☑ **Don't Miss**

Tasting the local specialities in the Old Town before trying to recreate them yourself.

Garlic, shallots and spices at a local market

MATT MUNRO/LONELY PLANET ©

visits. The half-day class focuses on local specialities, with rice-paper making and food decoration tips thrown in for good measure. The full-day class instructs participants in the fine art of *pho* (beef noodle soup).

As an added sweetener, there's a 20m swimming pool at the school. It's 4km east of the centre on the banks of the Thu Bon River.

A Hoi An Taster

Hoi An is a culinary hot bed and there are some unique dishes you should be sure to sample:

○ 'White rose' or *banh vac* is an incredibly delicate, subtly flavoured shrimp dumpling topped with crispy onions.

○ *Banh bao* is another steamed dumpling, this time with minced pork or chicken, onions, eggs and mushrooms that's said to be derived from Chinese dim sum.

○ *Cao lau* is an amazing dish – Japanese-style noodles seasoned with herbs, salad greens and bean sprouts, and served with slices of roast pork.

○ Other local specialities are fried *hoanh thanh* (wonton) and *banh xeo* (crispy savoury pancakes rolled with herbs in fresh rice paper).

Most restaurants serve these items, but quality varies widely.

Morning Glory Cooking School

This is the **cooking course** (☑0510-224 1555; www.msvy-tastevietnam.com; 106 Đ Nguyen Thai Hoc; half-day courses US$25-32) that launched Hoi An cooking courses. It's directed by Trinh Diem Vy, owner of several restaurants in town, or one of her protégés. Classes concentrate on local recipes including *cao lau* and 'white rose'. Classes can have up to 30 people and some participants feel the whole experience is a little too organised.

Red Bridge Cooking School

At this **school** (☑0510-393 3222; www.visit hoian.com/redbridge/cookingschool.html; Thon 4, Cam Thanh; per person US$32-52), going to class involves a relaxing 4km cruise down the river. There are half-day and full-day courses, both of which include market

Waterfront, Cham Islands

Tours Around Hoi An

The quintessentially Vietnamese countryside around Hoi An begs to be explored. Two-wheeled tours are very popular, as are paddle-boarding, kayaking and boat trips to the idyllic Cham Islands.

Great For...

☑ Don't Miss

Testing your two-wheel prowess on a motorbike tour around idyllic back roads.

Motorbike & Jeep

Vespa Adventures

Quite possibly the most fun and most stylish way to explore around Hoi An, **Vespa Adventures** (☏093-850 0997; www.vespaadventures.com; 134 Đ Tran Cao Van; per person $US65-76) offers the opportunity to ride pillion on classic retro two-wheelers with an Italian accent. There are morning and afternoon departures, and a popular after-dark 'Streets & Eats' option with lots of good food and cold beer.

Active Adventures Vietnam

Heading up into the hills, this place offers **tours** (☏090-51 01930; www.activeadventures-vietnam.com; 111 Ba Trieu) in original US jeeps to a Co Tu tribal village. There are hot springs and great hikes in the region.

villages, try **Cactus Tours Love of Life** (☎0510-350 5017; www.hoian-bicycle.com.vn; 66 Đ Phan Chu Trinh; tours US$29; ⏱9am-8.30pm). It also runs walking tours of Hoi An.

Boat & Kayak

Hoi An Kayak Center

This place offers **self-paddle rentals** (☎090-505 6640; www.hoiankayak.com; 125 Đ Ngo Quyen) for US$10 per hour, or two-hour guided paddles for US$25 per person.

Cham Islands

A breathtaking cluster of granite islands, set in aquamarine seas around 15km directly offshore from Hoi An, the Cham Islands make a wonderful excursion and Hoi An's two dive schools offer packages.

The islands were once closed to visitors and under close military supervision, but now day trips, diving or snorkelling the reefs and overnight stays are possible. The diving is not world class, but can be intriguing.

Blue Coral Diving (☎0510-627 9297; www. divehoian.com; 77 Đ Nguyen Thai Hoc; snorkelling trips US$40)

Cham Island Diving Center (☎0510-391 0782; www.vietnamscubadiving.com; 88 Đ Nguyen Thai Hoc; snorkelling day trips US$44, overnight snorkelling/diving trips US$82/112)

Hoi An Motorbike Adventures

This outfit specialises in **tours** (☎090-510 1930; www.motorbiketours-hoian.com; 111 Đ Ba Trieu) on cult Minsk motorbikes. The guides know the terrain, and the trips make use of beautiful back roads and riverside tracks.

Bicycle

Phat Tire Ventures

Offers a terrific **mountain-bike trip** (☎0510-653 9839; www.ptv-vietnam.com; 62 Đ Ba Trieu) to My Son ruins that takes in country lanes and temple visits. Pickup from hotels included. Also offers adventure thrills via rappelling and rock climbing.

Cactus Tours Love of Life

For good bicycle tours along quiet country lanes, past vegetable gardens and fishing

My Son Ruins

The site of Vietnam's most extensive Cham remains, My Son enjoys an enchanting setting in a lush jungle valley 55km west of Hoi An.

Great For...

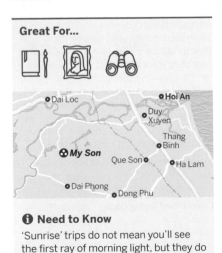

ℹ️ Need to Know

'Sunrise' trips do not mean you'll see the first ray of morning light, but they do beat the crowds.

★ **Top Tip**
Buildings D1 and D2 (once meditation halls) now house small displays of Cham sculpture.

History

My Son was once the most important intellectual and religious centre of the kingdom of Champa. It became a religious centre under King Bhadravarman in the late 4th century and was continuously occupied until the 13th century.

Most of the temples were dedicated to Cham kings associated with divinities, particularly Shiva, who was regarded as the founder and protector of Champa's dynasties.

My Son was rediscovered in the late 19th century by the French, who restored parts of the complex, but American bombing later devastated the temples.

Today it is a Unesco World Heritage site.

Touring the Site

Hotels in Hoi An arrange day trips to My Son (US$5 to US$10). Most minibuses depart at 8am and return between 1pm and 2pm. For the boat-ride option on the return leg, add an extra hour.

Archaeologists have divided My Son's monuments into 10 main groups, uninspiringly named A, A', B, C, D, E, F, G, H and K. Each structure within that group is given a number.

Only a handful of the monuments are properly labelled, but recent ongoing restoration has introduced a range of good information panels outlining the history of the site.

Sculpture remains, My Son

Group A

Group A was almost completely destroyed by US bombs. According to locals, the massive **A1**, considered the most important monument at My Son, remained impervious to aerial bombing and was intentionally finished off by a helicopter-borne sapper team. All that remains today is a pile of collapsed brick walls.

After the destruction of A1, Philippe Stern, an expert on Cham art, wrote a letter of protest to US president Nixon, who ordered US forces to stop damaging Cham monuments.

Group B

The main *kalan* (sanctuary), **B1**, was dedicated to Bhadresvara, which is a contraction of the name of King Bhadra-varman, who built the first temple at My Son, combined with '-esvara', which means Shiva. The first building on this site was erected in the 4th century, destroyed in the 6th century and rebuilt in the 7th century. Only the 11th-century base, made of large sandstone blocks, remains.

Group C

The 8th-century **C1** was used to worship Shiva, portrayed here in human form. In-side is an altar where a statue of Shiva, now in the **Museum of Cham Sculpture** (Bao Tang; 1 Đ Trung Nu Vuong; 40,000d; ⊘7am-5pm) in Danang, used to stand. Note the motifs, characteristic of the 8th century, carved into the brickwork of the exterior walls.

With the massive bomb crater in front of this group, it's amazing that anything's still standing.

My Son Museum

My Son's impressive **museum** (admission with entrance ticket; ⊘6.30am-4pm) has many statues from the site and information about how the temples were constructed. Cham culture, religion and way of life are also ex-plained, along with background information on the carvings, statues and architecture.

LANASAMOILOVA/SHUTTERSTOCK ©

⊙ SIGHTS

Museum of Trading Ceramics
Museum

(80 Đ Tran Phu; admission by Old Town ticket; ⊘7am-5.30pm) Occupies a restored wooden house and contains a small collection of artefacts from all over Asia, with oddities from as far afield as Egypt. While this reveals that Hoi An had some rather impressive trading links, it takes an expert's eye to appreciate the display. The exhibition on the restoration of Hoi An's old houses provides a useful crash course in Old Town architecture.

Chinese All-Community Assembly Hall
Historic Building

(Chua Ba; ☎0510-861 935; 64 Đ Tran Phu; ⊘8am-5pm) FREE Founded in 1773, this assembly hall was used by Fujian, Cantonese, Hainanese, Chaozhou and Hakka congregations in Hoi An. To the right of the entrance are portraits of Chinese resistance heroes in Vietnam who died during WWII. The well-restored main temple is a total assault on the senses, with great smoking incense spirals, demonic-looking deities, dragons and lashings of red lacquer – it's dedicated to Thien Hau.

Assembly Hall of the Chaozhou Chinese Congregation
Historic Building

(Trieu Chau Hoi Quan; opposite 157 Đ Nguyen Duy Hieu; admission by Old Town ticket; ⊘8am-5pm) Built in 1752, the highlight in this congregational hall is the gleaming woodcarvings on the beams, walls and altar – absolutely stunning in their intricacy. You could stand here for hours to unravel the stories, but if you're just popping by quickly, look for the carvings on the doors in front of the altar of two Chinese women wearing their hair in an unexpectedly Japanese style.

Chuc Thanh Pagoda
Buddhist Temple

(Khu Vuc 7, Tan An; ⊘8am-6pm) Founded in 1454 by a Buddhist monk from China, this is the oldest pagoda in Hoi An. Among the antique ritual objects still in use are several bells, a stone gong that is two centuries old and a carp-shaped wooden gong said to be even more venerable. To get to Chuc Thanh Pagoda, go north all the way to the end of Đ Nguyen Truong To and turn left. Follow the lane for 500m.

Handicraft Workshop
Workshop

(9 Đ Nguyen Thai Hoc; admission by Old Town ticket) Housed in a 200-year-old Chinese trading house, the Handicraft Workshop has artisans making silk lanterns and practising traditional embroidery in the back. In the front is your typical tourist-oriented cultural show with traditional singers, dancers and musicians. It makes a sufficiently diverting break from sightseeing.

Tran Duong House
Historic Site

(25 Đ Phan Boi Chau; admission 20,000d; ⊘9am-7pm) There's a whole block of colonnaded French colonial buildings on Đ Phan Boi Chau between nos 22 and 73, among them the 19th-century Tran Duong House. It's still a private home, so a family member will show you around. There's some antique French and Chinese furniture, including a sideboard buffet and a sitting room set with elaborate mother-of-pearl inlay. By contrast, the large, plain wooden table in the front room is the family bed.

Hoi An Museum of History & Culture
Museum

(7 Đ Nguyen Hue; admission by Old Town ticket; ⊘7am-5.30pm) Housed in the **Quan Am Pagoda**, this museum provides a sampling of pre-Cham, Cham and port-era artefacts, with some huge bells, historic photos, old scales and weights alongside plenty of ceramics.

✪ ACTIVITIES

There are many massage and treatment centres in Hoi An. Most are average, run by locals with minimal experience or training. A basic massage costs around US$12 an hour – there's a strip along Đ Ba Trieu. At the other end of the scale are indulgent places that offer a wonderful spa experience (with prices to match); these are mostly based in the luxury hotels.

Palmarosa Spa

(☑0510-393 3999; www.palmarosaspa.vn; 90 Đ
Ba Trieu; massages & treatments from 220,000d;
⊘10am-9pm) This highly professional
spa offers massages (including Thai and
Swedish), scrubs and facials, as well as
hand and foot care.

Ba Le Beauty Salon Spa

(☑0905-226 974; www.balewellbeautysalon.com;
45-11 Đ Tran Hung Dao; ⊘9am-7pm) Ba Le is run
by a fluent English speaker, who has trained
in the UK, and offers inexpensive threading,
waxing, facials, manicures and pedicures.

Countryside Charm Spa

(Duyen Que; ☑0510-350 1584; http://spahoian.
vn; 512 Đ Cua Dai; 1hr massages from US$20;
⊘8am-10pm) On the beach road, this
treatment centre has functional premises,
but staff are well trained. It also arranges
complimentary pickup from Hoi An.

🔒 SHOPPING

Hoi An has a history of flogging goods to
international visitors, and today's residents
haven't lost their commercial edge. Clothes
are the biggest lure: Hoi An has long been
known for fabric production. Hoi An has
over a dozen art galleries too and woodcarvings are a local speciality: head to Cam
Nam village and Cam Kim Island for these.

Villagecraft Planet Arts & Crafts

(www.facebook.com/VillagecraftPlanet; 37 Đ
Phan Boi Chau; ⊘10am-6pm) ✔ Shop here for
interesting homewares and fashion, often
using natural hemp and indigo, and crafted
incorporating fair-trade practices by the
Hmong, Black Thai and Lolo ethnic minority
people in the north of Vietnam.

Reaching Out Souvenirs, Clothing

(www.reachingoutvietnam.com; 103 Đ Nguyen
Thai Hoc; ⊘8.30am-9pm Mon-Fri, 9.30am-8pm
Sat & Sun) ✔ Excellent fair-trade gift shop
that stocks good-quality silk scarves,
clothes, jewellery, hand-painted Vietnamese hats, handmade toys and teddy bears.
The shop employs and supports artisans
with disabilities, and staff are happy to
show visitors through the workshop.

 ### Hoi An Photo Tour

Experienced and newbie photographers
are both catered for on the **Hoi An
Photo Tour** (☑090-567 1898; www.
hoianphototour.com; 42 Đ Phan Boi Chau;
per person US$45), which is coordinated
by professional cameraman Etienne
Bossot. Sunrise and sunset tours are
most popular, harnessing Hoi An's
delicate light for images of fisherfolk
and rice paddies.

Worker in rice fields near Hoi An
ANGELA OSTAFICHUK/SHUTTERSTOCK ©

Couleurs D'Asie Gallery Photography, Books

(www.facebook.com/couleurs.asie; 7 Đ Nguyen
Hue; ⊘9am-9pm) Superb images for sale
of Vietnam and Asia by Hoi An–based
photographer Réhahn. His portraits are
particularly stunning, and the best of his
images are collected in books also for sale.

Yaly Clothing

(☑0510-391 0474; www.yalycouture.com; 47
Đ Nguyen Thai Hoc; ⊘8am-9pm) Hoi An is
bustling with tailors; get something made
to order at this popular shop.

Metiseko Clothing

(www.metiseko.com; 86 Đ Nguyen Thai Hoc;
⊘9am-9.30pm) ✔ Winners of a Sustainable
Development award, this eco-minded store
stocks gorgeous clothing (including kids'
wear), accessories, and homewares such
as cushions using natural silk and organic
cotton. It is certified to use the Organic
Contents Standards label.

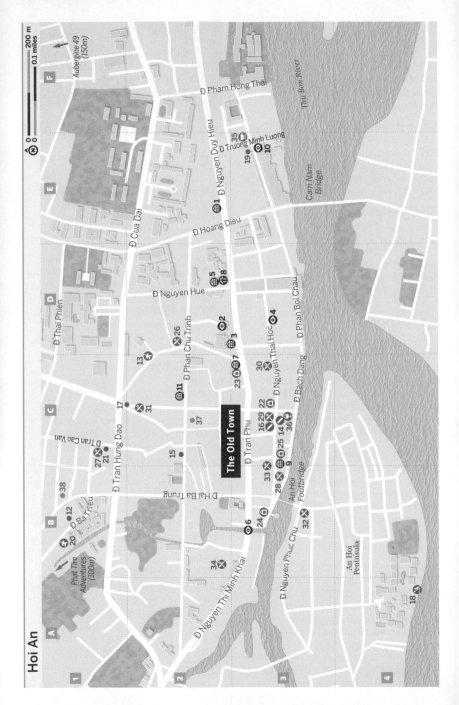

Hoi An

The Old Town

200 m
0.1 miles

Aubergine 49
(150m)

Phat Tire
Adventures
(100m)

An Hoi
Peninsula

Thu Bon River

Cam Nam
Bridge

Cam Nam Bridge

An Hoi
Footbridge

Đ Pham Hong Thai

Đ Nguyen Duy Hieu

Đ Truong Minh Luong

Đ Hoang Dieu

Đ Cua Dai

Đ Nguyen Hue

Đ Phan Chu Trinh

Đ Nguyen Thai Hoc

Đ Phan Boi Chau

Đ Bach Dang

Đ Tran Phu

Đ Tran Hung Dao

Đ Tran Cao Van

Đ Ba Trieu

Đ Hai Ba Trung

Đ Nguyen Phuc Chu

Đ Nguyen Thi Minh Khai

Đ Thai Phien

Avana   Clothing

(www.hoiandesign.com; 57 Đ Le Loi; ⊗8am-8pm)
Stylish boutique run by a European fashion
designer that stocks fab off-the-peg
dresses, blouses, shoes and accessories
(including great hats and bags).

Lotus Jewellery   Fashion, Accessories

(www.lotusjewellery-hoian.com; 82 Đ Tran Phu;
⊗8am-10pm) Very affordable and attractive handcrafted pieces loosely modelled
on butterflies, dragonflies, Vietnamese
sampans, conical hats and Chinese
symbols.

❌ EATING

The beauty of Hoi An is that you can snag
a spectacular cheap meal at the central
market and in casual eateries – or you can
splash out on a fine-dining experience.

Cocobox   Cafe $

(www.facebook.com/cocoboxvietnam; 94 Đ Le
Loi; juices & smoothies 60,000-75,000d; ⊗7am-
10pm) Refreshing cold-press juices are the
standout at this compact cafe–deli. Our
favourite is the Watermelon Man juice combining watermelon, passion fruit, lime and
mint. Coffee, salads and snacks are also
good – try the chicken pesto sandwich.

The attached 'farm shop' sells Vietnamese artisan produce including local honey
and cider from Saigon.

Bale Well   Vietnamese $$

(45-51 Đ Tran Cao Van; meals 150,000d;
⊗11.30am-10pm) Down a little alley near the
famous well, this local place is renowned
for one dish: barbecued pork, served up
satay-style, which you then combine with
fresh greens and herbs to create your own
fresh spring roll. A global reputation means
it can get busy.

Hoi An

 An Bang Beach

Just 4km east of Hoi An, An Bang is one of Vietnam's most happening and enjoyable beaches. Not being as impacted by the serious erosion evident at neighbouring Cua Dai, there's a wonderful stretch of fine sand and an enormous horizon, with only the distant Cham Islands interrupting the seaside symmetry. You'll find an expanding accommodation scene with several stylish holiday rental houses and a great selection of beachfront bar-restaurants.

Oceanfront restaurant **Soul Kitchen** (☏0906 440 320; www.soulkitchen.sitew. com meals 90,000-180,000d; ⊗10am-10pm Tue-Sun, 10am-6pm Mon; 🛜) has a grassy garden and thatched dining area where the daily menu could include tuna carpaccio, seafood salad or calamari. There are good wines and cocktails too, and on Sunday afternoons from around 4pm it's the place to be for gigs from a crew of talented locals and expats. There's also live music from 5.30pm from Thursday to Saturday

Shaded beach lounges, An Bang
SIMON POON/SHUTTERSTOCK ©

Little Menu   Vietnamese $$
(www.thelittlemenu.com; 12 Đ Le Loi; meals 115,000-225,000d; ⊗9.30am-11pm; 🛜) English-speaking owner Son is a fantastic host at this popular little restaurant with an open kitchen and short menu – try the fish in banana leaf or duck spring rolls, which feature on the set menu (225,000d). Flavours are made easy for most to like.

Nu Eatery   Fusion $$
(www.facebook.com/NuEateryHoiAn; 10a Đ Nguyen Thi Minh Khai; mains 80,000d; ⊗noon-9pm Mon-Sat) Don't be deceived by the humble decor at this compact eatery tucked away near the Japanese Bridge. There's a real wow factor to the seasonal small plates at this newish Hoi An favourite. Combine the pork belly steamed buns with a salad of grilled pineapple, coconut and pomelo, and don't miss the homemade lemongrass, ginger or chilli ice cream.

A well-chosen wine list – by the glass or the bottle – showcases Australian, French and South American varietals.

Cargo Club   International $$
(☏0510-391 1227; www.msvy-tastevietnam. com/cargo-club; 107 Đ Nguyen Thai Hoc; meals 70,000-160,000d; ⊗8am-11pm; 🛜) Remarkable cafe-restaurant serving Vietnamese and Western food, with a terrific riverside location (the upper terrace has stunning views). A relaxing day here munching your way around the menu would be a day well spent. The breakfasts are legendary (try the eggs Benedict), the patisserie and cakes are superb, and fine-dining dishes and good cocktails also deliver.

Morning Glory Restaurant   Vietnamese $$
(☏0510-224 1555; www.msvy-tastevietnam. com/morning-glory; 106 Đ Nguyen Thai Hoc; meals 60,000-160,000d; ⊗8am-11pm; 🛜🖉) An outstanding restaurant in historic premises that concentrates on street food and traditionally prepared dishes (primarily from central Vietnam). Highlights include the pork-stuffed squid, and shrimp mousse on sugar-cane skewers. There's an excellent vegetarian selection (try the smoked aubergine), including many wonderful salads. Prices are reasonable given the surrounds, ambience and flavours.

Aubergine 49   Fusion $$
(www.facebook.com/Aubergine49; 49a Đ Ly Thai Tho; three courses 250,000d; ⊗11am-3pm & 6-9.30pm) Three-course menus for 250,000d per person are a fine reason to

taxi around five minutes north of central Hoi An to this stylish restaurant crafting interesting fusion combinations of Asian and Western cuisine. There are also à la carte options and a decent wine list; menu standouts include stuffed squid and roast quail.

Mango Mango   Fusion $$$
(☎0510-391 0839; www.themangomango.com; 45 Đ Nguyen Phuc Chu, An Hoi; meals US$25-35; ☺7am-10pm; 🛜) Celebrity chef Duc Tran's most beautiful Hoi An restaurant enjoys a prime riverside plot and puts a global spin on Vietnamese cuisine, with fresh, unexpected combinations to the max. Perhaps at times the flavour matches are just a little too out there, but the cocktails are some of the best in town.

Green Mango   International $$$
(www.greenmango.vn; 54 Đ Nguyen Thai Hoc; meals 130,000-300,000d; ☺11.30am-9.30pm; ❄🛜) The setting, inside one of Hoi An's most impressive traditional wooden houses, is beautiful, and the accomplished cooking (both Western and Eastern) matches the surrounds.

There's also one of the only air-conditioned dining rooms in the Old Town upstairs.

🍷 DRINKING & NIGHTLIFE

Mia Coffee House   Cafe
(www.facebook.com/miacoffeehouse; 20 Đ Phan Boi Chau; ☺8am-5pm) Our favourite spot for an espresso, latte or cappuccino features a shaded corner location and good food, including grilled *panini* sandwiches and hearty baguettes.

Its own coffee blend sourced from Dalat arabica beans is the standout brew, and be sure to try the coffee *affogato*, a delicious blend of dessert and hot beverage.

Dive Bar   Bar
(88 Đ Nguyen Thai Hoc; ☺8am-midnight; 🛜) A top bar option in Hoi An with a great vibe thanks to the welcoming service, contemporary electronic tunes and sofas for lounging. There's also a cocktail garden and bar at the rear, a pool table and pub grub.

White Marble   Bar
(www.visithoian.com; 99 Đ Le Loi; ☺11am-11pm; 🛜) Wine-bar-cum-restaurant in historic premises with an unmatched selection of wines (many are available by the glass, from US$4) and refined ambience. Lunch and dinner set meals cost 230,000d.

Q Bar   Lounge
(94 Đ Nguyen Thai Hoc; ☺noon-midnight; 🛜) Q Bar offers stunning lighting, lounge music and electronica, and the best (if pricey, at around 120,000d) cocktails and mocktails in town. Draws a cool crowd.

ℹ INFORMATION

Sinh Tourist (☎0510-386 3948; www.thesinhtourist.vn; 587 Đ Hai Ba Trung; ☺6am-10pm) Books reputable open-tour buses.

Go Travel Vietnam (☎0510-392 9115; http://fb.me/GoTravelVietnam; 61a Đ Phan Chu Trinh; ☺9am-9pm) Airport transfers to Danang; can also arrange private cars and offers tours.

ℹ GETTING THERE & AWAY

AIR
The closest airport is 45 minutes away in Danang.

CAR & TAXI
Taxis cost approximately 400,000d to Danang. A trip in a car to Hue starts from US$100.

ℹ GETTING AROUND

Hoi An is best explored on foot; the Old Town is compact and highly walkable. To go further afield, rent a bicycle (25,000d per day). Reckon on about 70,000d for a taxi to An Bang beach.

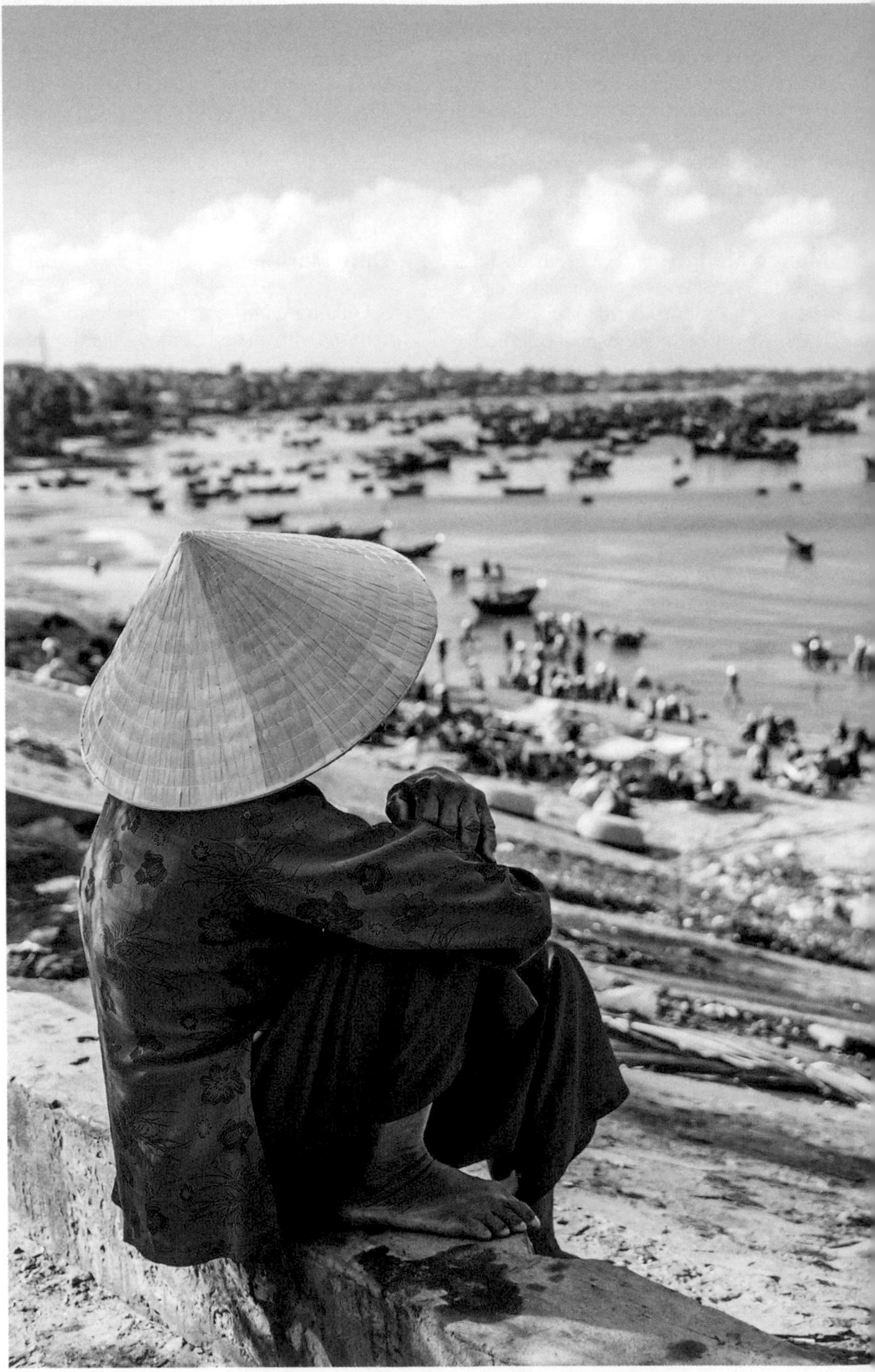

HEADHOG/SHUTTERSTOCK ©

MUI NE

In this Chapter

Mui Ne at a Glance...

Once upon a time, Mui Ne was an isolated stretch of beach where pioneering travellers camped on the sand. Times have changed and it's now an established beach resort forming one long coastal strip. Mui Ne is definitely moving upmarket, as more exclusive places open their doors, complemented by swish restaurants, but there is still a (kite) surfer vibe to the town. Sailing and windsurfing are also popular.

Mui Ne in One Day

Spend your first day with a morning walk or jog along Mui Ne's lovely sandy beach, followed by an afternoon trip to the **Fairy Spring** (p152), a massage, then dinner at **Sandals** (p153).

Mui Ne in Two Days

The next day sign up for a windsurfing, sailing or cooking course followed by a visit to the **Po Shanu Cham Towers** (p152) and a meal of ocean-fresh seafood at one of the beachside **Bo Ke** (p153).

Mui Ne Map (p154)

Arriving in Mui Ne

There's no airport, and the nearest train station is in Phan Thiet, so most visitors arrive by road via open-tour buses or private transport. There are good bus links to Ho Chi Minh City.

Where to Stay

Most accommodation is either right on the long coastal road or just off it, with a few good-value places in the hills behind town. Wherever you are, you won't be far from the beach.

Kitesurfing competition, Mui Ne

PATRIK DIETRICH/SHUTTERSTOCK ©

Adrenaline Sports

For kite- and windsurfers, late October to late April is peak season when gales blow. There's also some surf, good sailing and even a decent local golf course.

Mui Ne is the adrenaline capital of southern Vietnam. There's no scuba-diving or snorkelling to speak of, but when Nha Trang and Hoi An get the rains, Mui Ne gets the waves. Surf's up from August to December. For windsurfers, the gales blow as well, especially from late October to late April, when swells can stir things up big time. Kitesurfing has really taken off and the infinite horizon is often obscured by dozens of kites flapping in the wind. If this all sounds too much like hard work, you can simply lounge around on the beach, watching others take the strain.

Great For...

☑ Don't Miss

For a fun hour or so, check out Tropical Minigolf Mui Ne (p152).

Courses

Consider investing in a short kitesurfing lesson before opting for a multiday course, as it's a tricky skill to master.

> ★ **Top Tip**
>
> Many resorts east of Km 12 have almost completely lost their beaches due to coastal erosion.

Sankara Kitesurfing Academy

This **school** (☏0914 910 607; www.facebook.com/sankarakitesurfingacademy; 78 Đ Nguyen Dinh Chieu; ⊙9am-5pm) is run by experienced IKO (International Kiteboarding Organization) trained kitesurfers and offers instruction and equipment rentals. Lessons start at US$99 for two hours.

Manta Sail Training Centre

Excellent new **sailing school** (☏0908 400 108; http://mantasailing.org; 108 Đ Huynh Thuc Khang; sailing instruction per hr US$66) offering International Sailing Federation training (from beginner to advanced racing), wakeboarding (US$100 per hour including boat) and SUP rentals. Staff are very professional and they also have budget rooms available.

Surfpoint Kiteboarding School

With well-trained instructors and a friendly vibe, it's no surprise **Surfpoint** (☏0167-3422 136; www.surfpoint-vietnam.com; 52a Đ Nguyen Dinh Chieu; 3hr course incl all gear US$150; ⊙7am-6pm) is one of the best-regarded kite schools in town. A five-hour course costs US$250. Surfing lessons on softboards are also offered (from US$50) when waves permit and there are short boards for rent.

Jibes

Mui Ne's original kitesurfing school, **Jibes** (☏062-384 7405; www.windsurf-vietnam.com; 84-90 Đ Nguyen Dinh Chieu; ⊙7.30am-6pm) provides safety-conscious and patient instruction (US$60 per hour) and rents gear including windsurfs (US$35 per half-day), SUPs, surfboards, kitesurfs and kayaks.

From left: Street-food vendor, Mui Ne; Po Shanu Cham Towers; White sand dunes

◎ SIGHTS

Sand Dunes   Beach

Mui Ne is famous for its enormous red and white sand dunes. The 'red dunes' (*doi hong*) are convenient to Hai Long, but the 'white dunes' (*doi cat trang*) 24km northeast are the more impressive – the near-constant oceanic winds sculpt the pale yellow sands into wonderful Sahara-esque formations. But as this is Vietnam (not deepest Mali), there's little chance of experiencing the silence of the desert.

Prepare yourself for the hard sell as children press you to hire a plastic sledge to ride the dunes. Unless you're supermodel-light, it can be tricky to travel for more than a few metres this way.

Fairy Spring   River

(Suoi Tien) This stream flows through a patch of dunes with interesting sand and rock formations. It's a beautiful walk wading up the stream from the sea to its source, a spring. You can do the trek barefoot, but if you're heading out into the big

sand dunes afterwards, you'll need proper footwear.

Po Shanu Cham Towers   Hindu Site

(Km 5; 5000d; ☉7.30-11.30am & 1-4.30pm) West of Mui Ne, the Po Shanu Cham Towers occupy a hill near Phan Thiet, with sweeping views of the town and a cemetery filled with candy-like tombstones. Dating from the 9th century, this complex consists of the ruins of three towers, none of which are in very good shape. There's a small pagoda on the site, as well as a gallery and shop.

⚙ ACTIVITIES

Tropical Minigolf
Mui Ne   Minigolf

(97 Đ Nguyen Dinh Chieu; one round 100,000-120,000d; ☉10am-10.30pm) This attractive palm-shaded minigolf course is dotted with craggy rock formations to challenge your putting skills. Rates include a cold drink.

DETANAN/SHUTTERSTOCK ©

Sealinks Golf & Country Club

Golf

(062-374 1777; www.sealinksvietnam.com; Km 8, Mui Ne; 18 holes 1,350,000d) Fine 7671-yard course with ocean views and a challenging layout that includes lots of water hazards. Play a discounted twilight round from 2.30pm. The complex includes a resort hotel and driving range.

🍴 EATING

Periodically, the famous but illegally built seafront shacks – collectively known as the Bo Ke restaurants – are closed down by police.

Com Chay Vi Dieu

Vegetarian $

(15b Đ Huynh Thuc Khang; meals 25,000d; 7am-9pm;) This simple roadside place scores strongly for inexpensive Vietnamese vegetarian dishes, and serves great smoothies (20,000d). It's opposite the Eiffel Tower of the Little Paris resort. No English is spoken but you can point and choose.

Sindbad

Middle Eastern $

(www.sindbad.vn; 233 Đ Nguyen Dinh Chieu; mains 50,000-70,000d; 11am-1am;) A kind of kebab shack par excellence. Come here for inexpensive shawarma and shish kebabs and other Med favourites such as Greek salad. Very inexpensive and portions are generous; opens late.

Nhu Bao

Seafood $

(0914 531 767; 146 Đ Nguyen Dinh Chieu; mains 50,000-180,000d; 9am-9.30pm) A classic, no-nonsense Vietnamese seafood place: step past the bubbling tanks and there's a huge covered terrace which stretches down to the ocean. It's renowned for its crab.

Bo Ke

Seafood $$

(Đ Nguyen Dinh Chieu; mains 40,000-120,000d; 5-10pm) A group of seafood shacks on the beach.

Sandals

International $$

(062-384 7440; www.miamuine.com/dine; 24 Đ Nguyen Dinh Chieu, Mia Resort; meals 120,000-370,000d; 7am-10pm;) This outstanding hotel restaurant is the most

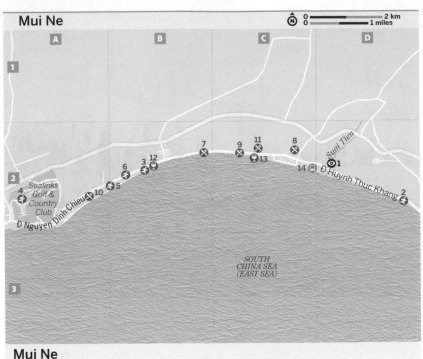

Mui Ne

atmospheric place in town. It's particularly romantic at night, with tables set around the shore-side pool or in the elegant dining rooms. Wait staff are knowledgeable, attentive and welcoming. The menu is superb with everything from pasta dishes to Vietnamese claypots executed and presented beautifully. Consider visiting for the wonderful breakfast buffet.

Villa Aria Mui Ne   International $$

(mains 95,000-200,000d; ⊙7am-9.30pm; 🛜)
The beautiful beachside location, with tables set on a shoreside deck, is the main attraction at this classy hotel restaurant. The menu takes in salads (from 75,000d), soups and pasta, and you'll find staff are attentive and eager to please.

🍷 DRINKING & NIGHTLIFE

PoGo   Bar
(📞0912 000 751; www.thepogobar.com; 138 Đ
Nguyen Dinh Chieu; ⊙8.30am-2am) A mighty
fine bar with a prime beach location, daybeds for lounging, DJs on weekends and
regular movie nights. Staff are very friendly
and there's a full menu too.

Joe's Café   Bar
(http://joescafemuine.com; 86 Đ Nguyen Dinh
Chieu; ⊙7am-1am; 🛜) If bangin' techno is
not your bag, Joe's is worth a try with live
music (every night at 7.30pm) and a pub-
like vibe. During the day it's a good place
to hang too, with a sociable bar area, lots
of drinks specials and an extensive food
menu.

Dragon Beach   Bar, Club
(120-121 Đ Nguyen Dinh Chieu; ⊙1pm-4am)
Western and local DJs play EDM, bass,
house and techno at this shoreside bar-
club. There's a chill-out deck with cushions
to one side and *shishas* for puffing. Happy
hour is 8pm to 10pm.

ℹ️ INFORMATION

Sinh Tourist (www.thesinhtourist.vn; 144 Đ
Nguyen Dinh Chieu; ⊙7am-10pm) Ever-reliable
and trustworthy agency for open-tour buses,
trips around Mui Ne and credit-card cash
advances.

ℹ️ GETTING THERE & AWAY

Open-tour buses are the most convenient
option for Mui Ne. Several companies have daily
services to/from HCMC (99,000d to 150,000d,
six hours), Nha Trang (from 122,000d, 5½ hours)
and Dalat (100,000d, four hours).

Phuong Trang (http://futabus.vn; 97 Đ Nguyen
Dinh Chieu) has four comfortable buses a day
running between Mui Ne and HCMC (135,000d).

ℹ️ GETTING AROUND

Scooters cost from 120,000d per day.

Mai Linh (📞062-389 8989) operates metered
taxis.

Fairy Spring (p152)

Pongour Falls, near Dalat

DALAT

In this Chapter

Dalat at a Glance...

This is Vietnam's alter ego: the weather is springlike cool instead of tropical hot, the town is dotted with elegant French-colonial villas rather than stark socialist architecture, and the farms around are thick with strawberries and flowers, not rice.

Dalat is small enough to remain charming and its countryside is blessed with lakes, waterfalls, evergreen forests and gardens. The town is a big draw for domestic tourists for whom it's a honeymoon capital. For travellers the moderate climate is ideal for adrenaline-fuelled activities – mountain biking, forest hiking, canyoning and climbing.

Dalat in One Day

Head straight for the **Hang Nga Crazy House** (p164) and marvel at its kitsch eccentricity, and then take in the **King Palace** (p164). In the afternoon book a toy train ride from the **Crémaillère Railway Station** (p164), and finish off with a stroll around **Xuan Huong Lake** (p164) and a meal at **Le Rabelais** (p167).

Dalat in Two Days

Sign up with a recommended adventure tour specialist for a day's trekking, mountain biking, kayaking, canyoning, abseiling or rock climbing. Or just explore the region's waterfalls by taxi if you're not feeling that active. If there's time in the late afternoon, catch the cable car to the **Truc Lam Pagoda** (p164). Make for the **Escape Bar** (p167) in the evening for live music and a good vibe.

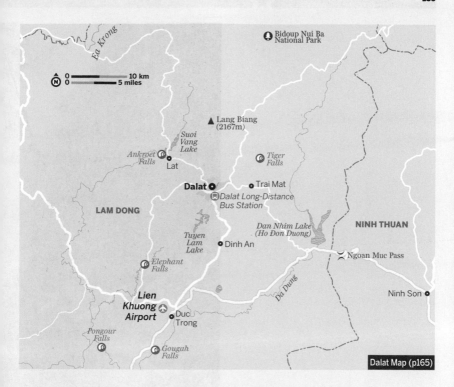

Dalat Map (p165)

Arriving in Dalat

Dalat airport (30km from town) has daily flights to Ho Chi Minh City, Hanoi, Danang and other cities.

Very efficient and regular bus services link Dalat with HCMC from the central terminal 1.5km south of Xuan Huong Lake. Other cities including Danang are also covered.

Where to Stay

Hotels and guesthouses are scattered around town and in the hills beyond. Many budget places are located in the streets north of Hoa Binh Square.

Rappelling at Datanla canyon (p162)

Adventure Sports

Dalat is Vietnam's highland adventure sports mecca, offering mountain biking and hiking, canyoning and rock climbing, white-water rafting, kayaking and motorbiking trips.

Great For...

ⓘ Need to Know

Stick to the recommended tour operators listed; accidents have occurred with unlicensed guides.

★ **Top Tip**

If considering an 'Easy Rider' motor-bike trip, test-drive the rider first before committing.

Tour Operators

○ Phat Tire Ventures (☎063-382 9422; www.ptv-vietnam.com; 109 Đ Nguyen Van Troi; ⊗8am-7pm) is a highly professional and experienced operator with mountain-biking trips from US$49, trekking from US$39, kayaking from US$39, canyoning (US$75), rappelling (US$57) and white-water rafting (US$67) in the rainy season. Multiday cycling trips are available.

○ Groovy Gecko Adventure Tours (☎063-383 6521; www.groovygeckotours.net; 65 Đ Truong Cong Dinh; ⊗8am-7pm) is an experienced agency operated by a lively young team with prices starting at US$38 for rock climbing, canyoning or mountain biking; day treks from US$25; and two-day treks from US$65.

○ Run by an enthusiastic local team, Pine Track Adventures (☎063-383 1916; www.pinetrackadventures.com; 72b Đ Truong Cong Dinh; ⊗8am-7pm) offers canyoning (from US$55), white-water rafting (from US$60), trekking, biking and some excellent multisport packages. A six-day exploration of the area around Dalat and bike ride down to Mui Ne is US$635.

Canyoning

A dramatic day out at the Datanla canyon involves negotiating several waterfalls using ropes and rappelling and a natural water slide. It usually culminates with a rinse in the infamous 'washing machine'. Only book this trip with the experienced operators we recommend.

Mountain Biking & Cycling

There's excellent biking around Dalat, which is ringed by hills and mountains. Trails run through pine forests and offer magnificent views. Road cycling is also rewarding, with light traffic and sublime vistas.

✕ **Take a Break**
Head to Da Quy (p166) for great, authentic food and service.

The routes to Nha Trang (one day including some rafting) and Mui Ne (two days) are wildly popular and involve serious descents.

White-Water Rafting & Kayaking

White-water rafting the Da Don River through remote terrain and taking in Class 2 and 3 rapids makes a fine day trip. Some operators offer combined hiking and rafting trips.

Motorbiking

For many travellers, the highlight of their trip in Vietnam is an off-the-beaten-track motorcycle tour with an 'Easy Rider'. Rider-guides can be found in hotels and cafes in Dalat. Read testimonials from past clients. Check the bike over. Discuss the route in detail – for scenery the highways that link Dalat to Mui Ne and Nha Trang are wonderful. Rates start at US$30 or so for

Motorbiking around Dalat

a day tour, or US$50 to US$75 per day for longer journeys.

Trekking

From day hikes through jungle rich with birdlife to extended trekking trips through tribal villages and over rolling hills and along lonely ridges, there's a fine choice of walks from Dalat. Troops of monkeys are sometimes encountered on some hikes.

Bidoup Nui Ba National Park

Occupying a densely forested highland plateau, this **national park** (☎063-374 7449; www.bidoupnuiba.gov.vn) encompasses evergreen and coniferous woodlands, bamboo groves and grasslands at altitudes between 650m and 2288m. Hill-tribe guides are available to guide you along trails, and there's an impressive visitor centre, 32km

north of Dalat, with interactive displays about the flora and fauna, and K'Ho hill-tribe crafts and culture.

Bidoup Nui Ba has 96 endemic plants, including the Dalat pine, and nearly 300 species of orchids. Yellow-cheeked gibbons can be heard in the early morning, while the park is also home to black bears and the vampire flying frog. The pleasant 3.5km trail from the visitor centre to a waterfall only fringes the park; to penetrate deep inside consider one of three other options, which include ascents of Lang Biang and Bidoup mountains. The longer trails don't start from the visitor centre, but staff there can organise guides.

☑ Don't Miss

The thrill of riding (like the locals) on two wheels; it's an essential Vietnam experience.

USJ/SHUTTERSTOCK ©

◉ SIGHTS

Hang Nga Crazy House Architecture

(☏063-382 2070; 3 Đ Huynh Thuc Khang; 40,000d; ⊙8.30am-7pm Mon-Fri) A free-wheeling architectural exploration of surrealism, Hang Nga Crazy House is a joyously designed, outrageously artistic private home. Imagine sculptured rooms connected by superslim bridges rising out of a tangle of greenery, an excess of cascading lava-flow-like shapes, wild colours, spiderweb windows and an almost organic quality to it all, with the swooping handrails resembling jungle vines. Think of Gaudí and Tolkien dropping acid together.

King Palace Palace

(Dinh 1; www.dinh1dalat.com; Hung Vuong; adult/child 20,000/10,000d; ⊙7.30am-5pm) Tastefully revamped, the main palace of Bao Dai, Vietnam's last emperor, beckons visitors with its beautiful tree-lined avenue and a surprisingly modest royal residence. Its peach-coloured rooms were once home to him, his wife and their five children before being taken over by Prime Minister Ngo Dinh Diem once Bao Dai went into exile in France in 1954.

Highlights are undoubtedly the family photos: Bao Dai playing with a dog and riding a horse, and well-scrubbed royal children with serious faces.

Crémaillère Railway Station Historic Building

(Ga Da Lat; 1 Đ Quang Trung; ⊙6.30am-5pm) FREE From Dalat's wonderful art-deco train station you can ride one of the five scheduled trains that run to Trai Mat (return 124,000d, 30 minutes) daily between 7.45am and 4pm; a minimum of 20 passengers is required.

A *crémaillère* (cog railway) linking Dalat and Thap Cham from 1928 to 1964 was closed due to VC attacks. A Japanese steam train is on display, and the classy waiting room retains a colonial feel.

Lam Dong Museum Museum

(☏063-382 0387; 4 Đ Hung Vuong; admission 10,000d; ⊙7.30-11.30am & 1.30-4.30pm Mon-Sat) This hillside museum is a stampede through Dalat's history, with a side trip into the natural history section, complete with outrageously bad taxidermy (look out for the angry wildcats!). Highlights include the wonderfully evocative photos of the Ma, K'Ho and Churu people, and displays of their traditional dress, musical instruments and ceremonial altars. Also, check out the remarkable stone xylophones dating back over 3000 years. Propaganda about the government support for local indigenous groups is hard to swallow, though.

Xuan Huong Lake Lake

Created by a dam in 1919, this banana-shaped lake was named after an anti-authoritarian 17th-century Vietnamese poet. It has become a popular icon of Dalat and a magnet for joggers and those in love. The lake can be circumnavigated along a scenic 7km sealed path that passes the flower gardens, golf club, night market and Dalat Palace hotel.

Truc Lam Pagoda & Cable Car Buddhist Temple

(Ho Tuyen Lam; cable car one way/return adult 50,000/70,000d, child 30,000/40,000d; ⊙cable car 7.30-11.30am & 1.30-5pm) The Truc Lam Pagoda enjoys a hilltop setting and has splendid gardens. It's an active monastery, though the grounds frequently teem with tour groups. Be sure to arrive by cable car (the terminus is 3km south of the centre), which soars over majestic pine forests.

The pagoda can be reached by road via turnoffs from Hwy 20.

⊘ TOURS

Dalat Happy Tours Food & Drink

(☏0912 893 091; www.dalathappytours.com; street-food tour US$4) After all the active exertions around Dalat, replenish your calories by going on an entertaining nightly street-food tour with friendly Lao. Start from the central Hoa Binh cinema at 6.30pm and proceed to sample *bahn xeo* (filled pancakes), buffalo-tail hotpot, delectable grilled skewers, 'Dalat pizza', rabbit curry, hot rice wine and more. Food prices not included.

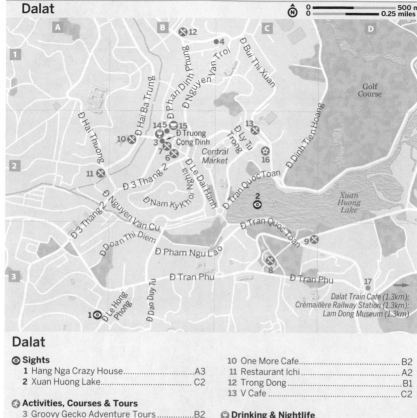

Dalat

◎ Sights
1 Hang Nga Crazy House.............................A3
2 Xuan Huong Lake.......................................C2

✚ Activities, Courses & Tours
3 Groovy Gecko Adventure Tours...............B2
4 Phat Tire Ventures...................................C1
5 Pine Track Adventures.............................B2

✕ Eating
6 Da Quy...B2
7 Goc Ha Thanh...B2
8 Le Rabelais...C3
9 Ming Dynasty...C3

10 One More Cafe...B2
11 Restaurant Ichi...A2
12 Trong Dong...B1
13 V Cafe...C2

🍷 Drinking & Nightlife
14 Hangout..B2
15 La Viet...B2

★ Entertainment
16 Escape Bar..C2

ℹ Transport
17 Vietnam Airlines......................................D3

✕ EATING

Trong Dong   Vietnamese **$**
(📞063-382 1889; 220 Đ Phan Dinh Phung;
meals 80,000-120,000d; ⏰11.30am-3pm &
5.30-9.30pm; 🛜) Intimate restaurant run
by a very hospitable team where the
creative menu includes spins on Vietnamese delights such as shrimp paste on a
sugar-cane stick, beef wrapped in *la lut* leaf,
and fiery lemongrass and chilli squid.

One More Cafe   Cafe **$**
(77 Đ Hai Ba Trung; cake 25,000d; ⏰8am-9pm
Thu-Tue; 🛜🍴) Comfy chairs to sink into,
eclectic peach walls and a glass display
case full of cakes greet you at this cosy,
Aussie-run cafe. Linger over an array of
teas, an espresso, an all-day breakfast or a
smoothie.

ZHUKOV OLEG/SHUTTERSTOCK ©

Hang Nga Crazy House (p164)

*A free-wheeling architectural
exploration of surrealism...*

Da Quy   Vietnamese $
(Wild Sunflower; 49 Đ Truong Cong Dinh; meals
from 50,000d; ⏾8am-10pm) Run by Loc, a
friendly English speaker, this place has a sophisticated ambience, yet accessible prices.
The traditional claypot dishes and hotpots
are more exciting than the Western menu.

Restaurant Ichi   Japanese $$
(☎063-355 5098; 1 Đ Hoang Dieu; meals 120,000-
300,000d; ⏾5.30-10pm Tue-Sun) Dalat's

only truly genuine Japanese restaurant is
compact, with subdued lighting and jazz in
the background. Spicy tuna rolls, chicken
yakitori and tempura are all fantastic, the
bento boxes are a bargain and there's even
natto (fermented soybeans) for aficionados.
Perch in front of the bar (with extensive
whisky offerings from around the world) to
watch sushi-master Tommo at work.

V Cafe   International $$
(☎063-352 0215; www.vcafedalatvietnam.com;
1/1 Đ Bui Thi Xuan; meals 99,000-145,000d;
⏾7am-10.30pm; 🛜🍴) Atmospheric bistro-
style place that serves international cuisine,

such as chicken curry Calcutta, veggie lasagne, Grandma's Hungarian goulash and Mexican-style quesadillas. The interior is decorated with atmospheric photography and there's live music every night 7.30pm to 8.45pm.

Goc Ha Thanh   Vietnamese $$
(53 Đ Truong Cong Dinh; meals 100,000-150,000d; ⊙7am-10pm; 🛜🖉) Casual place with attractive bamboo furnishings owned by a welcoming Hanoi couple. Strong on dishes such as coconut curry, hotpots, claypots, tofu stir-fries and noodles.

Dalat Train Cafe   International $$
(www.dalattrainvilla.com; 1 Đ Quang Trung; mains 79,000-155,000d; ⊙7am-10pm; 🛜🖉) Calling all trainspotters! Don't miss the opportunity to step inside this lovingly restored French-era railway carriage for a snack or meal in a unique setting, surrounded by images of trains worldwide. The blue-cheese burger, spicy tofu and veggie lasagne are all solid choices. From Dalat Train Station, turn right, walk 80m up the hill and look for the sign on the left.

Le Rabelais   French $$$
(🖉063-382 5444; www.dalatpalacehotel.com; 12 Đ Tran Phu; meals 600,000-1,700,000d; ⊙7am-10pm) The signature restaurant at the Dalat Palace hotel is *the* colonial-style destination with the grandest of dining rooms and a spectacular terrace that looks down to the lakeshore. Set dinner menus (1,700,000d) offer the full treatment; otherwise treat yourself to flawless à la carte dishes such as seared duck breast with orange or roast rack of lamb.

Ming Dynasty   Chinese $$$
(🖉063-381 3816; www.khaisilkorp.com; 7 Tran Hung Dao; mains 150,000-850,000d; ⊙noon-3pm & 7-10pm) Paintings of mountainous landscapes adorn the walls of this refined Chinese restaurant, with lake views from its terrace. Scroll through the iPad menu to select beautifully executed dishes such as Beijing duck, pork ribs with honey sauce, whole steamed grouper and flower crab with ginger and scallion.

🍸 DRINKING & NIGHTLIFE

Escape Bar   Live Music
(www.escapebardalat.com; Basement, Muong Thanh Hotel, 4 Đ Phan Boi Chau; ⊙4pm-midnight; 🛜) Outstanding live-music bar, owned by blues guitarist Curtis King who performs here nightly with a rotating band (from 9.15pm). Expect covers of Hendrix, the Eagles, the Doors and other classics, but the improvisation is such that each tune takes on a life of its own; travelling musicians are welcome to jam. The bar's decor, all 1970s chic, suits the sonics perfectly.

La Viet   Coffee
(82 Đ Truong Cong Dinh; ⊙7am-10pm) Is it an antique store? Is it a cafe? This cosy corner beguiles with its riot of plants, old bicycle parts, birdcages, vintage telephones and antique pianos. Find a corner to perch in to sip some seriously good coffee.

Hangout   Bar
(71 Đ Truong Cong Dinh; ⊙11am-midnight; 🛜) This late-night watering hole is popular with some of Dalat's Easy Riders, as well as visiting backpackers. It has a relaxed vibe, a pool table and inexpensive beers. The owner, a fluent English speaker, is an excellent source of local information.

ℹ️ GETTING THERE & AROUND

There are regular flights with **Vietnam Airlines** (🖉063-383 3499; www.vietnamairlines.com; 2 Đ Ho Tung Mau), VietJet Air and Jetstar, including a daily service to Danang (1¼ hours), four daily to Hanoi (1¾ hours) and HCMC (45 minutes), and two weekly to Can Tho (1¼ hours).

Lien Khuong Airport is 30km south of Dalat. Vietnam Airlines offers shuttle-bus transfers or a taxi is 180,000d to 200,000d.

Dalat is a major stop for open-tour buses. Sinh Tourist has daily buses to Mui Ne, Nha Trang and HCMC.

For reliable taxis try **Mai Linh** (🖉063-352 1111; http://www.mailinh.vn).

Golden-cheeked gibbon, Cat Tien National Park

ONDREJ PROSICKY/SHUTTERSTOCK ©

Cat Tien National Park

Cat Tien comprises an amazingly biodiverse area of lowland tropical rainforest. The Wild Gibbon Trek offers the chance to see (and hear!) one of Vietnam's rarest primates, the golden-cheeked gibbon, in the wild.

Great For...

❶ Need to Know

Cat Tien National Park (☏061-366 9228; www.namcattien.org; adult/child 50,000/20,000d; ☉7am-10pm) ✎

Biosphere Reserve

The 72,000-hectare Cat Tien National Park is one of the outstanding natural treasures in Vietnam, and the hiking, mountain biking and birdwatching here are outstanding. However, a word of caution: visitors have to be really lucky to see any of the larger mammals like tigers and elephants.

In 2001 Unesco added Cat Tien National Park to its list of biosphere reserves. Fauna in the park includes the bison-like guar, 79 types of reptile and 41 amphibian species, plus an incredible array of insects, including 400 or so butterfly species. Of the 350-plus birds, rare species include the orange-necked partridge and Siamese fireback.

Spend at least two full days here, if possible.

Brown hawk-owl, Cat Tien National Park

NITAT/SHUTTERSTOCK ©

❶ Getting There

Booking a tour takes the hassle out of transport arrangements.

To travel independently, all buses between Dalat and Ho Chi Minh City (every 30 minutes) pass a junction on Hwy 20 for the park. From this junction, hire a *xe om* (motorbike taxi; around 170,000d) to cover the remaining 24km. Lodges can also arrange transfers.

★ Top Tip

Book well ahead: the Wild Gibbon Trek is very popular, particularly on weekends.

Wild Gibbon Trek

The trek (US$60 per person, maximum four people) runs daily from the park HQ and involves a 5am start to get out to the gibbons in time for their dawn chorus; you have a chance to watch two separate gibbon families wake and greet the day.

The Wild Gibbon Trek is run by the park authorities, with the support of **Go East** (www.go-east.org), and requires you to stay in park-run accommodation the night before, as river crossings in the dark are too dangerous. All proceeds are ploughed back into the national park and assist the rangers in their protection efforts. To avoid disappointment, book in advance through cattienvietnam@gmail.com, or call ahead (☎061-366 9228).

The Gibbons

Golden-cheeked gibbons are only found in South Vietnam and Cambodia. As a result of habitat loss and hunting, the wild population is estimated at less than 20,000. Gibbons have been reintroduced into Cat Tien and this experience offers a rare insight into the lives of these charismatic primates.

Golden-cheeked gibbons are very territorial, with dominant females, and live in nuclear family groups, with the young staying with their mother for up to eight years. As with most other endangered creatures in Vietnam, they're hunted for the illegal pet trade, with parents killed and babies taken away, and also for dubious traditional medicine purposes.

The Gibbon Song

Guides string up hammocks from jungle trees at a 'listening station' so you can lounge in comfort while waiting for the melodious song of the gibbon. Once a call has been detected you'll have to hotfoot it across the jungle to find the gibbons.

The gibbons only sing for around 15 minutes, but it's a magical encounter as they sing a beautiful duet across the canopy.

Dao Tien

The trip includes a fully guided tour of the **Dao Tien Endangered Primate Species Centre** (www.go-east.org; adult/child incl boat ride 300,000/150,000d; ⊗tours 8.30am & 2pm), typically done at 8.30am, straight after the trek.

This centre, on an island in the Dong Nai River, is a rehabilitation centre hosting golden-cheeked gibbons, pygmy loris (both endemic to Vietnam and Cambodia), black-shanked douc and silvered langur that have been illegally trafficked. The eventual goal is to release the primates back into the forest. You can view gibbons in a semiwild environment and hear their incredible calls.

Hundreds of native fruit-tree saplings were planted on the island to provide the primates with foraging territory, and encourage them to learn the necessary skills to move around the forest canopy.

The centre's current focus is preserving the pygmy loris from extinction. Several of the rescued animals may never be released into the wild, as hunters tore out their poisonous teeth, without which they can't

Crocodile Lake

fend for themselves. The Dao Tien website allows you to 'adopt' individual animals.

Crocodile Lake

Crocodile Lake (Bau Sau; admission 200,000d, guide fee 500,000d, boat trip 450,000d) is one of the park highlights, reachable via two different routes.

The more straightforward option involves a 9km drive or bike ride from the park headquarters and a 5km trek to the swamp; the walk takes about three hours return. Alternatively, you can trek all the way with a guide along a tougher jungle route criss-crossed by streams.

Night treks are popular, as you've the chance of seeing crocs then, as well as other wildlife.

Cat Tien Bear & Wild Cat Rescue Station

Inside the national park, near the park headquarters, this rescue centre is home to nine sun bears and 25 black bears, rescued from poachers and/or bear bile farms. Other rescued animals include a small leopard and several golden-cheeked gibbons.

The conditions are not ideal, though the bears space-share a large outdoor area in which they're let loose every morning. The centre is due to relocate into new, larger premises 3km away soon.

Exploring the Park

Cat Tien National Park can be explored on foot, by mountain bike, by 4WD and also by boat along the Dong Nai River.

There are 14 well-established **hiking trails** in the park, colour-coded by the level of difficulty and ranging from 2km to 26km in length. Some are flat and paved, while others are demanding, muddy slogs that require crossing streams. Only the three most difficult trails require the services of a guide, as well as transport to and from the start of the trail.

If you need a guide, be sure to book one in advance; guides charge 800,000d for birdwatching excursions and 1,200,000d per day trek, regardless of group size. Take plenty of insect repellent. Leeches keep you company; you can rent 'leech socks' at the park HQ for a small fee.

RAE_THE_SPARROW/GETTY IMAGES ©

⮡ Where to Stay

The national park has accommodation that is handy for early-morning trekking. There are also an expanding number of lodges just outside the park entrance which are considerably more comfortable; all have restaurants.

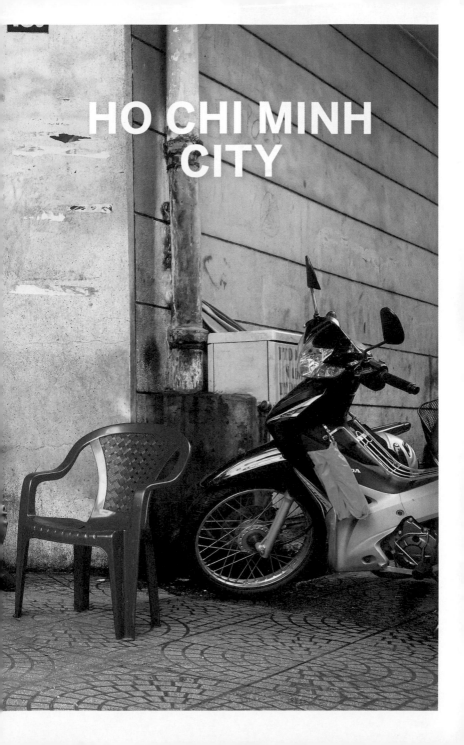

HO CHI MINH CITY

Ho Chi Minh City at a Glance...

Ho Chi Minh City (HCMC) is Vietnam at its most dizzying: a high-octane city of commerce and culture that has driven the country forward with its pulsating energy. A chaotic whirl, the city breathes life and vitality into all who settle here, and visitors cannot help but be hauled along for the ride. The ghosts of the past live on in buildings that one generation ago witnessed a city in turmoil, but now the real beauty of the former Saigon's urban collage is the seamless blending of these two worlds into one exciting mass.

Ho Chi Minh City in One Day

Explore old Saigon on foot (p180). After lunch at **Propaganda** (p202), head to the **War Remnants Museum** (p183) and then tour the **Reunification Palace** (p184). In the evening, catch sky-high sunset views from **Air 360** (p208), followed by a meal at the **Racha Room** (p202). Have a nightcap of bold craft beer at the **Pasteur Street Brewing Company** (p206), or punchy Asian-inspired cocktails at **Shrine** (p207).

Ho Chi Minh City in Two Days

Spend the morning in **Cholon** (p188), wandering around the market and historic temples. Catch a taxi up to District 3 for a cheap traditional lunch at **Banh Xeo 46A** (p203), then walk through Da Kao ward to the **Jade Emperor Pagoda** (p194) and **History Museum** (p182). In the evening, dine at **Cuc Gach Quan** (p203) and catch a band at **Acoustic** (p209).

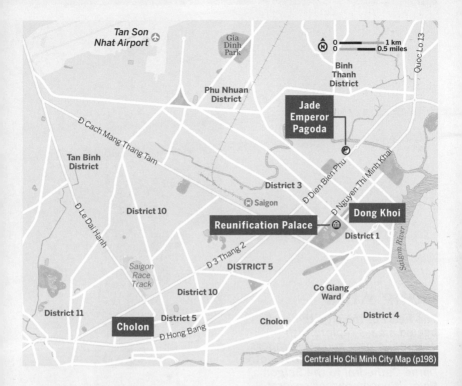

Central Ho Chi Minh City Map (p198)

Arriving in Ho Chi Minh City

Air Ho Chi Minh City's Tan Son Airport is 7km north of the central district and has a domestic and international terminal. Taxis to central districts (around 190,000d) take about 30 minutes. There's also an air-conditioned Route 152 bus (6000d, around 40 minutes, every 15 minutes, 6am to 6pm).

Train Trains arrive at Saigon station (Ga Sai Gon) just west of the centre. A taxi to the central district is around 50,000d.

Where to Stay

Within District 1, the Đ Dong Khoi area has smart hotels close to the city's best restaurants and bars, while Pham Ngu Lao scores for budget accommodation and cheap shopping. Around Ben Thanh Market has decent midrange options.

See p211 for more information.

Dong Khoi

The heart of the city, this well-heeled area is replete with designer stores and skyscrapers. Stretching from the august Notre Dame Cathedral to the Saigon River, it encompasses several tree-lined boulevards.

Great For...

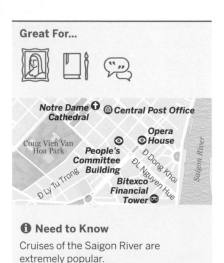

ⓘ Need to Know

Cruises of the Saigon River are extremely popular.

★ **Top Tip**
Escape the infernal HCMC traffic on the central pedestrianised section of ĐL Nguyen Hue.

Notre Dame Cathedral

Built between 1877 and 1883, **Notre Dame Cathedral** (Đ Han Thuyen) enlivens the heart of Ho Chi Minh City's government quarter, facing Đ Dong Khoi.

A brick, neo-Romanesque church with 40m-high square towers tipped with iron spires, the Catholic cathedral is named after the Virgin Mary. Interior walls are inlaid with devotional tablets and some stained glass survives.

English-speaking staff dispense tourist information from 9am to 11am Monday to Saturday. If the front gates are locked, try the door on the side facing the Reunification Palace.

Central Post Office

Right across the way from Notre Dame Cathedral, Ho Chi Minh City's striking French **post office** (2 Cong Xa Paris; ⊘7am-9.30pm) is a period classic, designed by Gustave Eiffel and built between 1886 and 1891.

Painted on the walls of its grand concourse are fascinating historic maps of South Vietnam, Saigon and Cholon, while a mosaic of Ho Chi Minh takes pride of place at the end of its barrel-vaulted hall. Note the magnificent tiled floor of the interior and the copious green-painted wrought iron.

Opera House interior detail

Opera House

Gracing the intersection of Đ Dong Khoi and ĐL Le Loi, this grand colonial edifice with a sweeping staircase was built in 1897 and is one of the city's most recognisable buildings. Officially known as the Municipal Theatre, the **Opera House** (Nha Hat Thanh Pho; ☎08-3823 7419; www.hbso.org.vn; Lam Son Sq) captures the flamboyance of France's belle époque. Performances range from ballet and opera to modern dance and musicals. Check the website for English-language listings and booking information.

> ☑ **Don't Miss**
> A performance of ballet or opera at the Opera House.

BILL PERRY/SHUTTERSTOCK ©

A popular event is the **AO Show** (www.aoshowsaigon.com; Opera House, Lam Son Sq; from 504,000d; ⊙either 6pm or 8pm most days), a one-hour performance combining music, dance and acrobatics.

People's Committee Building

The glorious **People's Committee Building** (Hôtel de Ville; ĐL Nguyen Hue), one of the city's most prominent landmarks, is home to the Ho Chi Minh City People's Committee.

Built between 1901 and 1908, the former Hôtel de Ville decorates the northwestern end of ĐL Nguyen Hue, but unfortunately the ornate interior is not open to the public. In 2015 the centre of ĐL Nguyen Hue was turned into a vibrant pedestrian-only mall bookended by a new statue of Ho Chi Minh to commemorate his 125th birthday.

Road access around the thoroughfare still courses with a kinetic river of two-wheeled traffic, especially on weekends. At the northeastern edge of ĐL Nguyen Hue adjoining Đ Dong Khoi, construction is ongoing for a central city station for Saigon's new metro system.

Bitexco Financial Tower

The 68-storey, 262m-high, Carlos Zapata–designed **skyscraper** (www.saigonskydeck.com; 2 Đ Hai Trieu; adult/child 200,000/130,000d; ⊙9.30am-9.30pm) dwarfs all around it. It's reportedly shaped like a lotus bulb, but also resembles a CD rack with a tambourine shoved into it. That tambourine is the 48th-floor **Saigon Skydeck**, with a helipad on its roof.

Choose a clear day and aim for sunset, or down a drink in the **Eon Heli Bar** (52nd fl, Bitexco Financial Tower, 2 Đ Hai Trieu; ⊙11.30am-2am) instead.

> ✗ **Take a Break**
> Soak up the Saigon views and enjoy a tasty meal in Secret Garden (p201).

Walking Tour: Old Saigon

Ho Chi Minh City may be rapidly modernising but this tour strips back the layers of modern lacquer to reveal the fascinating historic city beneath.

Start 23/9 Park
Distance 4km
Duration Three hours

7 Stately **Notre Dame Cathedral** (p178) sits just across the way from the magnificent Gustave Eiffel–designed **Central Post Office** (p178).

7
FINISH

Ð Le Duan

Ð Nguyen Du

DISTRICT 1

Ð Ngo Thoi Nhiem

Ð Vo Van Tan

Ð Nguyen Thi Dieu

Ð Truong Dinh

Ð Cach Mang Thang Tam

Cong Vien Van Hoa Park

1 23/9 Park borders the backpacker district and owes its shape to a former tenure as a railway terminus.

START **1**

2

Ð Pham Ngu Lao

Ð Nguyen Thai Hoc

ĐL Tran Hung Dao

Ð Yersin

Ð Ky Con

Ð Calmette

2 The lovely Sino-French **Fine Arts Museum** (p183) is stuffed with period details (and great art).

Classic Photo: The People's Committee Building is one of the city's most prominent landmarks.

Botanic Gardens

Saigon River

6 The **People's Committee Building** (p179) is a triumph of French colonial architecture. Its illuminated exterior attracts geckos at night.

5 HCMC's most famous hotel is the **Continental**, built in 1880 and featured in *The Quiet American*.

4 The landmark **Caravelle Hotel** housed foreign news bureaux and embassies during the American War.

Đ Dong Khoi

ĐL Hai Ba Trung

ĐL Nguyen Hue

Đ Ho Tung Mau

Đ Pasteur

Đ Ton Duc Thang

Đ Ham Nghi

Đ Nguyen Cong Tru

Đ Ban Chuong

Ben Nghe Channel

Take a break... Stop for a drink in the Eon Heli Bar (p179) on the 52nd floor and savour the views.

3 The Skydeck at the dramatic, contemporary **Bitexco Financial Tower** (p179) affords the ultimate vista.

2 NIGELSPIERS/SHUTTERSTOCK © 3 LE TU/SHUTTERSTOCK © 6 R M NUNES/SHUTTERSTOCK © 7 EFIRED SHUTTERSTOCK ©

Aircraft on display, War Remnants Museum

MILOSZ MASLANKA/SHUTTERSTOCK ©

City of Culture: HCMC's Museums

Ho Chi Minh City boasts a fascinating history. Fortunately the city has a roster of excellent museums where you can learn about its colonial past and wartime period.

Great For...

☑ Don't Miss

The Cham art inside the Fine Arts Museum.

Ho Chi Minh Museum

Nicknamed the 'Dragon House' (Nha Rong), this former customs house was built by the French authorities in 1863. The **museum** (Bao Tang Ho Chi Minh; 1 Ð Nguyen Tat Thanh, District 4; 10,000d; ⊗7.30-11.30am & 1.30-5pm Tue-Sun) houses many of Ho Chi Minh's personal effects, including some of his clothing, his sandals and spectacles. On the waterfront, just across Ben Nghe Channel from District 1, the museum is easily reached on foot by heading south along the river on Ð Ton Duc Thang and crossing the bridge.

History Museum

Built in 1929 by the Société des Études Indochinoises, this notable Sino-French **museum** (Bao Tang Lich Su; Ð Nguyen Binh Khiem; 15,000d; ⊗8-11.30am & 1.30-5pm

History Museum

Saigon
War Remnants Museum

Đ Điện Biên Phủ

Đ Nguyễn Thị Minh Khai

Saigon River

Fine Arts Museum

ĐL Lê Lợi

Ho Chi Minh Museum

❶ Need to Know

Some museums close for a lengthy lunch break.

✕ Take a Break

Nha Hang Ngon (p203) is a popular and stylish street-food cafe.

★ Top Tip

Check out the Requiem Exhibition (compiled by legendary war photographer Tim Page) in the War Remnants Museum.

Tue-Sun) houses a rewarding collection of artefacts illustrating the evolution of the cultures of Vietnam, from the Bronze Age Dong Son civilisation (which emerged in 2000 BC) and the Funan civilisation (1st to 6th centuries AD), to the Cham, Khmer and Vietnamese. The museum is just inside the main gate to the city's botanic gardens and zoo.

War Remnants Museum

Formerly the Museum of Chinese and American War Crimes, the **War Remnants Museum** (Bao Tang Chung Tich Chien Tranh; ☑08-3930 5587; http://warremnantsmuseum. com; 28 Đ Vo Van Tan, cnr Đ Le Quy Don; 15,000d; ☺7.30am-noon & 1.30-5pm) is consistently popular with Western tourists. Few museums anywhere convey the brutality of war and its civilian victims quite this clearly.

Many of the atrocities documented here were well-publicised but rarely do Westerners hear the victims of US military action tell their own stories, as they do here.

While some displays are one-sided, many of the most disturbing photographs illustrating US atrocities are from US sources, including those of the infamous My Lai Massacre.

Fine Arts Museum

With its airy corridors and verandas, this elegant 1929 colonial-era yellow-and-white **building** (Bao Tang My Thuat; 97a Đ Pho Duc Chinh; 10,000d; ☺9am-5pm Tue-Sun) is stuffed with period details; it is exuberantly tiled throughout and home to some fine (albeit deteriorated) stained glass, as well as one of Saigon's oldest lifts.

Hung from the walls is an impressive selection of art, including thoughtful pieces from the modern period. As well as contemporary art, much of it (unsurprisingly) inspired by war, the museum displays historical pieces dating back to the 4th century.

Meeting room, Reunification Palace

Reunification Palace

Surrounded by royal palm trees, the dissonant 1960s architecture of this government building and its historic significance make it an essential sight.

Great For...

ℹ Need to Know

Reunification Palace (Dinh Thong Nhat; 📞08-3829 4117; www.dinhdoclap. gov.vn; Đ Nam Ky Khoi Nghia; adult/child 30,000/5000d; ⊘7.30-11am & 1-5pm)

★ **Top Tip**
English- and French-speaking guides are on duty during opening hours.

KANOKRATNOK/SHUTTERSTOCK ©

Wartime Role

The first Communist tanks to arrive in Saigon rumbled here on 30 April 1975 and it's as if time has stood still since then. The building is deeply associated with the fall of the city in 1975, yet it's the kitsch detailing and period motifs that steal the show.

After crashing through the wrought-iron gates – in a dramatic scene recorded by photojournalists and shown around the world – a soldier ran into the building and up the stairs to unfurl a VC flag from the balcony. In an ornate reception chamber, General Minh, who had become head of the South Vietnamese state only 42 hours before, waited with his improvised cabinet. 'I have been waiting since early this morning to transfer power to you,' Minh said to the VC officer who entered the room. 'There is no question of your transferring power,' replied the officer. 'You cannot give up what you do not have.'.

Historical Background

In 1868 a residence was built on this site for the French governor-general of Cochinchina and gradually it expanded to become Norodom Palace. When the French departed, the palace became home to the South Vietnamese president Ngo Dinh Diem. So unpopular was Diem that his own air force bombed the palace in 1962 in an unsuccessful attempt to kill him.

The president ordered a new residence to be built on the same site, this time with a sizeable bomb shelter in the basement. Work was completed in 1966, but Diem did not get to see his dream house as he was killed by his own troops in 1963.

Antique radio transmitters

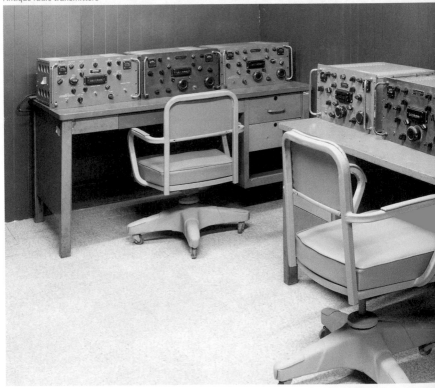

Independence Palace

The new building was named Independence Palace and was home to the successive South Vietnamese president, Nguyen Van Thieu, until his hasty departure in 1975. Designed by Paris-trained Vietnamese architect Ngo Viet Thu, it is an outstanding example of 1960s architecture, with an airy and open atmosphere.

Visiting the Palace

The ground floor is arranged with meeting rooms, while upstairs is a grand set of reception rooms, used for welcoming foreign and national dignitaries. In the back of the structure are the president's living quarters; check out the model boats, horse tails and severed elephants' feet. The 2nd floor contributes a shagadelic card-playing room, complete with a cheesy round leather banquette, a barrel-shaped bar, hubcap light fixtures and groovy three-legged chairs set around a flared-legged card table. There's also a cinema and a rooftop nightclub, complete with helipad: James Bond/Austin Powers – eat your heart out.

Perhaps most fascinating of all is the basement with its telecommunications centre, war room and warren of tunnels, where hulking old fans chop the air and ancient radio transmitters sit impassively.

Towards the end are rooms where videos appraise the palace and its history in Vietnamese, English, French, Chinese and Japanese. The national anthem is played at the end of the tape and you are expected to stand up – it would be rude not to.

☑ **Don't Miss**

The basement is fascinating, with its telecommunications centre, war room and warren of tunnels.

WORLDPICS/SHUTTERSTOCK ©

✗ **Take a Break**

Cyclo Resto (p204) offers fine-value local food.

Thien Hau Pagoda (p190)

Cholon

Rummage through Cholon (District 5) and lift the lid on a treasure trove of historic temples, impressive pagodas, a fine market and Chinese flavours.

Great For...

Phung Son Pagoda

ⓟ Khanh Van Nam Vien Pagoda

Quan Am Pagoda

Đ Hong Bang

Cha Tam Church ⓘ

Thien Hau Pagoda

Binh Tay Market ◉

ⓘ Need to Know

A taxi from Pham Ngu Lao to Cholon costs around 100,000d or hop on bus 1 from Ben Thanh Market.

★ **Top Tip**

For in-depth tours of Cholon, contact local expert **Tim Doling** (www.historic vietnam.com).

惠
土成
方會
館

歐風亞雨雨調和

慕鼓晨鐘同覺悟

天功至善承總我先賢怨怨赤誠匡教化

惠福夫人戴業少近

大帝

Background

Ho Chi Minh City's Chinatown is less Chinese than it once was, largely due to the 1978–79 anticapitalist and anti-Chinese campaign, when many ethnic Chinese fled the country, taking with them their money and entrepreneurial skills. A lot of those refugees have since returned (with foreign passports) to explore investment possibilities. Full-form written Chinese characters (as opposed to the simplified system used in mainland China) decorate shopfronts and temples in abundance, adding to the sensation that you have strayed into a forgotten corner of China.

Cholon means 'big market' and during the American War it was home to a thriving black market. Like much of HCMC, Cholon's historic shopfronts are swiftly disappearing under advertising hoardings or succumbing to developers' bulldozers, but some traditional architecture survives and an atmospheric strip of traditional herb shops thrives between Đ Luong Nhu Hoc and Đ Trieu Quang Phuc, providing both a visual and an olfactory reminder of the old Chinese city.

Binh Tay Market

Cholon's **main market** (Cho Binh Tay; www.chobinhtay.gov.vn; 57a ĐL Thap Muoi; ⊘6am-7.30pm) has a great clock tower and a central courtyard with gardens. Much of the business here is wholesale but it's popular with tour groups. The market was originally built by the French in the 1880s; Guangdong-born philanthropist Quach Dam paid for its rebuilding and was commemorated by a statue that is now in the Fine Arts

Museum. Expect a friendly welcome when you sit down for breakfast or coffee with the market's street-food vendors.

Thien Hau Pagoda

This gorgeous 19th-century **temple** (Ba Mieu, Pho Mieu, Chua Ba Thien Hau; 710 Đ Nguyen Trai) FREE is dedicated to the goddess Thien Hau, and always attracts a mix of worshippers and visitors who mingle beneath the large coils of incense suspended overhead. It is believed that Thien Hau can travel over the oceans on a mat and ride the clouds to save people in trouble on the high seas.

Phung Son Pagoda

Built between 1802 and 1820 on the site of structures from the Funan period, dating back at least to the early centuries of Christianity, this **Buddhist temple** (Phung Son Tu,

Fruit and vegetable stall, Bin Tay Market

☑ Don't Miss

Cha Tam Church's interior is decorated with images of the Stations of the Cross, while holy water is dispensed from huge clam shells.

✕ Take a Break

Binh Tay Market has some terrific food stalls.

Chua Go; 1408 ĐL 3 Thang 2, District 11; ⊘prayers 4-5am, 4-5pm & 6-7pm) is extremely rich in gilded, painted and beautifully fashioned bronze, wood, ceramic and beaten copper statuary. The **main dais**, with its many levels, is dominated by a large gilded A Di Da Buddha (the Buddha of Infinite Light; Amitābha). The main entrances are usually locked most of the time, but the side entrance is open during prayer times.

Khanh Van Nam Vien Pagoda

Built between 1939 and 1942, this **temple** (269/2 Đ Nguyen Thi Nho) is said to be the only pure Taoist temple in Vietnam and is unique for its colourful statues of Taoist disciples. Features to seek out include the unique 150cm-high statue of Laotse – the supreme philosopher of Taoism and author of the *Dao De Jing* (The Classic of the Way and its Power) – located upstairs.

Quan Am Pagoda

One of Cholon's most active and colourful temples, this **shrine** (Chua Quan Am; 12 Đ Lao Tu) FREE was founded in the early 19th century. It's named after the Goddess of Mercy, whose full name is Quan The Am Bo Tat, literally 'the bodhisattva who listens to the cries of the world', in reflection of her compassionate mission.

Cha Tam Church

Built around the turn of the 19th century, this decaying light-caramel-painted **church** (25 Đ Hoc Lac; ⊘7am-noon, 2-6pm & 7-9pm) FREE exudes a sleepy, tropical feel. A pew in the church is marked with a small plaque identifying the spot where President Ngo Dinh Diem was seized after taking refuge here with his brother Ngo Dinh Nhu on 2 November 1963, after fleeing the Presidential Palace.

A guide demonstrates a concealed tunnel

Day Trip: Cu Chi Tunnels

The tunnel network of Cu Chi became legendary for its role in facilitating Viet Cong (VC) control of a large rural area during the American War. Tours are justifiably very popular.

Great For...

☑ Don't Miss

An M-41 tank and a bomb crater are near the exit of the Ben Dinh tunnels.

Extent

At its peak the tunnel system stretched from the South Vietnamese capital to the Cambodian border; in the district of Cu Chi alone more than 250km of tunnels honeycomb the ground. The network, parts of which were several storeys deep, included countless trapdoors, constructed living areas, storage facilities, weapon factories, field hospitals, command centres and kitchens.

History

The tunnels of Cu Chi were built over a period of 25 years, beginning sometime in the late 1940s. They were the improvised response of a poorly equipped peasant army to its enemy's high-tech ordnance, helicopters, artillery, bombers and chemical weapons.

Inside one of the enlarged tunnels

XUANHUONGHO/SHUTTERSTOCK ©

ⓘ Need to Know

Cu Chi Tunnels (adult/child 110,000/30,000d)

✕ Take a Break

Snack vendors can be found around the tunnels.

★ Top Tip

Cu Chi tours often include a trip to the **Cu Chi Wildlife Rescue Station** (www. wildlifeatrisk.org; adult/child US$5/free; ⊙ 7.30-11.30am & 1-4.30pm).

The Viet Minh built the first tunnels in the red earth of Cu Chi during the war against the French. The tunnel system later assumed enormous strategic importance when the area came under VC control.

Cu Chi Tunnels

Two sections of this remarkable tunnel network (which are enlarged and upgraded versions of the real thing) are open to the public. One is near the village of Ben Dinh and the other is 15km beyond at Ben Duoc.

Most tourists visiting the tunnels end up at Ben Dinh, as it's easier for tour buses to reach. Even if you stay above ground, it's still an interesting experience learning about the region's ingenious and brave resistance activities.

Ben Dinh

The most visited of the tunnel sites, this small, renovated section is near the village of Ben Dinh, about 50km from HCMC.

In one of the classrooms at the visitors centre a large map shows the extent of the network while another shows cross-section diagrams of the tunnels. The section of the tunnel system presently open to visitors is a few hundred metres south of the visitors centre. It snakes up and down through various chambers along its 50m length.

Ben Duoc

The tunnels here have been enlarged to accommodate tourists, although they're still a tight squeeze. Inside the underground chambers are bunkers, a hospital and a command centre that played a role in the 1968 Tet Offensive. The set pieces include tables, chairs, beds, lights, and dummies outfitted in guerrilla gear.

Worshippers burn incense, Jade Emperor Pagoda

SALA JEAN/SHUTTERSTOCK ©

Jade Emperor Pagoda

Built in 1909 to honour the supreme Taoist god, this is one of the most spectacularly atmospheric temples in the city, stuffed with statues of phantasmal divinities and grotesque heroes.

Main Temple Structure

Inside the main building are two especially fierce and menacing Taoist figures. On the right (as you face the altar) is a 4m-high statue of the general who defeated the Green Dragon (depicted underfoot). On the left is the general who defeated the White Tiger, which is also being stepped on.

Worshippers mass before the ineffable Jade Emperor, who presides – draped in luxurious robes and shrouded in a dense fug of incense smoke – over the main sanctuary. He is flanked by his guardians, the Four Big Diamonds (Tu Dai Kim Cuong), so named because they are said to be as hard as diamonds.

Great For...

☑ Don't Miss

A small pond in the compound seethes with turtles, some of which have shells inscribed with auspicious inscriptions.

Statue detail, Jade Emperor Pagoda

TRAN THI HAI YEN/SHUTTERSTOCK ©

Thi Nghe Channel

Đ Tran Quang Khai **Jade Emperor Pagoda**

Đ Vo Thi Sau

Đ Dien Bien Phu

Đ Nguyen Binh Khiem

❶ Need to Know

Jade Emperor Pagoda (Phuoc Hai Tu, Chua Ngoc Hoang; 73 Đ Mai Thi Luu; ☺7am-6pm, 1st & 15th of lunar month 5am-7pm) FREE

✕ Take a Break

Check out the arty hang-out **Decibel** (www.decibel.vn; 79/2/5 Đ Phan Kê Binh; ☺7.30am-midnight Mon-Sat) for a drink.

★ Top Tip
The temple's statues, depicting characters from Buddhist and Taoist lore, are made from papier-mâché.

The Chief of Hell

Off the Jade Emperor's chamber is another room presided over by Thanh Hoang, the Chief of Hell; to the left is his red horse. Other figures here represent the gods who dispense punishments for evil acts and rewards for good deeds. The room also contains the famous Hall of the Ten Hells, carved wooden panels illustrating the varied torments awaiting evil people in each of the Ten Regions of Hell. Women queue up at the seated effigy of the City God, who wears a hat inscribed with Chinese characters that announce 'At one glance, money is given'. In a mesmerising ritual, worshippers first put money into a box, then rub a piece of red paper against his hand before circling it around a candle flame.

Women's Chamber

This fascinating little room has the ceramic figures of 12 women, overrun with children and wearing colourful clothes, sitting in two rows of six. Each of the women exemplifies a human characteristic, either good or bad (as in the case of the woman drinking alcohol from a jug). Each figure represents a year in the 12-year Chinese astrological calendar. Presiding over the room is Kim Hoa Thanh Mau, the Chief of All Women. Upstairs is a hall to Quan Am, the Goddess of Mercy, opposite a portrait of Dat Ma, the bearded Indian founder of Zen Buddhism.

⊙ SIGHTS

Saigon Central Mosque   Mosque

(66 Đ Dong Du) Built by South Indian Muslims in 1935 on the site of an earlier mosque, lime-green Saigon Central Mosque is an immaculately clean and well-tended island of calm in the bustling Dong Khoi area. In front of the sparkling white and blue structure, with its four decorative minarets, is a pool for the ritual ablutions required by Islamic law before prayers.

Take off your shoes before entering the building.

Mariamman Hindu Temple   Hindu Temple

(Chua Ba Mariamman; 45 Đ Truong Dinh; ⊘7.30am-7.30pm) Only a small number of Hindus live in HCMC, but this colourful slice of southern India is also considered sacred by many ethnic Vietnamese and Chinese. Reputed to have miraculous powers, the temple was built at the end of the 19th century and dedicated to the Hindu goddess Mariamman. Remove your shoes before stepping onto the slightly raised platform and ignore any demands to buy joss sticks and jasmine. The temple is three blocks west of Ben Thanh Market.

❸ ACTIVITIES

Les Rives   Boating

(☑0128-592 0018; www.lesrivesexperience. com; Bach Dang jetty; sunset cruises adult/child 1,399,00/980,000d, Mekong Delta cruises adult/ child 2,499,000/1,799,000d) Runs sunset boat tours (minimum two people) at 4pm along canals beyond the city edges, and a Mekong Delta cruise which departs at 7.30am and takes seven to nine hours.

It can also convey you to the Cu Chi Tunnels (adult/child 1,899,000/1,299,000d) and Can Gio (adult/child 2,399,000/ 1,799,000d) by boat. Other options include incorporating *cyclo* excursions or cooking classes.

> *Saigon Central Mosque is an immaculately clean and well-tended island of calm...*

Saigon Central Mosque

MATYAS REHAK/SHUTTERSTOCK ©

L'Apothiquaire   Spa
(La Maison de L'Apothiquaire; ☑08-3932 5181; www.lapothiquaire.com; 64a Ð Truong Dinh, District 3; ◷8.30am-9pm) Long considered the city's most elegant spa, L'Apothiquaire is housed in a beautiful white mansion tucked down a quiet alley, with a pool and sauna. Guests enjoy body wraps, massages, facials, foot treatments and herbal baths, and L'Apothiquaire makes its own line of lotions and cosmetics.

Other branches are located in **District 1** (☑08-3822 2158; www.lapothiquaire.com; 100 Ð Mac Thi Buoi, District 1) and **Saigon South** (☑08-5413 6638; 103 Ð Ton Dat Thien, District 7).

Aveda   Spa
(☑08-3519 4679; www.facebook.com/aveda herbal; Villa 21/1 Ð Xuan Thuy; ◷9am-8pm) Across in District 2, but worth the journey for its intensely soothing Indian-influenced Ayurvedic spa and massage treatments.

Aqua Day Spa   Spa
(☑08-3827 2828; www.aquadayspasaigon.com; Sheraton Saigon, 88 Ð Dong Khoi; ◷10am-11pm; ⊕) One of HCMC's smartest hotel spas, this beautiful space offers a range of treatments, including warm-stone massage, foot pampering and facials.

🎓 COURSES

GRAIN Cooking Classes   Cooking
(☑08-3827 4929; www.grainbyluke.com; Level 3, 71-75 ÐL Hai Ba Trung; per person from US$48; ◷9am-noon & 2-5pm Mon-Sat) These cooking classes are designed and coordinated by Vietnamese-Australian celebrity chef Luke Nguyen. Four-course menus change regularly to reflect seasonal produce, and Luke himself is on hand for some classes throughout the year. Check the website for timings.

Saigon Cooking Class   Cooking
(☑08-3825 8485; www.saigoncookingclass.com; 74/7 ÐL Hai Ba Trung; per adult/child under 12yr US$39/25; ◷10am & 2pm Tue-Sun) Learn from the chefs at Hoa Tuc restaurant as they prepare three mains (including *pho bo* – beef noodle soup – and some of their signature

War Surplus Market

Dan Sinh Market (104 Ð Yersin; ◷7am-6pm) Also known as the War Surplus Market, this is the place to find authentic combat boots or rusty (and perhaps less authentic) dog tags among the hardware stalls. There are also handy gas masks, field stretchers, rain gear, mosquito nets, canteens, duffel bags, ponchos, boots and flak jackets.

dishes) and one dessert. A market visit is optional (per adult/child under 12 years US$45/28, including a three-hour class).

🎓 TOURS

Detoured   Tours
(☑0168-597 6136; www.detouredasia.com; per person US$55-65) Excellent walking tours with an inquisitive and fun Saigon expat discovering hidden secrets of the city. Highlights include funky street art, hip cafes and shops concealed in art-deco apartment blocks, good street snacks, and lunch in a chic Vietnamese restaurant. Additional transport between walking stops is by taxi or motorbike.

Vespa Adventures   Tours
(☑0122-299 3585; www.vespaadventures. com; 169a Ð De Tham; per person from US$69) Zooming out of **Café Zoom** (www.facebook. com/cafezoomsaigon; 169a Ð De Tham), Vespa Adventures offers entertaining, guided city tours on vintage scooters, as well as multiday trips around southern Vietnam. Embracing food, drink and music, the Saigon After Dark tour is brilliant fun.

Sophie's Art Tour   Tour
(☑0121-830 3742; www.sophiesarttour.com; per person US$55; ◷9am-1pm Tue-Sat) Highly engaging and informative four-hour tour from expert Sophie Hughes, who has her finger on the pulse of the HCMC art scene. Tours visit the Fine Arts Museum, private collections and contemporary art spaces,

Central Ho Chi Minh City

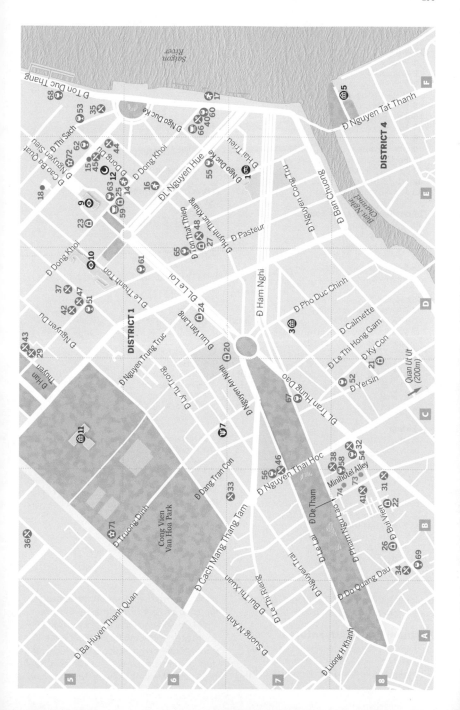

Saigon River

Đ Tôn Đức Thắng

DISTRICT 4

Đ Nguyễn Tất Thành

DISTRICT 1

Công Viên Văn Hoa Park

Đ Cách Mạng Tháng Tám

Central Ho Chi Minh City

explaining the influence of recent Vietnamese history on artistic style and technique.

Vietnam Photo Adventures Tours

(📞0913 236 876; www.vietnamphotoadventures.com; per person US$29-59) Get creative with your camera and produce your own photographic memories on various tours focusing on Saigon landmarks, the street life of Cholon and local neighbourhoods. Tours are conducted by an experienced photographer who is also a long-term resident of Vietnam. Longer one- and two-night trips in the Mekong Delta are also available.

🔒 SHOPPING

🔒 Dong Khoi Area

Ben Thanh Market   Market
(Cho Ben Thanh; ĐL Le Loi, ĐL Ham Nghi, ĐL Tran Hung Dao & Đ Le Lai; ☺5am-6pm) Centrally located, Ben Thanh and its surrounding streets comprise one of Saigon's liveliest areas. Everything that's commonly eaten, worn or used by the Saigonese is piled high, and souvenir items can be found in equal abundance. Vendors are determined and prices usually higher than elsewhere (restaurant stalls are reasonable), so bargain vigorously and ignore any 'Fixed Price' signs.

Good restaurant stalls are usually open until midafternoon. It's an area where it pays to be extra vigilant about looking after personal items and electronics.

Once the indoors market closes, a small night market just outside takes over until midnight.

Mekong Quilts   Arts & Crafts
(📞08-2210 3110; www.mekong-quilts.org; 1st fl, 68 ĐL Le Loi; ☺9am-7pm) 🖊 Beautiful handmade silk quilts, sewn by the rural poor in support of a sustainable income.

Giant Step
Urban Art Gallery   Art
(📞0126-415 4338; 3a Đ Ton Duc Thang; ☺11am-6pm Mon-Sat) Excellent gallery and retail outlet focusing on street art. Find it on Facebook to see what exhibitions are scheduled. The surrounding laneways are also packed with street art.

Saigon Kitsch   Gifts & Souvenirs
(33 Đ Ton That Thiep; ☺9am-10pm) This colourful French-run shop specialises in reproduction propaganda items, emblazoning its revolutionary motifs on coffee mugs, coasters, jigsaws and T-shirts. Also cool laptop and tablet covers fashioned from recycled Vietnamese packaging.

Mai Lam   Clothing
(www.mailam.com.vn; 132-134 Đ Dong Khoi; ☺9am-9pm) Vibrant, colourful, creative and highly inspiring, Mai Lam carries beautiful (but pricey) hand-stitched men and women's clothing and accessories.

Mystere   Arts & Crafts
(141 Đ Dong Khoi; ☺9am-10pm) Attractive lacquerware, fabrics and jewellery sourced from ethnic minority peoples and hill tribes.

🔒 Pham Ngu Lao Area

Hanoi Gallery   Propaganda Posters
(79 Đ Bui Vien; ☺9am-10pm) Fans of socialist realism should visit this very cool little store selling both original (or so we're told) propaganda posters (US$600) and A3 prints (US$10).

Orange   Fashion & Accessories
(180 Đ Bui Vien; ☺9am-10pm) Funky T-shirts and bags.

🍴 EATING

Ho Chi Minh City is Vietnam's culinary capital. Delicious regional fare is complemented by a well-developed choice of international restaurants, with Indian, Japanese, Thai, Italian and East–West fusions well represented. Unsurprisingly, given its heritage, HCMC has a fine selection of French restaurants, from the casual bistro to haute cuisine.

🍴 Dong Khoi Area

Secret Garden   Vietnamese $
(8th fl, 158 Đ Pasteur; meals 55,000-80,000d; ☺8am-10pm; 🖊) Negotiate the stairs in this faded Saigon apartment building to arrive at Secret Garden's wonderful rooftop restaurant. Rogue chickens peck away in the herb garden, Buddhist statues add Asian ambience, and delicious homestyle dishes are served up with city views. Service can sometimes be a little *too* casual, but it's worth persevering for the great flavours.

5Ku Station   Barbecue $
(29 Đ Le Thanh Thon; meals around 100,000d; ☺4pm-late) Hopping with evening diners, this chain of makeshift-looking *al fresco* barbecue restaurants is fun, boisterous,

Porcelain figure, Mariamman Hindu Temple (p196)

...this colourful slice of India is also considered sacred by many ethnic Vietnamese...

outgoing and tasty. Grab yourself a wooden box seat, a cold beer and chow down on barbecue and hotpot alongside a mix of locals, travellers and expats.

Huong Lai   Vietnamese $
(🕿08-3822 6814; www.huonglai2001saigon. com; 38 Đ Ly Tu Trong; meals 70,000-180,000d; ⏰noon-3pm & 6-10pm) A must for finely presented, traditional Vietnamese food, the airy and high-ceilinged loft of an old French-era shophouse is the setting for dining with a difference. Staff are from disadvantaged families or are former street children and receive on-the-job training, education and a place to stay.

Racha Room   Thai $$
(🕿0908 791 412; www.facebook.com/theracha-room; 12-14 Đ Mac Thi Buoi; shared plates 195,000-320,000d; ⏰11.30am-midnight) The Racha Room is one of the city's most hip eateries.

Thai street food underpins the diverse menu of bar snacks (40,000d to 150,000d) and shared plates, but it effortlessly stretches to include neighbouring countries as well. Asian-inspired cocktails ensure the Racha Room is also one of the city's best bars. Pop in for happy hour from 5pm to 7.30pm.

Propaganda   Vietnamese $$
(🕿08-3822 9048; www.propagandasaigon. com; Đ 21 Han Thuyen; meals 105,000-185,000d; ⏰7.30am-10.30pm) Colourful murals and retro socialist posters brighten up this popular bistro with park views. The menu focuses on street-food classics from around Vietnam, all enjoyed with a bustling and energetic ambience. Salads are particularly good – try the wild pepper and green mango salad with barbecue chicken – and retreat to the 1st floor if downstairs is too crowded.

Nha Hang Ngon   Vietnamese $$
(🕿08-3827 7131; 160 Đ Pasteur; meals 60,000-260,000d; ⏰7am-10pm; 🛜) Thronging with locals and foreigners, this is one of HCMC's most popular spots, with a large

THOR JORGEN UDVANG/SHUTTERSTOCK ©

range of the very best street food in stylish surroundings across three levels. Set in a leafy garden ringed by food stalls, each cook serves up a specialised traditional dish, ensuring an authentic taste of Vietnamese, Thai, Japanese or Chinese cuisine.

Hum Lounge & Restaurant   Vegetarian $$

(☑08-3823 8920; www.humvietnam.vn; 2 Đ Thi Sach; meals 80,000-190,000d; ⊙10am-10pm; 🛜🖊) This new opening brings the excellent Vietnamese-inspired vegetarian cuisine of the city's long-established **Hum Vegetarian Cafe & Restaurant** (☑08-3930 3819; 32 Đ Vo Van Tan) to a central garden location. Settle into the elegant and verdant space and enjoy dishes including papaya and banana-flower salads, mushrooms steamed in coconut, and the subtle combination of braised tofu with star anise and cinnamon.

Temple Club   Vietnamese $$

(☑08-3829 9244; www.templeclub.com.vn; 29 Đ Ton That Thiep; meals 120,000-210,000d; ⊙noon-midnight; 🛜🖊) This classy establishment, on the 2nd floor of a beautiful colonial-era villa decorated with spiritual motifs and elegant Chinese characters, offers a huge selection of delectable Vietnamese dishes, including vegetarian specialities, alongside a spectrum of spirited cocktails.

Au Parc   Cafe $$

(☑08-3822 3080; www.auparcsaigon.com; 23 Đ Han Thuyen; meals 125,000-275,000d; ⊙7am-11pm; 🛜) The laptop and tablet crowd flocks to this slender two-floor cafe for its Mediterranean and Middle Eastern–inflected selection of salads, quiches, baguettes, focaccia, pasta, mezze and light grills, from breakfast and brunch to dinner. Many ingredients are homemade, and the smoothies, juices and views of the park are all sublime. There's a nonsmoking lounge upstairs.

Relish & Sons   Bistro $$

(☑012 0721 4294; www.facebook.com/relishandsons; 44 Đ Dong Du; meals 100,000-170,000d; ⊙8am-midnight; 🛜) Relish & Sons brings a versatile Melbourne vibe to Saigon. Kick off with good coffee and eggs lots of ways,

before returning for gourmet burgers, bar snacks, and craft beer and cider on tap. Later in the evening, cocktails with an Asian spin become most people's drink of choice. Try the Sugar 'n' Spice with Vietnamese mint and fresh pomelo.

Maxim's Nam An   Vietnamese $$$

(☑08-3829 6676; www.maxims.com.vn; 15 Đ Dong Khoi; meals 190,000-400,000d; ⊙7pm-late) Something of a Saigon legend, this supper club is distinguished more for its over-the-top jazz club ambience and live music than for the food, which is fine if not jaw-dropping. If you're after a memorable experience though, you could do a lot worse.

✪ Da Kao & Around

Banh Xeo 46A   Vietnamese $

(☑08-3824 1110; 46a Đ Dinh Cong Trang; regular/extra large 70,000/110,000d; ⊙10am-9pm; 🖊) Locals will always hit the restaurants that specialise in a single dish and this renowned spot serves some of the best *banh xeo* in town. These Vietnamese rice-flour pancakes stuffed with bean sprouts, prawns and pork (vegetarian versions available) are legendary. Other dishes available include excellent *goi cuon* (fresh summer rolls with pork and prawn).

Cuc Gach Quan   Vietnamese $$

(☑08-3848 0144; www.cucgachquan.com.vn/en; 10 Đ Dang Tat; meals 75,000-200,000d; ⊙9am-midnight) It comes as little surprise that the owner is an architect when you step into this cleverly renovated old villa. The decor is rustic and elegant at the same time, which is also true of the food. Despite its tucked-away location in the northernmost reaches of District 1, this is no secret hideaway: book ahead.

Tib   Vietnamese $$

(☑08-3829 7242; www.tibrestaurant.com.vn; 187 Đ Hai Ba Trung; mains 125,000-285,000d; 🛜) Visiting presidents and prime ministers have slunk down this lantern- and fairy-light-festooned alley and into this atmospheric old house to sample Tib's imperial Hue cuisine. Although you could probably find similar food for less money elsewhere, the setting is wonderful. **Tib Vegetarian** (11 Đ Tran Nhat Duat; mains 40,000-60,000d; 🍴) offers a more relaxed alternative with a cheaper and less formal spin on the vegetarian menu.

✖ Reunification Palace & Around

Cyclo Resto   Vietnamese $
(📞0975 513 011; www.cycloresto.com.vn; 6.28 Đ Cach Mang Thang Tam; 5 courses US$6; ⏰11am-10pm) This place offers some of the best-value food in town. For US$6 you get five fabulous Vietnamese dishes. The popular cooking course – incorporating five dishes is US$29 – and US$10 *cyclo* tours of the city are also available.

San Fu Lou   Dim Sum $$
(📞08-3823 9513; www.sanfulou.com; Ground fl, AB Tower, 76a Đ Le Lai; dim sum 45,000-175,000d; ⏰7am-3am) Always bustling, the modern San Fu Lou offers a fine array of Cantonese dim sum shared plates. Highlights include duck and black-truffle dumplings and beef short ribs with ginger

and black pepper. Bring along a few friends so you can sample more of the huge menu, and be ready to linger longer than first planned.

Marina   Vietnamese, Seafood $$
(📞08-3930 2379; 172 Đ Nguyen Dinh Chieu; meals 100,000-500,000d; ⏰11am-11pm) Ask a sample of well-to-do Saigonese where to go for seafood and the chances are they will recommend this place. It's definitely geared to local tastes (bright lights, TVs playing sports, and bad piped music), but the food is delicious, particularly squid and the soft-shell crabs.

✖ Pham Ngu Lao Area

Five Oysters   Vietnamese $
(www.fiveoysters.com; 234 Đ Bui Vien; meals from 35,000d; ⏰9am-11pm) With a strong seafood slant and friendly service, light and bright Five Oysters in backpackerland is frequently packed with travellers feasting on oysters (30,000d), grilled octopus, seafood soup, snail pie, *pho,* fried noodles, grilled mackerel with chilli oil and more.

From left: Iced coffees; *Goi cuon* (rice-paper rolls); Papaya salad from a street stall

Bargain-priced beer also makes it a popular spot along the PNL strip.

Margherita International $

(175/1 Đ Pham Ngu Lao; meals 35,000-100,000d; ⊙8am-10pm) A golden oldie, Margherita cooks up Vietnamese, Italian and Mexican food at a steal. Secure an outdoor table, order a freshly squeezed juice, and watch the world go by on one of PNL's busier side streets.

Coriander Thai $

(16 Đ Bui Vien; meals 75,000-180,000d; ⊙11am-2pm & 5-11pm) The blond-wood furniture and cheap bamboo wallpaper do Coriander few favours, but the menu is stuffed with authentic Siamese delights. The lovely fried *doufu* (tofu) is almost a meal in itself, the green curry is zesty, and the claypot seafood fried rice is excellent.

Mon Hue Vietnamese $

(www.nhahangmonhue.vn; 201 Đ De Tham; meals 45,000-120,000d; ⊙6am-11pm; ❄️📶🍴) Hue's famous cuisine comes to HCMC's hungry hordes through this chain of eight restaurants. This handy branch offers a good,

air-conditioned introduction for travellers who don't make it to the old capital.

Quan Ut Ut Barbecue $$

(📞08-3914 4500; www.quanutut.com; 168 Đ Vo Van Kiet; meals 180,000-300,000d; ⊙4-11.30pm) With a name roughly translating to the 'Oink Oink Eatery', this casual place with river views celebrates everything porcine with an American-style barbecue spin. Huge street-side grills prepare great ribs, spicy sausages and pork belly, and tasty sides include charred sweetcorn and grilled pineapple. Huge burgers are also good, and the owners even make their own flavour-packed craft beers.

Thao Dien (District 2)

Boat House Bistro $$

(📞08-3744 6790; www.facebook.com/boathousevietnam; 40 Lily Rd, APSC Compound, 36 Đ Thao Dien; bar snacks 65,000-165,000d, meals 145,000-195,000d; ⊙8am-11pm) This versatile spot features many riverside options. Enjoy a leisurely lunch at the outside tables, sit at the bar for a few beers, or graduate to cocktails on the daybeds. Food runs from

DORY F/SHUTTERSTOCK ©

Fruit seller, Ho Chi Minh City

bar snacks to burgers, salads and wraps, and weekdays from 4.30pm to 6.30pm there are good happy-hour specials. Look forward to occasional live music too.

The MAD House   Bistro $$
(📞08-3519 4009; www.facebook.com/mad-saigon; 6/1/2 Đ Nguyen U Di; meals 150,000-300,000đ; ⏰5-10pm Mon, 11.30am-10pm Tue-Fri, 9am-10pm Sat & Sun; 🛜) The MAD House is a popular option for the expat denizens of District 2. Highlights include excellent coffee, robust cocktails, and an innovative menu blending Scandinavian and Vietnamese influences – MAD House translates to Food House in Danish. Look forward to stunning tropical decor and a lovely garden area that's a perfect retreat from the bustle of the city.

Trois Gourmands   French $$$
(📞08-3744 4585; http://3gourmandsaigon.com; 39 Đ Tran Ngoc Dien; meals from 400,000đ; ⏰noon-3pm & 6-10.30pm Tue-Sun) An elegant villa-with-swimming-pool setting is the venue for this impressive restaurant, overseen by the warm and welcoming former

sommelier and Frenchman Gils Brault. Champions of fine food served through indulgent set menus, Trois Gourmands is worth the trek: cheese lovers can come for the selection alone, made in-house, while the wine choice is naturally strong.

🍷 DRINKING & NIGHTLIFE

Happening Ho Chi Minh City is concentrated around the Dong Khoi area, with everything from dives to designer bars.

Check out **Everyone's a DJ** (www.facebook.com/everyonesadj) for notifications of various gigs and events around town.

🍺 Dong Khoi Area

Pasteur Street
Brewing Company   Craft Beer
(www.pasteurstreet.com; 144 Đ Pasteur; small/large beers from 45,000/95,000đ; ⏰11am-10pm; 🛜) Proving there's hoppy life beyond 333 lager, Pasteur Street Brewing turns out a fine selection of excellent craft beer. Brews utilise local ingredients including lemongrass, rambutan and jasmine, and up

to six different beers are always available. Great bar snacks – try the spicy Nashville fried chicken – are also served in Pasteur Street's hip upstairs tasting room.

L'Usine   Cafe
(www.lusinespace.com; 151/1 Đ Dong Khoi; ⊗7.30am-10.30pm; 🛜) Tucked away in a colonial building with high ceilings, marble-topped tables, photos of old Saigon and an appetising cafe menu (sandwiches from 95,000d). A designer homewares and clothing store is attached; head through the Art Arcade, turn right along the lane between the buildings and zip upstairs.

The Workshop   Coffee
(www.facebook.com/the.workshop.coffee; 10 Đ Ngo Duc Ke; coffee from 45,000d; ⊗8am-8pm; 🛜) Coffee-geek culture comes to HCMC at this spacious upstairs warehouse space that's also perfect if you need to do some writing or other work. Single-origin fair-trade roasts from Dalat feature, and there's a great display of B&W photos of old Saigon to peruse while you're waiting for your Chemex or cold brew.

Vesper   Bar
(www.facebook.com/vespersaigon; Ground fl, Landmark Bldg, 5b Đ Ton Duc Thang; ⊗11am-late Mon-Sat) From the sinuous curve of the hardwood bar to the smoothly arranged bottles on the shelves, soft chill-out rhythms, funky caramel leather furniture and fine tapas menu, Vesper is a cool spot by the river. There's a roadside terrace, but traffic noise is epic.

Shrine   Cocktail Bar
(✆0916 806 093; www.shrinebarsaigon.com; 64 Đ Ton That Thiep; ⊗11am-1am Mon-Sat, 4pm-midnight Sun) Decked out with replica Khmer sculptures, Shrine is a chic and sophisticated alternative to more rowdy sports and hostess bars nearby. There's a proud focus on creating interesting – and very potent – cocktails (100,000d to 200,000d) from the team behind the bar, and pan-Asian flavours infuse a versatile food menu stretching from bar snacks

Gay Saigon

There are few openly gay venues in town, but most of Ho Chi Minh City's popular bars and clubs are generally gay-friendly. **Apocalypse Now** (p207) sometimes attracts a small gay contingent, and **Republic** (63/201 Đ Dong Du; ⊗10am-2am) just off Đ Dong Khoi and **Babylon Pub** (24-26 Đ Bui Vien; ⊗6pm-4am) in Pham Ngu Lao are also both popular.

(85,000d to 230,000d) to larger shared plates (220,000d to 460,000d).

Plantrip Cha   Teahouse
(www.facebook.com/PlantripCha; 3a Đ Ton Duc Thang; tea from 30,000d; ⊗9am-9pm) After perusing the galleries and street art of the emerging **3A Alternative Art Area** district, recharge and revive at this funky teahouse with brews from around the planet. Our favourite is the refreshing Tra Mojito iced tea.

2Go   Juice Bar
(www.2gosaigon.vn; 91 Đ Pasteur; juices 23,000-39,000d; ⊗7am-11pm) Excellent juices, smoothies and Vietnamese snacks (23,000d to 31,000d) are served up from this funky and colourful shipping container. It's a handy refuelling stop if you're exploring nearby museums and Notre Dame Cathedral. Try the super-refreshing, nonalcoholic Apple Mojito.

Apocalypse Now   Club
(✆08-3824 1463; www.facebook.com/apocalypsenowsaigon; 2c Đ Thi Sach; ⊗7pm-2am) 'Apo' has been around since 1991 and remains one of the must-visit clubs. A sprawling place with a big dance floor and an outdoor courtyard, the bar's eclectic cast combines travellers, expats, Vietnamese movers and shakers, plus the odd working girl. The music is thumping and it's apocalyptically rowdy. The 150,000d weekend charge gets you a free drink.

Broma: Not a Bar   Bar
(www.facebook.com/bromabar; 41 Đ Nguyen
Hue; ⏱5pm-2am) Compact and bohemian
rooftop bar overlooking the busy pedes-
trian mall of Đ Nguyen Hue. Look forward
to a good selection of international beers,
live gigs, and DJs with a funk, hip-hop and
electronica edge.

🔵 Da Kao & Around

Decibel   Bar
(www.decibel.vn; 79/2/5 Đ Phan Kê Bính;
⏱7.30am-midnight Mon-Sat) This small, two-
floor restaurant-cafe-bar is a super-relaxed
choice for a coffee or cocktail, with a fine
cultural vibe, film nights and art events.

🔵 Pham Ngu Lao Area

View   Bar
(www.ducvuonghotel.com; 8th fl, Duc Vuong
Hotel, 195 Đ Bui Vien; ⏱10am-midnight Mon-Fri,
to 2am Sat & Sun) Not as elevated as other
rooftop bars around town, but less preten-
tious and a whole lot easier on the wallet.
It's still a good escape to look down on the
heaving backpacker bustle of Pham Ngu
Lao, and the food menu is also good value.

Le Pub   Pub
(📞08-3837 7679; www.lepub.org; 175/22 Đ Pham
Ngu Lao; ⏱9am-2am; 📶) The name says it
all – British pub meets French cafe-bar –
and the pomegranate-coloured result,
ranging over three floors, is a hit. An extensive beer list, nightly promotions, cocktail
jugs and pub grub draw in the crowds. The
surrounding lane is becoming popular with
a local after-dark crowd.

🔵 Reunification Palace & Around

Vespa Sofar   Bar
(www.vespasofar.com; 99 Đ Pham Ngu Lao;
⏱11am-midnight; 📶) This cool Vespa and
Mod-themed cafe-bar combo is a short
walk from Pham Ngu Lao. Look forward
to good coffee, juice and smoothies, well-
priced cocktails, and a decent beer list
including a few Belgian brews. Look for the
cool VW Kombi van that's the main bar, and
the retro Vespas parked outside. Happy
hour runs from 6pm to 8pm.

Air 360   Bar
(www.air360skybar.com; 21st fl, Ben Thanh Tower,
136-138 Đ Le Thi Hong Gam; ⏱5.30pm-2am)
Happy hour runs from 5pm to 8pm at this

Neo-Romanesque Notre Dame Cathedral (p178)

modern sky bar – perfect to make the most of sunset and secure a good discount on the pricey drinks menu. Pâtés, terrines and charcuterie selections underpin the food menu. It's just a short walk from the heaving backpacker bars on Pham Ngu Lao.

Chill Skybar   Cocktail Bar
(www.chillsaigon.com; 26 & 27th fl, AB Tower, 76a Đ Le Lai; ☾5.30pm-late) The most upmarket of Saigon's sky bars – it's very popular with local high rollers working their way through a bottle of Hennessy cognac or Johnnie Walker Blue Label – and the only one to enforce a pretty strict dress code. Dig out your cleanest long trousers and maybe leave the Beer Lao or Vang Vieng rafting T-shirt in your backpack.

🚇 Thao Dien (District 2)
Saigon Outcast   Bar
(www.saigonoutcast.com; 188 Đ Nguyen Van Huong; ☾10am-11.45pm) Head across to District 2 for this venue's diverse combo of live music, DJs, cinema nights and good times amid funky street art. Cocktails, craft beer and local ciders are available in the raffish garden bar, and there's a cool outdoor market occasionally on Sunday mornings. Check the website for what's on. From District 1, it's around 150,000d in a taxi.

BiaCraft   Bar
(www.biacraft.com; 90 Đ Xuan Thuy, Thao Dien; ☾11am-midnight) Excellent craft beer bar across the river in the District 2 area. Look forward to locally brewed beers, plus the best of hoppy and distinctive imported brews. Bar snacks complete a tasty offering that may well see you kicking on for 'just one more round'.

⭐ ENTERTAINMENT
Acoustic   Live Music
(☎08-3930 2239; www.facebook.com/acoustic barpage; 6e1 Đ Ngo Thoi Nhiem; ☾7pm-midnight; 🛜) Don't be misled by the name: most of the musicians are fully plugged-in and dangerous when they take to the intimate stage of the city's leading live-music venue. And

Sky Bars

There's something madly exciting about gazing over the neon city at night, preferably with a cocktail in hand. It's well worth the extra dong to enjoy the frenetic pace of life on the streets from the lofty vantage point of a rooftop bar. Bars with great sunset and after-dark vistas include Air 360, Chill Skybar and View.

Our favourite spots:

EON Heli Bar (p179) Secure a window seat and catch the sun going down from this snappy 52nd-floor vantage point over town.

Shri (☎08-3827 9631; 23rd fl, Centec Tower, 72-74 Đ Nguyen Thi Minh Khai; ☾10.30am-midnight Mon-Sat, 4.30pm-midnight Sun) On the Centec Tower's 23rd floor, Shri's stylish terrace has a separate area for nondiners reached by stepping stones over a tiny stream.

M Bar (http://www.majesticsaigon.com/mb.php; 1 Đ Dong Khoi; ☾4pm-1am) On the 8th floor of the Majestic Hotel, this is a great spot for a sundowner, with panoramic views of the river and a certain colonial-era cachet.

Saigon Saigon Bar (www.caravellehotel.com; 19 Lam Son Sq; ☾11am-2am; 🛜) For excellent views in the city centre, stop by Saigon Saigon for a drink around dusk. This fancy bar has live music, cool breezes and a casually upscale feel.

judging by the numbers that pack in, the local crowd just can't get enough. It's at the end of the alley by the up-ended VW Beetle, and the cocktails are deceptively strong.

Municipal Theatre   Concert Venue
(Opera House; ☎08-3829 9976; Lam Son Sq) The French-era Opera House is home to the HCMC Ballet and the **Ballet & Symphony Orchestra** (www.hbso.org.vn), and hosts performances by visiting artists.

Motorcycle traffic on a city street

Golden Dragon
Water Puppet Theatre Water Puppets
(✆08-3930 2196; 55b Đ Nguyen Thi Minh Khai;
ticket US$7.50) Saigon's main water-puppet
venue, with shows starting at 5pm, 6.30pm
and 7.45pm, and lasting about 50 minutes.

ℹ INFORMATION

DANGERS & ANNOYANCES

Be careful at all times but especially in the Dong
Khoi area, around Pham Ngu Lao and the Ben
Thanh Market, and along the Saigon riverfront.
Motorbike 'cowboys' specialise in bag-, camera-,
laptop- and tablet-snatching. Be careful when
you use your smartphone on the street.

TRAVEL AGENCIES

Go Go Vietnam (✆08-3920 9297; www.
gogo-vietnam.com; 40/7 Đ Bui Vien) Well-run
tour company and travel agency with excellent
credentials in visa extensions and renewals, and
good-value day trips.

Sinh Tourist (✆08-3838 9593; www.thesin-
htourist.vn; 246 Đ De Tham; ◷6.30am-10.30pm)
Popular budget travel agency.

ℹ GETTING THERE & AWAY

Ho Chi Minh City is served by Tan Son Nhat
Airport, 7km from the centre of town. Domestic
airlines include **Vietnam Airlines** (✆08-3832
0320; www.vietnamairlines.com), **VietJet Air**
(✆1900 1886; www.vietjetair.com), **Jetstar
Pacific Airlines** (✆1900 1550; www.jetstar.
com/vn/en/home) and **Vietnam Air Service
Company** (VASCO; ✆08-3845 8017; www.vasco.
com.vn) for the Con Dao Islands.

Trains from **Saigon train station** (Ga Sai Gon;
✆08-3823 0105; 1 Đ Nguyen Thong, District 3;
◷ticket office 7.15-11am & 1-3pm) head north to
destinations including Danang. Purchase tickets
from travel agents for a small booking fee.

ℹ GETTING AROUND

Metered taxis cruise the streets and are very
affordable. Expect to pay around 25,000d (US$1)
from Dong Khoi to Pham Ngu Lao. **Mai Linh Taxi**
(✆08-3838 3838) and **Vinasun Taxi** (✆08-3827
2727) can be trusted. Uber is also popular.

Where to Stay

Central Ho Chi Minh City is the obvious lodging choice given its proximity to almost everything of interest, its relative closeness to the airport and its tempting array of establishments across all price ranges.

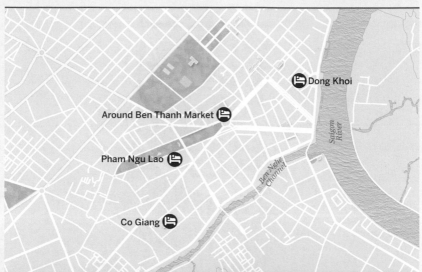

Neighbourhood	Atmosphere
Dong Khoi Area	Well-heeled area with grand thoroughfares and French colonial elegance; home to the city's top-notch hotels and sprinkled with attractive midrange options; good foodie neighbourhood.
Pham Ngu Lao Area	The budget and backpacker zone; more than 100 accommodation choices, including countless family-run guesthouses and minihotels, and even a few dorms; midrange travellers can also find excellent deals here; good-value eateries and cheap shopping.
Around Ben Thanh Market	Has decent midrange options; one of Saigon's liveliest areas, with market shopping and food stalls.
Co Giang	For a quieter and slightly cheaper alternative to Pham Ngu Lao, there's a string of guesthouses in a quiet alley connecting Đ Co Giang and Đ Co Bac; popular with long-timers; you'll need to book well ahead; preference goes to longer term bookings; further from major sights.

CON DAO
ISLANDS

In this Chapter

Con Dao Islands at a Glance...

Isolated from the mainland, the Con Dao Islands are one of Vietnam's star attractions. Long the Devil's Island of Indochina, the preserve of political prisoners and undesirables, they are now turning heads thanks to their striking natural beauty and tranquillity.

Con Son, the largest of this chain of 15 islands and islets, is ringed with lovely beaches, coral reefs and scenic bays, and remains partially covered in thick forests. In addition to hiking, diving and exploring deserted coastal roads and beaches, there are excellent wildlife-watching opportunities.

Con Dao Islands in One Day

Head straight to the beautiful beach of **Bai Dat Doc** (p216) for a morning swim, then into Con Son Town for lunch at **Infiniti Cafe & Lounge** (p220), Stroll the seafront promenade then spend the rest of the afternoon acquainting yourself with Con Dao's sombre history, starting with the **Bao Tang Con Dao Museum** (p220), followed by the **Tiger Cages** (p219).

Con Dao Islands in Two Days

Rise early the next day to catch the local **market** faround the intersection of Đ Tran Huy Lieu and Đ Nguyen An Ninh at its busiest. Tour the rest of the island's historic sites, including **Phu Hai Prison** (p219) and peaceful **Hang Duong Cemetery** (p219). Then take a trek through the dense rainforest of Con Son Island's interior, or join a diving or snorkelling trip out to the island reefs.

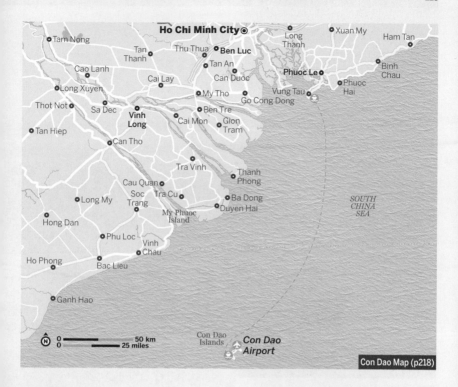

Con Dao Map (p218)

Arriving in the Con Dao Islands

Con Dao Airport The tiny airport is about 15km from the town centre. There are three to five daily flights between Con Son and Ho Chi Minh City and four weekly flights between Con Son and Can Tho in the Mekong Delta.

Ben Dam Port There are two ferries connecting Con Son Island with Vung Tau (12 hours), with sailings three to four times a week.

Where to Stay

Accommodation options have greatly improved in Con Dao over the last few years and there are now about 20 guesthouses and minihotels in Con Son Town.

However, expect to pay about double the rate for the equivalent place on the mainland.

Fishing boat off the Con Dao Islands

CAO TRAN THO/SHUTTERSTOCK ©

Best Beaches

Blessed with stunning beaches and loaded with natural allure, the islands are the ultimate castaway experience in Vietnam.

Great For...

☑ **Don't Miss**

The grave of Vo Thi Sau in Con Son's cemetery, a place of pilgrimage.

Bai Dat Doc

The best beach on Con Son Island, Bai Dat Doc is a simply beautiful cove, consisting of a kilometre-long crescent of pale sand, backed by green hills. It has a gently shelving profile and no pollution, so it's ideal for swimming. Though it's backed by the luxury bungalows of the Six Senses hotel, it's not a private beach and there are access points close to the road. Very rarely dugongs have been seen frolicking in the water off the nearby cape.

Bai Dram Trau

Reached via a dirt track 1km before the airport on Con Son Island, Bai Dram Trau

Other Islands

Bay Canh Island

Perhaps the best all-round island to visit is Bay Canh, to the east of Con Son Island, which has lovely beaches, old-growth forest, mangroves, coral reefs and sea turtles (seasonal).

There is a fantastic two-hour walk to a functioning French-era lighthouse on Bay Canh's eastern tip, although it involves a steep climb of 325m. Once at the summit, the panoramic views are breathtaking.

Tre Lon Island

Some of the more pristine beaches are on the smaller islands, such as the beautiful white-sand beach on Tre Lon, to the west of Con Son Island.

is a sublime but remote 700m half-moon crescent of soft sand, fringed by casuarina trees and bookended by forest-topped rocky promontories. It's best visited at low tide.

There's some snorkelling on reefs offshore and three very simple seafood shacks (all open noon till dusk only).

Bai Loi Voi

On the north side of Con Son Town, Bai Loi Voi is a broad sand-and-shingle beach with lots of seashells and casuarinas for shade.

There's a good stretch of sandy beach right in the centre of Con Son, around the Con Dao Resort.

Con Dao

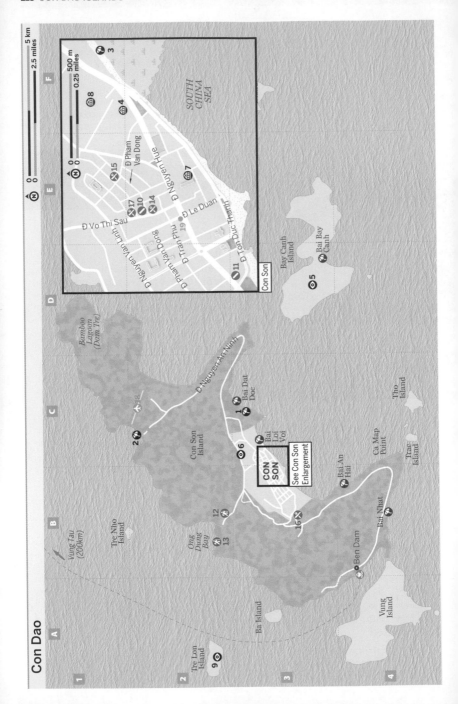

0   5 km
0   2.5 miles

Con Son (enlargement)

0   500 m
0   0.25 miles

SOUTH CHINA SEA

Bamboo Lagoon (Dam Tre)

Con Son Island

Đ Nguyen An Ninh

Bai Dat Doc

Bai Loi Voi

CON SON
See Con Son Enlargement

Bai An Hai

Ca Map Point

Tho Island

Trac Island

Vung Island

Ba Island

Ben Dam

Bai Nhat

Ong Dung Bay

Tre Nho Island

Vung Tau (200km)

Tre Lon Island

Bay Canh Island
Bai Bay Canh

Con Son

Đ Pham Van Dong

Đ Nguyen Hue

Đ Vo Thi Sau

Đ Nguyen Van Linh

Đ Phan Van Dong

Đ Tran Phu

Đ Le Duan

Đ Ton Duc Thanh

⊙ SIGHTS

There's nowhere quite like Con Son Town in all Vietnam. This delightful pocket-sized island capital has litter-free streets, well-kept municipal buildings and an air of calm and prosperity.

Of course, the town's genteel appearance and character is tempered considerably by the presence of several prisons, cemeteries and reminders of the islands' historic role as a penal colony. There are ghosts everywhere in Con Son.

Phu Hai Prison　　　Historic Building

(⊘7-11.30am & 1-5pm) The largest of the 11 jails on the island, this prison dates from 1862. Thousands of prisoners were held here, with up to 200 prisoners crammed into each detention building. During the French era, all prisoners were kept naked, chained together in rows, with one small box serving as a toilet for hundreds. One can only imagine the squalor and stench. Today, emaciated mannequins that are all too lifelike recreate the era.

Tiger Cages　　　Historic Building

(⊘7-11.30am & 1-5pm) The notorious cells dubbed 'tiger cages' were built in 1940 by the French to incarcerate nearly 2000 political prisoners. There are 120 chambers with ceiling bars, where guards could poke at prisoners like tigers in a Victorian zoo. Prisoners were beaten with sticks from above, and sprinkled with quick lime and water (which burnt their skin, and caused blindness).

Hang Duong Cemetery　　Cemetery

Some 20,000 Vietnamese prisoners died on Con Son and 1994 of their graves can be seen at the peaceful Hang Duong Cemetery, located at the eastern edge of town. Sadly, only 700 of these graves bear the name of the victims.

Vietnam's most famous heroine, Vo Thi Sau (1933–52), was buried here, the first woman executed by a firing squad on Con Son, on 23 January 1952.

⊕ ACTIVITIES

There are lots of **treks** around Con Son Island, as much of the interior remains heavily forested. For more information on treks and boat trips, visit www.condaopark.com.vn.

It's a steep uphill hike to the old fruit plantations of **So Ray**, following a slippery but well-marked trail through dense rainforest. The plantation is home to a sociable troop of long-tailed macaques, with sweeping views. The return hike takes about 90 minutes.

Con Dao is the most pristine marine environment in the country, perfect for **scuba-diving** and snorkelling. There's abundant healthy coral and marine life includes turtles, rays, triggerfish and parrotfish.

Con Dao

Bao Tang Con Dao Museum

This impressive new **museum** (⊘7-11am & 1.30-5pm) has more than 2000 exhibits, including many rare documents, dioramas and excellent photographs, which comprehensively record the islands' history, including the French-colonial era and of course the 'prison period'. Modern displays including audiovisuals are used.

Ong Dung Bay   Hiking
A hike that you can do yourself is a 1km walk (about 30 minutes each way) through rainforest to Ong Dung Bay. The trail begins a few kilometres north of town passing **Ma Thien Lanh Bridge**.

The bay has only a rocky beach, although there is a good coral reef about 300m offshore.

Dive! Dive! Dive!   Diving
(☑064-383 0701; www.dive-condao.com; Đ Nguyen Hue; ⊘8am-9pm) 🏄 Instructor Larry has been in Con Dao since 2011 and has vast experience diving the island reefs. This is an experienced, conservation-minded operation, offering RAID courses and the dive shop is a great source of general information on the Con Daos.

The company constantly monitors reefs to remove fishing nets and trash from corals.

Con Dao Dive Center   Diving
(☑0903 700 8483; http://divecondao.com; Bar200, Pham Van Dong; ⊘7.30am-10pm) A very friendly and professional PADI dive resort, offering fine instruction and courses, (Open Water is US$550), fun dives (two-dive trips US$160), snorkelling and freediving trips. Owner Rhys is happy to chat about diving options and things to do on Con Dao.

It's based at Bar200.

🍴 EATING & DRINKING

All the following places are in Con Son Town.

Bar200 Con Dao   Cafe $
(http://divecondao.com; Đ Pham Van Dong; meals from 35,000d; ⊘8am-10.30pm; 🛜) Popular place to hang for travellers in town, with a relaxed, sociable vibe; the owners are clued-up when it comes to island info. There's great coffee (including espresso and cappuccino) and Western comfort grub including burgers, pizza, sandwiches and breakfast cereals.

After dark the beers and cocktails start flowing.

Infiniti Cafe & Lounge   Cafe $$
(Đ Pham Van Dong; meals 70,000-150,000d; ⊘7am-10pm; 🛜) A lot of effort has gone into this hip cafe-bar with its artistic, reclaimed furnishings and lovely pavement terrace with bench seating. Cocktails are chalked up on a board and you'll find plenty of interest on the menu, including great pizza and pasta.

Thu Ba   Vietnamese, Seafood $$
(☑064-3830 255; Đ Vo Thi Sau; meals 75,000-200,000d) Serving creatively prepared, beautifully presented Vietnamese cuisine, Thu Ba is strong on seafood, hotpots and curries. The gregarious owner speaks great English and is happy to make suggestions based upon what's seasonal and fresh.

Quan Thanh Huyen   Vietnamese $$
(Khu 3, Hoang Phi Yen; meals 70,000-160,000d; ⊘noon-9pm) South of town by a water-lily-filled lake, this lovely little restaurant enjoys a great setting, with little gazebos next to the water and an orchestra of croaking frogs.

Offers authentic Vietnamese cuisine including hotpots and snakehead fish straight from the lake.

Hang Duong Cemetery (p219)

ℹ️ GETTING THERE & AROUND

There are three to five daily flights between Con Son and HCMC jointly operated by **Vasco** (📞038-330 330; www.vasco.com.vn; 44 Đ Nguyen Hue) and Vietnam Airlines. Con Son is also connected to Can Tho in the Mekong Delta.

The tiny **airport** (Co Ong Airport) is about 15km from the town centre. All of the big hotels

Some 20,000 Vietnamese prisoners died on Con Son...

on the island provide free transport both to and from the airport.

Con Son Island has several **taxis** (📞064-361 6161); hotels rent motorbikes and bicycles.

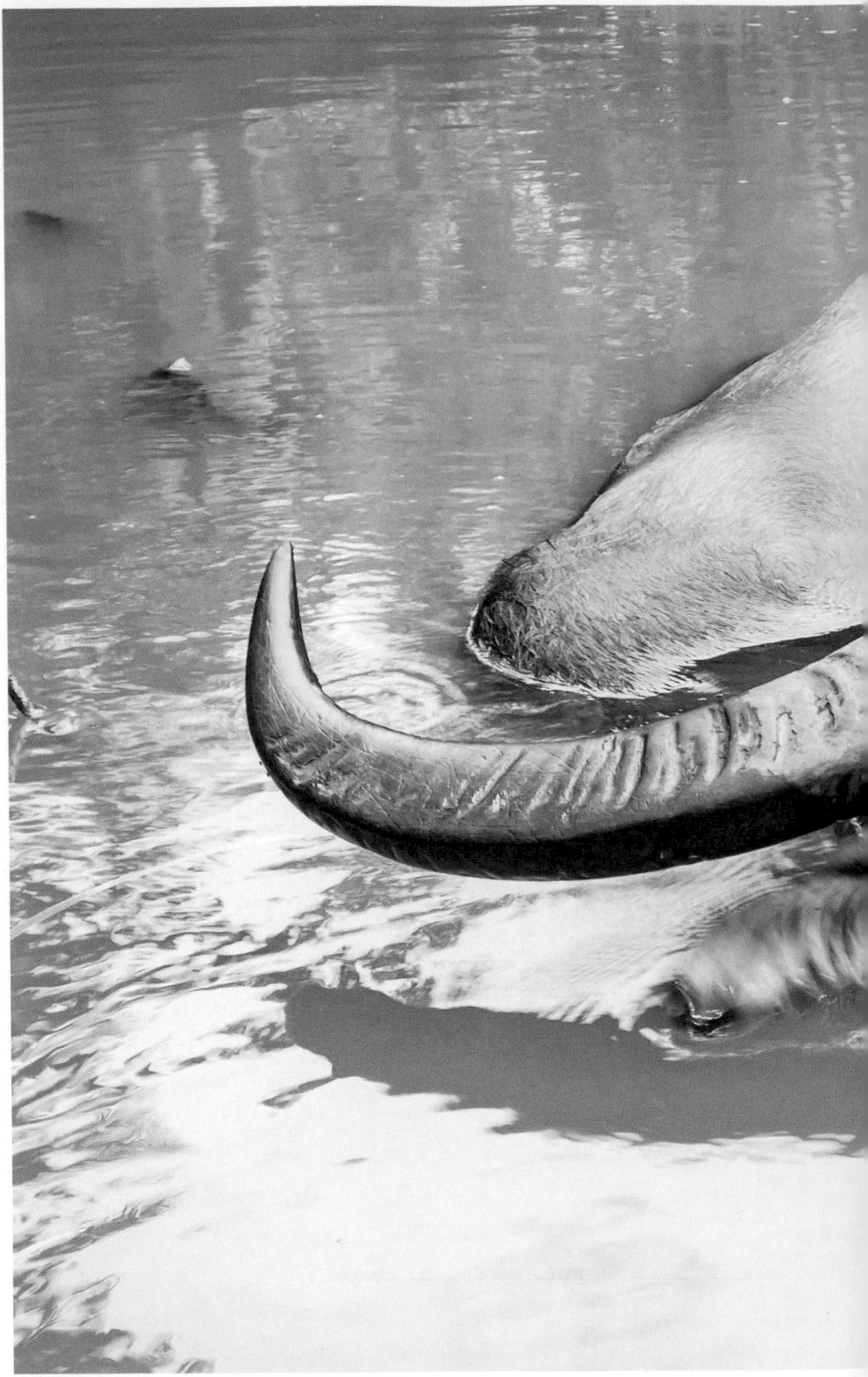

KRZYSZTOF KRAWCZYK/SHUTTERSTOCK ©

Water buffalo, Mekong Delta

MEKONG DELTA

Mekong Delta at a Glance...

The 'rice bowl' of Vietnam, the delta is carpeted in a dizzying variety of greens. It's a water world that moves to the rhythms of the mighty Mekong, where boats, houses and markets float upon the innumerable rivers, canals and streams that criss-cross the landscape like arteries.

The bustling commerce of its towns contrasts sharply with the languid, almost soporific pace of life in the countryside. Mangrove forests teem with a wealth of birdlife and bristle with the remains of Viet Cong bunkers, ornate Khmer pagodas and Buddhist temples reaching for the sky.

Mekong Delta in Two Days

Join the throngs amid the bustling floating markets on a boat trip from **Can Tho**, then explore the city's temples, museums and pagodas, and enjoy an evening meal at **L'Escale** (p231). The following day, head to nearby **Vinh Long** (p232) for a homestay experience with a local family.

Mekong Delta in Four Days

Head to **Chau Doc** (p232) close to the border with Cambodia, a likeable town with significant Chinese, Cham and Khmer communities, and explore its cultural sights and market. Eat at **Memory Delicatessen** (p234). The next day head to sacred **Sam Mountain** (p234), then enjoy a sundowner at **Bamboo Bar** at 32 Đ Le Loi and a memorable meal at **Bassac Restaurant** (p234).

Floating Markets

Can Tho Map (p231)
Chau Doc Map (p233)

Arriving in Mekong Delta

The cities of Can Tho, Ben Tre, My Tho and Vinh Long are all very accessible by bus (or on tours) from Ho Chi Minh City. Can Tho also has a busy airport, with flights to HCMC, Dalat, Danang, Hanoi and Phu Quoc.

Where to Stay

The towns and cities all have a decent selection of good-value midrange (and some luxury) hotels, but also consider a stay in a homestay to get to know rural life in the Mekong: Vinh Long has a good selection.

Unloading watermelons, Cai Rang Floating Market (p228)

Floating Markets

For many visitors, experiencing a Mekong Delta floating market is a highlight of their trip. There are many in the region, but those around Can Tho are the most famous.

Great For...

❶ Need to Know

Visit floating markets as early as possible in the morning.

MATT MUNRO/LONELY PLANET ©

★ **Top Tip**

Taking a well-organised tour like Hieu's Tour (p230) will save a lot of hassle

Can Tho has two huge floating markets, but Chau Doc and Vinh Long are two other possibilities.

Cai Rang Floating Market

Just 6km from Can Tho in the direction of Soc Trang is Cai Rang, the biggest **floating market** (☺5am-noon) in the Mekong Delta. There is a bridge here that serves as a great vantage point for photography. The market is best around 6am to 7am, and it's well worth getting here early to beat boatloads of tourists. This is a wholesale market, so look at what's tied to the long pole above the boat to figure out what they're selling to smaller traders.

Cai Rang can be seen from the road, but getting here is far more interesting by boat (US$10 to US$15). From the market area in Can Tho it takes about 45 minutes by river, or you can drive to the Cau Dau Sau boat landing (by the Dau Sau Bridge), from where it takes only about 10 minutes to reach the market.

Phong Dien Floating Market

The Mekong Delta's most intimate and best **floating market** (☺5am-noon), Phong Dien has fewer motorised craft and more stand-up rowing boats, with local vendors shopping and exchanging gossip. Less crowded than Cai Rang, there are also far fewer tourists. It's at its bustling best between 5am and 7am. The market is 20km southwest of Can Tho; you can get there by road but many operators now offer a six-hour combined Cai Rang–Phong Dien tour, returning to Can Tho through quieter backwaters.

Boat stocked with produce at a floating market

Cai Be Floating Market

This **river market** (⏰5am-noon) is still the principal attraction on a boat tour from Vinh Long, though it has shrunk considerably due to the building of bridges in the delta and the subsequent transportation of goods by road rather than river. The market is at its best around 6am. Wholesalers on big boats moor here, each specialising in different types of fruit or vegetable, hanging samples of their goods from tall wooden poles. It's an hour by boat from Vinh Long.

A notable sight is the huge and photogenic Catholic cathedral on the riverside.

Most people make detours on the way there or back to see the canals or visit orchards. For those travelling on an organised tour of the delta, it is customary to board a boat here, explore the islands and moor in Vinh Long before continuing to Can Tho.

To Market, To Market

Can Tho is the only place in the delta where you may experience hassle from would-be guides. Some may accost you as soon as you get off the bus and even turn up at your lodgings after asking your *xe om* (motorbike taxi) driver where you're headed. To choose who you go with, consider the following:

○ What does the tour include? Is it a 40-minute dash to Cai Rang, returning to Can Tho straight away, or a half-day tour taking in smaller waterways?

○ How big is the boat? Larger boats come equipped with life jackets, have roofs and get to the markets faster, but you'll be in a large group. Smaller boats make for a more intimate experience, but not all carry life jackets and may have flimsy roofs (or none at all), so you may end up doing a wet rat impression in a downpour.

○ When does the tour depart? If you start out after 6.30am, you've missed the best of the action.

○ Does the guide speak good English? Small boats along the riverside near the giant statue of Ho Chi Minh offer the cheapest deals, but you won't get a commentary on riverside life.

○ Costs range from around 120,000d per hour (depending on your negotiating skills) for a small boat with the operator speaking a few words of English to around US$30 per person for a seven-hour tour taking in both markets, with a fluent English-speaking guide.

> ☑ **Don't Miss**
> The Bang Lang bird sanctuary between Can Tho and Vinh Long.

BANANA REPUBLIC IMAGES/SHUTTERSTOCK ©

> ✕ **Take a Break**
> Mekong (p231) caters for all tastes and wallets.

Can Tho

The epicentre of the Mekong Delta, Can Tho is the largest city in the region. As the political, economic, cultural and transportation centre of the delta, it's a buzzing town with a lively waterfront lined with sculpted gardens, an appealing blend of narrow backstreets and wide boulevards. It is also the perfect base for nearby floating markets, the major draw for tourists who come here to boat along the many canals and rivers leading out of town.

◎ SIGHTS

Ong Temple   Temple

(32 Đ Hai Ba Trung; ⊘6am-8pm) FREE In a fantastic location facing the Can Tho River, this Chinese temple is set inside the **Guangzhou Assembly Hall**, and wandering through its incense-coil-filled interior is very enjoyable. It was originally built in the late 19th century to worship Kuang Kung, a deity symbolising loyalty, justice, reason, intelligence, honour and courage, among other merits.

Approaching the engraved screen, the right side is dedicated to the Goddess of Fortune and the left side is reserved for the worship of General Ma Tien. In the centre of the temple is Kuang Kung flanked by the God of Earth and the God of Finance.

Can Tho Museum   Museum

(Bao Tang Can Tho; 1 ĐL Hoa Binh; ⊘8-11am & 2-5pm Tue-Thu, 8-11am & 6.30-9pm Sat & Sun) FREE This large, well-presented museum brings local history to life with mannequins and life-size reproductions of buildings, including a Chinese pagoda and a house interior. Displays (with ample English translations) focus on the Khmer and Chinese communities, plant and fish specimens, rice production and, inevitably, the war.

Bang Lang   Bird Sanctuary

(admission 8000d; ⊘5am-6pm) On the road between Can Tho and Long Xuyen, this is a magnificent 1.3-hectare bird sanctuary with astonishing views of thousands of resident storks and snowy egrets. There is a tall viewing platform to see the birds filling the branches; the best times to view this incredible sight are around dawn and dusk.

Bang Lang is 46km northwest of Can Tho; join a tour, or take a *xe om* or a bus to Thoi An hamlet and then a *xe om*.

ⓖ TOURS

Hieu's Tour   Cultural

(📱093 966 6156; www.hieutour.com; 27a Đ Le Thanh Ton) Young, enthusiastic, English-speaking guide Hieu offers excellent tours around Can Tho – from early-morning jaunts to the floating markets (US$23 to Cai Rang, US$30 to Cai Rang and Phong Dien) to cycling tours, food tours and even visits to **Pirate Island** (Quan Dao Ha Tien; Hai Tac) further afield. Hieu is keen to show visitors true delta culture and a floating homestay is in the works.

Mekong Tours   Cultural

(📱090 785 2927; www.mekongtours.info; 93 Đ Mau Than) Based at Xoai Hotel, this operator offers highly recommended tours of the floating markets, as well as an entertaining nightly street-food tour that departs the hotel at 6.30pm.

⊗ EATING

Nem Nuong
Thanh Van   Vietnamese $

(📱071-0382 7255; cnr Nam Ky Khoi Nghia & 30 Thang 4; meals 45,000d; ⊘8am-9pm) The only dish this locally acclaimed little spot does is the best *nem nuong* in town. Roll your own rice rolls using the ingredients provided: pork sausage, rice paper, green banana, starfruit, cucumber and a riot of fresh herbs, then dip into the peanut-and-something-else sauce, its secret jealously guarded. Simple and fantastic!

Quan Com Chay Cuong   Vegetarian $

(9 Đ De Tham; meals from 20,000d; ⊘11am-10pm; 🖋) Located around the back of the Munireangsey pagoda, this is one of the

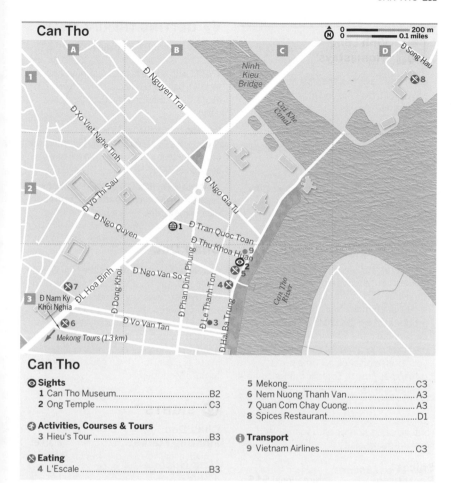

Can Tho

better *com chay* (vegetarian) eateries in the city. The vegetable, rice and mock-meat dishes (including mock-chicken hotpot) are nicely prepared and the service is friendly. Order from the English menu or point at what you like at the buffet.

Mekong   Vietnamese, International $
(38 Đ Hai Ba Trung; meals from 60,000d; ⊙7am-8pm; ⌨) Looking onto busy Hai Ba Trung, this travellers' favourite has a good blend of local and international food at reasonable prices, though it's a case of quantity over

quality. Try the tangy sour soup with fish and the passion-fruit crème brûlée.

L'Escale   Vietnamese, International $$
(☎071-381 9139; http://nambocantho.com; 1 Đ Ngo Quyen, Nam Bo Boutique Hotel; meals 200,000-500,000d; ⊙6am-10.30pm; ⌨) With tantalising river views from the top of the Nam Bo hotel and subdued romantic lighting, this is the place to canoodle with your sweetie over glasses of wine from the strong wine list and beautifully executed dishes such as claypot fish with pineapple,

Vinh Long 'Homestays'

For many travellers, the chance to experience river life and get to know a local family is a highlight of a Mekong visit. Perhaps 'homestay' is the wrong word: in most cases you will actually be staying in specially constructed rustic hostels and guesthouses.

Some homestays have large communal rooms with bunks, while others offer basic bungalows with shared facilities and some even have rooms with en suites. Breakfast is usually included; in some places you'll share a meal with the family, while in bigger places there are simple restaurants. The only constant is a verdant, rustic setting and a taste of rural life.

Although many tourists book through group tours in Ho Chi Minh City, you can just take the ferry from Vinh Long and then a *xe om* (motorbike taxi) to your preferred choice. Some hosts don't speak much English, but welcome foreign guests just the same.

sautéed garlic shrimp with spinach and smoked-duck salad.

Spices Restaurant
International $$$

(☑071-0381 0111; Cai Khe, Ninh Kieu, Victoria Can Tho Resort; meals 200,000-680,000d; ☺6am-10pm; 🛜☑) Go for a table overlooking the river at this fine restaurant, which is refined without being stuffy, and opt for the beautifully presented trio of salads (green papaya, banana flower, green mango) or the assortment starter for two, and follow up with deep-fried elephant fish or pork-stuffed squid.

Lamb shanks and seared duck cater to homesick palates and the desserts are magnificent.

ℹ️ GETTING THERE & AWAY

Can Tho is served by **Vietnam Airlines** (☑071-384 4320; 64 Đ Nguyen An Ninh), Vietjet Air and VASCO, with flights to Dalat (one hour, twice weekly), Danang (1½ hours, daily), Hanoi (2¼ hours, three daily) and Phu Quoc (one hour, daily).

Can Tho International Airport (www.cantho airport.com; Đ Le Hong Phong) is 10km northwest of the city centre. A taxi into town will cost around 220,000d.

All buses (to HCMC and other Mekong towns) depart from the main bus station, 2.5km northwest of the centre.

Chau Doc

Draped along the banks of the Hau Giang River (Bassac River), Chau Doc sees plenty of travellers washing through on the river route between Cambodia and Vietnam. Chau Doc's cultural diversity – apparent in the mosques, temples, churches and nearby pilgrimage sites – makes it fascinating to explore. It's also a good base for trips to Sam Mountain.

◎ SIGHTS

Chau Doc Floating Market
Market

(☺5am-noon) You need to get up at the crack of dawn to see the best of this floating market. The action is busiest around 5am to 6am, when locals gather to buy fresh produce wholesale. Less colourful and much calmer than other floating markets.

Floating Houses
House

These houses, whose floats consist of empty metal drums, are both a place to live and a livelihood for their residents. Under each house, fish are raised in suspended metal nets. The fish flourish in their natural river habitat; the family can feed them whatever scraps are handy. You can get a close-up look by hiring a boat.

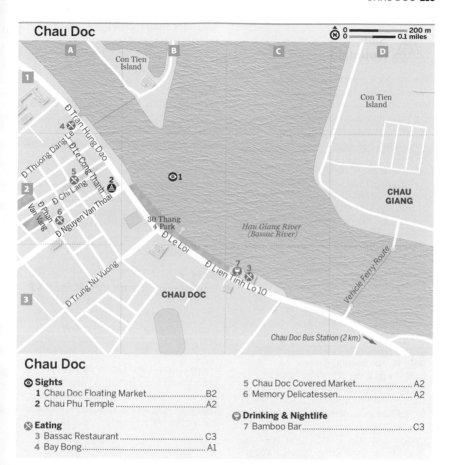

Chau Doc

Chau Phu Temple Buddhist Temple

(Dinh Than Chau Phu; cnr Ð Nguyen Van Thoai & Ð Gia Long; ☼dawn-dusk) In 1926 this temple was built to worship the Nguyen dynasty official Thoai Ngoc Hau, buried at Sam Mountain. The structure is decorated with both Vietnamese and Chinese motifs; inside are funeral tablets bearing the names of the deceased as well as biographical information about them. There's also a shrine to Ho Chi Minh.

Chau Giang Mosque Mosque

Domed, arched Chau Giang Mosque, in the hamlet of Chau Giang, serves the local Cham Muslims. To get there, take the car ferry from Chau Giang ferry landing across the Hau Giang River. From the ferry landing, walk inland from the river for 30m, turn left and walk 50m.

 TOURS

Xuan Mai Cultural

(✆0855 8896 11847, 0849 1891 0477; maixuanvn2001@yahoo.com) Friendly English-speaking Mai arranges tours of the area, either on motorbike or by car. She also makes bookings for speedboat transfers to Cambodia.

Sam Mountain

A sacred place for Buddhists, Sam Mountain (Nui Sam, 284m) and its environs are crammed with dozens of pagodas and temples. A strong Chinese influence makes it particularly popular with ethnic Chinese but Buddhists of all ethnicities visit here. The views from the top are excellent (weather permitting), ranging deep into Cambodia. There's a military outpost on the summit, a legacy of the days when the Khmer Rouge made cross-border raids and massacred Vietnamese civilians.

Along with the shrines and tombs, the steep path to the top is lined with the unholy clamour of commerce and there are plenty of cafes and stalls at which to stop for a drink or a snack. Walking down is easier than walking up (a not particularly scenic 45-minute climb), so you can get a motorbike to drop you at the summit (about 30,000d from the base of the mountain).

Many people get here by rented motorbike or on the back of a *xe om* (motorbike taxi; about 50,000d one way from Chau Doc). The most rewarding way to get here, however, is to rent a bicycle and to take the new road that runs towards the Cambodian border through peaceful rice-paddy scenery.

 EATING

Chau Doc Covered Market   Vietnamese $
(Cho Chau Doc; Đ Bach Dang; meals 20,000-40,000d; ⏱7am-9pm; 🖋) Try delicious local specialities, such as grilled glutinous rice filled with banana, and other stall food in this busy fresh-food market.

Bay Bong   Vietnamese $
(22 Đ Thuong Dang Le; meals 50,000-100,000d; ⏱9am-8pm) Informal spot with metal tables and chairs and so-so service, but the food is something, with tasty fish-and-vegetable hotpot, stir-fried rice with seafood, snake-head fish soup, garlicky morning glory and more.

Memory Delicatessen   International $$
(57 Đ Nguyen Huu Canh; meals 60,000-200,000d; ⏱7am-10pm; 🖾🛜🖋) This sophisticated cafe-restaurant that attracts local trendies is memorable for its wonderful melange of international dishes, from the excellent pizzas topped with imported ingredients to the fragrant vegetable curry with coconut milk and lemongrass, accompanied by an array of fresh juices and imaginative shakes. Skip dessert, though, unless it's the homemade ice cream.

Bassac Restaurant   French, Vietnamese $$$
(🖀076-386 5010; 32 Đ Le Loi; meals 170,000-450,000d; ⏱6am-10pm; 🖋) Chau Doc's most sophisticated dining experience is at the Victoria Chau Doc Hotel where the menu veers between wonderful international dishes (roast rack of lamb, seared duck breast), dishes with a French accent (provençale tart, gratin dauphinoise) and beautifully presented Vietnamese dishes, such as grilled squid with green peppercorns. The apple pie with cinnamon ice cream makes for a sublime ending.

 GETTING THERE & AWAY

The most comfortable long-distance buses to Can Tho and HCMC are **Phuong Trang** (www.futaexpress.com), which depart from the main bus station, and **Hung Cuong** (www.hungcuonghotel.com), which depart from in front of Hung Cuong Hotel.

The **bus station** (Ben Xe Chau Doc; Đ Le Loi) is on the eastern edge of town, around 2km out of the centre.

XUANHUONGHO/SHUTTERSTOCK ©

SALAJEAN/SHUTTERSTOCK ©

PETER STUCKINGS/SHUTTERSTOCK ©

Clockwise from top: Child tending cattle at a rice plantation; Gateway of Chau Phu Temple (p233); Incense offerings, Ong Temple (p230)

PHU QUOC

Phu Quoc at a Glance...

Fringed with white-sand beaches and with large tracts still cloaked in dense, tropical jungle, Phu Quoc has rapidly morphed from a sleepy island backwater to a must-visit beach escape. Beyond the resorts lining Long Beach and development beginning on the east coast, there's still ample room for exploration and escaping. Dive the reefs, kayak in the bays, eat up the back-road miles on a motorbike, or just lounge on the beach, indulge in a massage and dine on fresh seafood.

Phu Quoc in Two Days

Savour the tropical life by enjoying a day relaxing on **Long Beach** (p244), strolling along the powdery white sand, swimming and perhaps indulging in a massage. Dine at **Spice House at Cassia Cottage** (p246). The next day book a tour of the gorgeous **An Thoi Islands** (p244), which are perfect for snorkelling.

Phu Quoc in Four Days

Investigate **Duong Dong town**, and take in the (infamous) **Fish Sauce Factory** (p244), **Cau Castle** (p244) and **Coi Nguon Museum** (p244). In the afternoon head to beautiful **Sao Beach** (p242). On day four explore the island by motorbike (or join a tour), visiting remote coves such as Cua Can Beach and Dai Beach. Round off the day with a meal at **Itaca Resto Lounge** (p247).

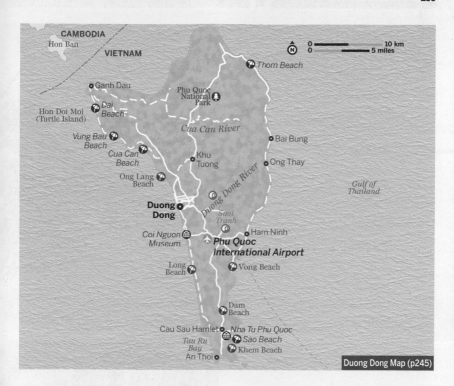

Map caption: Duong Dong Map (p245)

Arriving in Phu Quoc

Air Phu Quoc airport has excellent connections to Ho Chi Minh City, Can Tho and Hanoi plus two flights per week to Singapore.

Boat There are fast boats to Phu Quoc from the mainland towns of Ha Tien (1½ hours) and Rach Gia (2½ hours), and also car ferries.

Where to Stay

Long Beach has an excellent selection of accommodation, while coves including Ong Lang and Sao Beach also offer a great beach base.

Sao Beach, at the southern tip of Phu Quoc

Beach-Hopping on Phu Quoc

Phu Quoc is liberally sprinkled with picture-perfect white-sand beaches and lovely coves. Saddle up and explore the island on a scooter, or join an island tour.

Great For...

❶ Need to Know

The island is 48km long and hilly in the north, so set off early if you want to do the entire loop described here.

From Duong Dong, head north along the coastal road and you'll pass a succession of lovely sandy bays perfect for chilling. If you've time, you can also take in a ride through the national park and some of the scenery on the remote east coast too before returning via a waterfall to Duong Dong.

Sao Beach

With picture-perfect white sand, the delightful curve of beautiful **Sao Beach** (Bai Sao) bends out alongside a sea of mineral-water clarity just a few kilometres from An Thoi, the main shipping port at the southern tip of the island. There are a couple of beachfront restaurants, where you can settle into a deckchair or partake in water sports.

If heading down to Sao Beach by motorbike, fill up with petrol before the trip.

Cua Can Beach

The most accessible of the northern beaches, **Cua Can** (Bai Cua Can) is about 11km from Duong Dong. It remains mercifully quiet during the week, but can get busy at weekends.

A ride through the villages around Cua Can is interesting, with the road crossing the river several times on rickety wooden bridges.

Vung Bau Beach

This appealing northern **beach** (Bai Vung Bau) is reachable via the coastal road. The waves are rough and it's a little neglected,

Suoi Tranh waterfall

but it means that you can have the beach without the crowds. Be quick: development is in the works.

Dai Beach

A relatively isolated northern **beach** (Bai Dai) that retains its remote tropical charm.

Phu Quoc National Park

About 90% of Phu Quoc is forested, and the trees and adjoining marine environment enjoy official protection. This is the last large stand of forest in the south, and in 2010 the park was declared a Unesco Biosphere Reserve. The forest is densest in northern Phu Quoc, in the Khu Rung Nguyen Sinh forest reserve; you'll need a motorbike or mountain bike to tackle the bumpy dirt roads that cut through it. There are no real hiking trails.

Thom Beach

The road from Dai Beach to **Thom Beach** (Bai Thom) via Ganh Dau is very beautiful, passing through dense forest with tantalising glimpses of the coast below.

Suoi Tranh

Compared with the waterlogged Mekong Delta, Phu Quoc has very little surface moisture, but there are several springs originating in the hills. The most accessible of these is **Suoi Tranh** (admission 5000d); look for the entrance sign and concrete tree from the Duong Dong–Vong Beach road.

From the ticket counter it's a 10-minute walk through the forest to the falls.

> ☑ **Don't Miss**
> The Suoi Tranh waterfall is perfect for a cooling dip after a hot day on the road.

FRANK FISCHBACH/SHUTTERSTOCK ©

> ✕ **Take a Break**
> Check out **Sakura** (meals from 100,000d; ⊘10am-10pm) on Ong Lang beach for great seafood.

⊙ SIGHTS

Long Beach
Beach

(Bai Truong) Long Beach is draped invitingly along the west coast from Duong Dong almost to An Thoi port. Development concentrates in the north near Duong Dong, where the recliners and rattan umbrellas of the various resorts rule; these are the only stretches that are kept garbage-free. With its west-facing aspect, sunsets can be stupendous.

A motorbike or bicycle is necessary to reach some of the remote stretches flung out towards the southern end of the island.

There should be no problem for beach-combers to stretch out their towels on the sand, but you may get moved on quickly if you get too close to the paying guests.

There are several small lanes heading from the main Đ Tran Hung Dao drag down to Long Beach that shelter some of the nicest places to stay and eat. You can buy drinks from a few bamboo huts, but bring water if planning a long hike along the beach.

An Thoi Islands
Island

(Quan Dao An Thoi) Just off the southern tip of Phu Quoc, these 15 islands and islets can be visited by chartered boat. It's a fine area for sightseeing, fishing, swimming and snorkelling. Hon Thom (Pineapple Island) is about 3km in length and is the largest island in the group.

Most boats depart from An Thoi on Phu Quoc, but you can make arrangements through hotels on Long Beach, as well as dive operators. Boat trips generally do not run during the rainy season.

Other islands here include Hon Dua (Coconut Island), Hon Roi (Lamp Island), Hon Vang (Echo Island), Hon May Rut (Cold Cloud Island), the Hon Dams (Shadow Islands), Chan Qui (Yellow Tortoise) and Hon Mong Tay (Short Gun Island). As yet, there is no real development on the islands, but expect some movement in the future.

Coi Nguon Museum
Museum

(www.coinguonphuquoc.com; 149 Tran Hung Dao; 20,000d; ⊘8am-5pm) With displays on Vietnamese medicines, Stone Age tools, a boatful of barnacle-encrusted ceramics, oddly compelling shell-covered furniture and a small room devoted to the island prison, this private museum is an oddball introduction to Phu Quoc history and culture. But did the marine fauna section really require the untimely demise of 14 hawksbill turtles?

Nha Tu Phu Quoc
Museum

(⊘7.30-11am & 1.30-4pm) **FREE** Not far from Sao Beach in the south of the island, Phu Quoc's notorious old prison, built by the French in the late 1940s, contains a small museum that narrates the gruesome history of the jail. A war memorial stands south of the prison on the far side of the road.

Dinh Cau Temple
Taoist Temple

(Cau Castle; Đ Bach Dang, Duong Dong) **FREE** This combination temple and lighthouse was built in 1937 to honour Thien Hau, the Goddess of the Sea, who provides protection for sailors and fishers. Sometimes called a 'castle', Dinh Cau gives you a good view of the harbour entrance and the promenade is popular with locals taking a stroll at sunset.

Fish Sauce Factory
Factory

(www.hungthanhfishsauce.com.vn; Duong Dong; ⊘8-11am & 1-5pm) **FREE** The distillery of Nuoc Mam Hung Thanh is the largest of Phu Quoc's fish-sauce makers, a short walk from the market in Duong Dong. At first glance, the giant wooden vats may make you think you've arrived for a wine tasting, but one sniff of the festering *nuoc mam* essence jolts you back to reality. Take a guide along unless you speak Vietnamese.

Most of the sauce produced is exported to the mainland for domestic consumption, though an impressive amount finds its way abroad to kitchens in Japan, North America and Europe.

Duong Dong

⊚ Sights
1 Dinh Cau Temple B1
2 Fish Sauce Factory B1
3 Long Beach B2

⊕ Activities, Courses & Tours
4 Flipper Diving Club B2
5 Jerry's Jungle Tours C3
6 John's Tours B1

⊗ Eating
7 Dinh Cau Night Market B1
8 Itaca Resto Lounge C3
9 Nha Ghe Phu Quoc Crab House B1
10 Spice House at Cassia Cottage B3
11 Winston's Burgers & Beer C3

⊚ Drinking & Nightlife
12 Le Bar B3

⊕ ACTIVITIES

Flipper Diving Club   Diving
(☏077-3994 924; www.flipperdiving.com; 60 Đ
Tran Hung Dao; ⊗7am-7pm) Centrally located,
multilingual PADI dive centre for everything
from novice dive trips to full instructor
courses. Very professional, with plenty
of diving experience worldwide, and with
instructors who put you at ease if you're a
newbie.

⊕ TOURS

Jerry's
Jungle Tours   Boat Tour, Hiking
(☏0938 226 021; www.jerrystours.wixsite.com/
jerrystours; 112 Đ Tran Hung Dao; day trips from
US$30) Archipelago explorations by boat,
snorkelling, fishing, one-day and multiday
trips to islands, motorbike tours, boulder-
ing, birdwatching, hiking and cultural tours
around Phu Quoc.

From left: Raw pepper; Seafood on display at the night market; Hot corn for sale at a farmer's market

John's Tours   Boating
(☎0918 939 111; www.johnsislandtours.com; 4 Đ Tran Hung Dao; tour per person US$12-40) Well represented at hotels and resorts; cruises include snorkelling, island-hopping, sunrise fishing and squid-fishing trips.

🍴 EATING

Dinh Cau
Night Market   Vietnamese $
(Đ Vo Thi Sau; meals from 70,000d; ☺5pm-midnight; 🖊) The most atmospheric place to dine on the island, Duong Dong's night market has around a dozen stalls serving a delicious range of Vietnamese seafood, grills and vegetarian options. It's geared towards tourists and quality can be a mixed bag, so look for a local crowd, as they are a discerning bunch.

Nha Ghe Phu Quoc
Crab House   Seafood $$
(☎077-384 5067; 21 Đ Tran Hung Dao; meals 200,000-780,000d; ☺11am-10pm; ❄🛜) At this crustacean sensation you won't be crabby once you get your claws into the likes of soft-shell crab with green-peppercorn salsa, *com ghe* (jasmine rice with crab meat and fish sauce) or Cajun-style blue crab. Extra hungry? Don't be shellfish and share the mega squid-crab-shrimp-sausage combo with your nearest and dearest.

Winston's
Burgers & Beer   Burgers $
(☎0126 390 1093; 121 Đ Tran Hung Dao; burgers from 70,000d; ☺1-10pm) The name says it all: this bar is all about (really good) burgers, beer and a large selection of cocktails, mixed by the eponymous Winston. Linger for a chat or challenge your drinking companions to a game of Connect 4. It has few vegetarian options.

Spice House at
Cassia Cottage   Vietnamese $$
(www.cassiacottage.com; 100c Đ Tran Hung Dao; meals 190,000-300,000d; ☺7-10am & 11am-10pm) Nab a beachside high table, order a papaya salad, grilled garlic prawns, cinnamon-infused okra, a delectable fish curry or grilled beef skewers wrapped in betel leaves, and time dinner to catch the sunset at this excellent restaurant.

MIEL.NICK/STUDIO/SHUTTERSTOCK ©

Itaca Resto Lounge   Fusion $$$

(www.itacalounge.com; 125 Đ Tran Hung Dao; tapas 90,000-195,000d, meals 175,000-220,000d; ⊙6-11pm Tue-Sun Nov-Apr; 🛜) This much-applauded restaurant has a winning Mediterranean-Asian fusion menu (with tapas), a much-enjoyed al fresco arrangement and friendly, welcoming hosts. Don't expect sea views, but do expect wagyu beef burgers, seared tuna with passion fruit, wild-mushroom risotto and a charming ambience.

🍷 DRINKING & NIGHTLIFE

Le Bar   Bar

(118/9 Đ Tran Hung Dao; ⊙6am-11pm; 🛜) With its gorgeous tiled floor, art-deco furniture and colonial charms, this highly elegant and well-poised upstairs lounge-bar at **La Veranda** (📞077-398 2988; www.laveranda resort.com) is a superb spot for a terrace sundowner.

Rory's Beach Bar   Bar

(118/10 Đ Tran Hung Dao; ⊙9am-late) Phu Quoc's liveliest and most fun beach bar draws a steady torrent of travellers and island residents down the path to its seaside perch. Expect bonfires on the beach, great happy-hour specials and staff happy to chat.

ℹ️ GETTING THERE & AROUND

Phu Quoc International Airport is 10km southeast of Duong Dong.

Motorbikes and bicycles can be hired from most hotels. **Mai Linh** (📞077-397 9797) is a reliable taxi operator.

Street vendors, Hoi An (p123)

In Focus

Two-wheeled traffic in Ho Chi Minh City

Vietnam Today

A period of sustained growth has transformed Vietnam. Change is most apparent in the big cities, where steel-and-glass high-rises define skylines and a burgeoning middle class now has the spending power to enjoy air-conditioned living and overseas travel. Yet, in rural and highland areas the nation's new-found prosperity is less evident.

The Big Picture

Forty years since the end of the American War, Vietnam has made giant strides. Per-capita income has grown from US$98 in 1993 to over US$2000 by 2015, and today Vietnam is one of the 10 fastest-growing economies in the world. Start-up business numbers are booming. And yet this rapid development is disjointed as the state sector remains huge, controlling around two-fifths of the economy.

The spectre of corruption casts a shadow over development every step of the way. Transparency International ranked Vietnam the lowest of all the Asia-Pacific countries it measured in 2014. For most Vietnamese people corruption is simply a part of day-to-day life, as they have to pay backhanders for everything from securing a civil service job to arranging an internet connection.

belief systems
(% of population)

80 | 10 | 6 | 2 | 1 | 1
None | Buddhist | Catholic | Hoa Hao | Cao Dai | Other

if Vietnam were 100 people

86 would be Kinh
3 would be Thai & Muong
2 would be Khmer Krom
2 would be Tay
1 would be Hoa
6 would be Other

population per sq km

👤 ≈ 30 people

Vietnam | UK | USA

Tourism Woes: a Blip or a Trend?

In mid-2015, the Vietnamese government did what its tourism industry had been urging them to do for years – it (partially) relaxed visa regulations, allowing easier access to the country for several European nationalities. After years of exponential growth, tourist arrivals were on the slide, with a knock-on effect for the nation's important service sector. Further visa reforms may or may not boost tourism.

As tourism chiefs pondered the stats, an EU-funded study found that just 6% of tourists surveyed said they would want to return to Vietnam, provoking a barrage of newspaper headlines. The clearly alarmed Vietnam Tourism authority quickly ordered a counter-survey (which suggested higher approval ratings). But an underlying message was clear: overseas visitors considered road transport dangerous and the nation's infrastructure poor, felt hassled by street vendors and overcharged by shopkeepers, and were frustrated by the lack of reliable travel information.

Uneasy Neighbours

On the surface, Vietnam and its northern neighbour China have much in common, with a shared heritage, common frontier and all-powerful ruling Communist parties. But for the Vietnamese, China represents something of an overbearing big brother (and 1000 years of subordination). The nations fought a recent on-off border war that rumbled on for years, only ending in 1990, and there are concerns that another conflict could erupt over offshore islands in the South China Sea (always the 'East Sea' in Vietnam). China claims virtually the whole area, and is busy constructing port facilities and airstrips. In May 2014, anti-Chinese riots erupted in several provinces, resulting in at least 21 deaths and thousands of Chinese nationals fleeing the country. By November 2015 tensions remained, but the situation had calmed enough for President Xi Jinping to visit Hanoi as the countries sought to repair ties.

The two nations have plenty of mutual ground. Trade has continued to boom (though more one-way than the Vietnamese would like), reaching US$66 billion in 2015, and Chinese is the second most popular foreign language studied in Vietnam. Ultimately, Presidents Trong and Xi signed various cooperation agreements concerning investment and infrastructure but little progress was evident over territorial disputes.

Statues at the Tomb of Khai Dinh (p115)

History

The Vietnamese trace their roots back to the Red River Delta where farmers first cultivated rice. Millennia of struggle against the Chinese then followed. Vietnam only became a united state in the 19th century, but quickly faced the ignominy of French colonialism and then the devastation of the American intervention. The Vietnamese nation has survived tempestuous, troubled times, but its strength of character has served it well.

2789 BC
The Van Lang kingdom, considered the first independent Vietnamese state, is founded by the Hung Vuong kings.

2000 BC
The Bronze Age Dong Son culture emerges in the Red River Delta around Hanoi, renowned for its rice cultivation and bronzeware.

111 BC
The Han emperors of China annex the Red River Delta region of Vietnam, heralding 1000 years of Chinese rule.

A MiG-21 fighter jet used during the American War

EQROY/SHUTTERSTOCK ©

The Early Days

Humans first inhabited northern Vietnam about 500,000 years ago, though it took until 7000 BC for these hunter-gatherers to practise rudimentary agriculture. The sophisticated Dong Son culture, famous for its bronze *moko* drums, emerged sometime around the 3rd century BC. The Dong Son period also saw huge advances in rice cultivation and the emergence of the Red River Delta as a major agricultural centre.

From the 1st to 6th centuries AD, southern Vietnam was part of the Indianised Cambodian kingdom of Funan – famous for its refined art and architecture. Funan's principal port city was Oc-Eo in the Mekong Delta, and archaeological excavations here suggest there was contact with China, Indonesia, Persia and even the Mediterranean.

The Hindu kingdom of Champa emerged around present-day Danang in the late 2nd century AD. Like Funan, it adopted Sanskrit as a sacred language and borrowed heavily from Indian art and culture. By the 8th century, Champa had expanded southward to

AD 40	602	1010
The Trung Sisters vanquish the Chinese and proclaim themselves queens of an independent Vietnam.	Rebellions by leaders including Ly Bon and Trieu Quang Phuc against Chinese rule ultimately fail.	Thang Long (City of the Soaring Dragon), known today as Hanoi, is founded and becomes the new capital of Vietnam.

include what is now Nha Trang and Phan Rang. The Cham were a feisty bunch who conducted raids along the entire coast of Indochina, and thus found themselves in a perpetual state of war with the Vietnamese to the north and the Khmers to the south. Ultimately this cost them their kingdom, as they found themselves squeezed between these two great powers.

One Thousand Years of Chinese Domination

The Chinese conquered the Red River Delta in the 2nd century BC. Over the following centuries, large numbers of Chinese settlers, officials and scholars moved south, seeking to impress a centralised state system on the Vietnamese.

In the most famous act of resistance, in AD 40, the Trung Sisters (Hai Ba Trung) rallied the people, raised an army and led a revolt against the Chinese. The Chinese counter-attacked, but, rather than surrender, the Trung Sisters threw themselves into the Hat Giang River.

The early Vietnamese learned much from the Chinese, including the advancement of dykes and irrigation works – reinforcing the role of rice as the 'staff of life'. As food became more plentiful the population expanded, forcing the Vietnamese to seek new lands south along the coast.

During this era, Vietnam was a key port of call on the sea route between China and India. The Chinese introduced Confucianism, Taoism and Mahayana Buddhism to Vietnam, while the Indian influence brought Theravada Buddhism and Hinduism.

Liberation from China

In the early 10th century, the Tang dynasty collapsed, provoking the Vietnamese to launch a revolt against Chinese rule. In AD 938 popular patriot Ngo Quyen defeated Chinese forces by luring the Chinese fleet up the Bach Dang River in a feigned retreat, only to counter-attack and impale their ships on sharpened stakes hidden beneath the waters.

From the 11th to 13th centuries, Vietnamese independence was consolidated under the emperors of the Ly dynasty, founded by Ly Thai To. This was a period of progress that saw the introduction of an elaborate dyke system for flood control and cultivation, and the establishment of the country's first university. During the Ly dynasty, the Chinese, the Khmer and the Cham launched attacks on Vietnam, but all were repelled.

The Chinese took control of Vietnam again in the early 15th century, taking the national archives and some of the country's intellectuals back to Nanjing – a loss that was to have a lasting impact on Vietnamese civilisation. Heavy taxation and slave labour were also typical of the era.

But in 1418 wealthy philanthropist Le Loi sparked the Lam Son Uprising by refusing to serve as an official for the Chinese Ming dynasty. By 1425 local rebellions had erupted in

1427	**16th century**	**1516**
Le Loi triumphs over the Chinese, declaring himself emperor, the first in the long line of the Le dynasty.	HCMC begins life as humble Prey Nokor, a backwater Khmer village in what was then the eastern edge of Cambodia.	Portuguese traders land at Danang, sparking the start of European interest in Vietnam.

several regions and Le Loi travelled the countryside to rally the people, and eventually defeat the Chinese.

Le Loi and his successors launched a campaign to take over Cham lands to the south, which culminated in the occupation of its capital Vijaya, near present-day Quy Nhon in 1471.

Division & Unity

Vietnam found itself divided in two throughout much of the 17th and 18th centuries. The powerful Trinh Lords ruled the North. To the south were the Nguyen Lords. By this time, several European nations were interested in Vietnam's potential and were jockeying for influence, while China again contested control of the North.

In 1802 Nguyen Anh proclaimed himself Emperor Gia Long, thus beginning the Nguyen dynasty. When he captured Hanoi, his work was complete and, for the first time in two centuries, Vietnam was united, with Hue as its new capital city.

Street Names

All Vietnamese street names are controlled by an intensely patriotic Communist Party. These reflect important dates, battles, heroes and heroines.

o **30 Thang 4** The date (30 April) Communist forces captured Saigon.

o **Hai Bai Trung** Two sisters who led a revolt against Chinese rule in AD 40.

o **Le Loi** Robin Hood–style rebel leader; vanquished the Chinese in 1426.

o **Nguyen Thai Hoc** Led the Yen Bai revolt against the French.

o **Quang Trung** Ruthless 18th-century military leader, emperor and reformer.

o **Tran Hunh Dao** Defeated Kublai Khan and invading Mongol forces.

The French Takeover

France's military activity in Vietnam began in 1847, when the French Navy attacked Danang harbour. Saigon was seized in early 1859 and, in 1862, Emperor Tu Duc signed a treaty that gave the French the three eastern provinces of Cochinchina.

In 1872 Jean Dupuis, a merchant seeking to supply salt and weapons via the Red River, seized the Hanoi Citadel. A French conquest of the North followed, and in 1883 they attacked Hue and the Treaty of Protectorate was imposed on the imperial court.

The French colonial authorities carried out ambitious public works, such as the construction of the Saigon–Hanoi railway and draining of the Mekong Delta swamps. These projects were funded by heavy government taxes which had a devastating impact on the rural economy.

1802
Emperor Gia Long takes the throne and the Nguyen dynasty is born, ruling over Vietnam until 1945.

1883
The French impose the Treaty of Protectorate on the Vietnamese, marking the start of 70 years of colonial control.

1941
Ho Chi Minh forms the Viet Minh, a liberation movement seeking independence from France and fighting the Japanese occupation.

Visiting a war museum, Hue

★ The American War

Four million Vietnamese killed or injured

15 million tonnes of US ammunition expended

4857 US helicopters downed

3689 US fixed-wing aircraft lost

Fight for Independence

Throughout the colonial period, the desire of many Vietnamese for independence simmered below the surface. Nationalist aspirations often erupted into open defiance of the French.

Leading patriots soon realised that modernisation was the key to an independent Vietnam. Vietnamese intellectuals favoured the education of the masses, the modernisation of the economy and working with the French towards independence.

The most successful of the anticolonialists were the Communists who were able to tune into the frustrations and aspirations of the population – especially the peasants. In 1941 Ho Chi Minh formed the Viet Minh, which resisted the Vichy French government, as well as Japanese forces, and carried out extensive political activities during WWII. As well as being a Communist, Ho appeared pragmatic, patriotic and populist, and understood the need for national unity.

For a time, Vietnam was spared the ravages of Japanese occupation. However, as WWII drew to a close, Japanese rice requisitions, combined with floods and breaches in the dykes, caused a horrific famine in which perhaps two million North Vietnamese people starved to death.

By the spring of 1945 the Viet Minh controlled large swathes of the country, particularly in the North. In mid-August, Ho Chi Minh called for a general uprising, later known as the August Revolution, then on 2 September 1945 he declared independence. Throughout this period, he wrote eight letters to the US asking for aid, but received no replies.

With near anarchy in the South and the Chinese occupying the North, Ho decided to accept a temporary return of the French, deeming them less of a long-term threat than the Chinese. But the détente quickly began to unravel as fighting broke out in Hanoi, and Ho Chi Minh and his forces fled to the mountains to regroup, where they would remain for the next eight years.

Conflict between the French and Viet Minh rumbled on for years. But on 7 May 1954, after a 57-day siege, more than 10,000 starving French troops surrendered to the Viet

---

1945
Ho Chi Minh proclaims Vietnamese independence on 2 September in Ba Dinh Square in central Hanoi.

1954
French forces surrender to Viet Minh fighters as the siege of Dien Bien Phu comes to a dramatic close on 7 May.

1955
Vietnam is 'temporarily' divided into North Vietnam and South Vietnam, and people are given 300 days to relocate.

Minh at Dien Bien Phu. This defeat brought an end to the French colonial adventure in Indochina.

Resolutions included the 'temporary' division of Vietnam into two zones at the Ben Hai River (near the 17th Parallel) until nationwide elections could be held. The South was ruled by a government led by Ngo Dinh Diem, a fiercely anti-Communist Catholic. Nationwide elections were never held, as the Americans rightly feared that Ho Chi Minh would win with a massive majority.

As time went on Diem became increasingly tyrannical, closing Buddhist monasteries, imprisoning monks, banning opposition parties and doling out power to family members. The US began to see Diem as a liability and threw its support behind a military coup, launched by a group of young generals in November 1963.

War with the Americans

The Communists' campaign to liberate the South began in 1959. The Ho Chi Minh Trail reopened for business, universal military conscription was implemented and the National Liberation Front (NLF), later known as the Viet Cong (VC), was formed.

As the NLF launched its campaign, the Diem government quickly lost control of the countryside. By early 1965 the Saigon government was on its last legs. The army was getting ready to evacuate Hue and Danang, and the central highlands seemed about to fall.

First US Troops Arrive

The Americans saw France's war in Indochina as an important element in the worldwide struggle against Communist expansion. Vietnam was the next domino and could not topple.

A decisive turning point in US strategy came with the August 1964 Gulf of Tonkin incident. Two US destroyers claimed to have come under unprovoked attack off the North Vietnamese coast. On US president Lyndon Johnson's orders, 64 sorties unleashed bombs on the North – the first of thousands of such missions that would hit every single road and rail bridge in the country, as well as 4000 of North Vietnam's 5788 villages.

As the military situation of the Saigon government reached a new nadir, the first US combat troops splashed ashore at Danang in March 1965. By December 1965, there were 184,300 US military personnel in Vietnam and 636 Americans had died. By December 1967, the figures had risen to 485,600 US soldiers in the country and 16,021 dead. There were 1.3 million soldiers fighting for the Saigon government, including the South Vietnamese and other allies.

By 1966 the buzz words in Washington were 'pacification', 'search and destroy' and 'free-fire zones'. Pacification involved developing a pro-government civilian infrastructure in each village. To protect the villages from VC raids, mobile search-and-destroy units of

1960	1963	1965
The National Liberation Front launch a guerrilla war against the Diem government, sparking the 'American War'.	South Vietnam's president Ngo Dinh Diem is overthrown and killed in a coup backed by the USA.	To prevent collapse of the Saigon regime, the US bombs North Vietnam and dispatches combat troops to the South.

soldiers moved around the country hunting VC guerrillas. In some cases, villagers were evacuated so the Americans could use heavy weaponry such as napalm and tanks in areas that were declared free-fire zones.

These strategies were only partially successful: US forces could control the countryside by day, while the VC usually controlled it by night. Even without heavy weapons, VC guerrillas continued to inflict heavy casualties in ambushes and through extensive use of mines and booby traps.

Tet Offensive

In January 1968 North Vietnamese troops launched a major attack on the US base at Khe Sanh in the Demilitarised Zone (DMZ). This battle, the single largest of the war, was in part a massive diversion from the Tet Offensive.

The Tet Offensive marked a decisive turning point in the war. On the evening of 31 January, as the country celebrated the Lunar New Year, the VC broke an unofficial holiday ceasefire with a series of coordinated strikes in more than 100 cities and towns. As the TV cameras rolled, a VC commando team took over the courtyard of the US embassy in central Saigon. However, the Communists miscalculated the mood of the population, as the popular uprising they had hoped to provoke never materialised.

Although the US were utterly surprised – a major failure of military intelligence – they immediately counter-attacked with massive firepower, bombing and shelling heavily populated cities. The counter-attack devastated the VC, but also traumatised the civilian population.

The VC may have lost the battle, but were on the road to winning the war. Watching the killing and chaos in Saigon beamed into their living rooms, public tolerance of the war and its casualties reached breaking point.

Simultaneously, stories began leaking out of Vietnam about atrocities and massacres carried out against unarmed Vietnamese civilians, including the infamous My Lai Massacre.

Peace Talks & Accords: Beginning of the End

The first half of 1969 saw the conflict escalate further as the number of US soldiers in Vietnam reached an all-time high of 543,400. Australia, New Zealand, South Korea, the Philippines and Thailand also sent military personnel to South Vietnam as part of what the Americans called the 'Free World Military Forces', whose purpose was to help internationalise the American war effort in order to give it more legitimacy.

While the fighting raged, Nixon's chief negotiator, Henry Kissinger, pursued peace talks in Paris with his North Vietnamese counterpart Le Duc Tho.

1968	1969	1972
The Viet Cong launches the Tet Offensive. Hundreds of Vietnamese civilians are killed in the My Lai Massacre.	After a lifetime dedicated to revolution, Ho Chi Minh dies in Hanoi in September of heart failure.	The North Vietnamese cross the Demilitarized Zone (DMZ) at the 17th Parallel to attack South Vietnam and US forces.

In 1969 the Americans began secretly bombing Cambodia in an attempt to flush out Vietnamese Communist sanctuaries. This new escalation provoked violent anti-war protests in the US and elsewhere. A peace demonstration at Kent State University in Ohio resulted in four protesters being shot dead. It was clear that the war was tearing America apart.

In the spring of 1972, the North Vietnamese launched an offensive across the 17th Parallel; the USA responded with increased bombing of the North. Eventually, the Paris Peace Accords were signed by the USA, North Vietnam, South Vietnam and the VC on 27 January 1973, which provided for a ceasefire, the total withdrawal of US combat forces and the release of 590 American POWs.

Victory & Reunification

Most US military personnel departed Vietnam in 1973, leaving behind a small contingent of technicians, advisors and CIA agents. Still the war rumbled on, only now the South Vietnamese were fighting alone.

In January 1975, the North Vietnamese launched a massive ground attack across the 17th Parallel. The invasion provoked panic in the South Vietnamese army as whole brigades fled southward, joining hundreds of thousands of civilians clogging Hwy 1. City after city – Hue, Danang, Quy Nhon, Nha Trang – were simply abandoned with hardly a shot fired.

The North Vietnamese pushed on to Saigon and on the morning of 30 April 1975, their tanks smashed through the gates of Saigon's Independence Palace (now called Reunification Palace). General Duong Van Minh, president for just 42 hours, formally surrendered, marking the end of the war.

Just a few hours before the surrender, the last Americans were evacuated by helicopter from the US embassy roof. Harrowing images of US Marines booting Vietnamese people off their helicopters were beamed around the world. And so more than a quarter of a century of American military involvement came to a close. Throughout the entire conflict, the USA never actually declared war on North Vietnam.

The Americans weren't the only ones who left. Hundreds of thousands of Vietnamese fled the country as 'boat people', refugees risking everything to undertake perilous journeys on the South China Sea.

China & the Khmer Rouge

Relations with China to the north and the Khmer Rouge in Cambodia were rapidly deteriorating. War-weary Vietnam felt encircled by enemies. An anti-capitalist campaign was launched in March 1978, seizing private property and businesses. Most of the victims were ethnic Chinese – hundreds of thousands of whom fled as 'boat people' – and relations with China soured further.

1975	1978	1986
On 30 April 1975, Saigon falls to the North Vietnamese. Saigon is renamed Ho Chi Minh City.	Vietnamese forces invade Cambodia on Christmas Day 1978, sweeping through the shattered country.	*Doi moi* (economic reform) is launched with a rash of economic reforms.

After repeated attacks on Vietnamese border villages by the Khmer Rouge, Vietnamese forces entered Cambodia on Christmas Day 1978. They succeeded in driving the Khmer Rouge from power on 7 January 1979 and set up a pro-Hanoi regime in Phnom Penh. China viewed the attack on the Khmer Rouge as a serious provocation. In February 1979 Chinese forces invaded Vietnam and fought a brief, 17-day war before withdrawing.

Liberation of Cambodia from the Khmer Rouge soon turned to occupation and a long civil war, which exacted a heavy toll on Vietnam economically.

Embracing Change

In 1985 President Mikhail Gorbachev came to power in the Soviet Union. *Glasnost* (openness) and *perestroika* (restructuring) were in, radical revolutionaries were out. Vietnam followed suit in 1986 by choosing *doi moi* (economic reform). The Vietnamese decided to unilaterally withdraw from Cambodia in September 1989, as they could no longer afford the occupation. The party in Vietnam was on its own and needed to reform to survive.

Dramatic changes in Eastern Europe in 1989 and the collapse of the Soviet Union in 1991 forced the pace of change. Economically the Vietnamese decided to embrace the market. Capitalism has since taken root, and Vietnam joined ASEAN in 1995.

Relations with Vietnam's old nemesis, the USA, have also vastly improved. In early 1994 the USA lifted its economic embargo. Full diplomatic relations were restored and presidents Bill Clinton, George W Bush and Barack Obama have subsequently visited Vietnam.

1994
The US trade embargo on Vietnam, in place in the North since 1964 and extended to the reunified nation since 1975, is revoked.

2009
Pro-democracy activists are jailed for 'spreading propaganda against the government'.

2016
Economy grows at around 6%, driven by strong export growth and private consumption.

Outdoor market, Hoi An

SINSEEHO/SHUTTERSTOCK ©

People & Culture

Industrious, proud, stubborn and yet mischievous, quick to laugh and fond of a joke, the Vietnamese are a complicated bunch. For Westerners, the national character can be difficult to fathom: direct questions are frequently met with evasive answers. A Vietnamese person would never tell a relative stranger their life story or profound personal thoughts. Their deep respect for tradition, family and the state reflects core Confucian principles.

The National Psyche

Historically the national mentality has been to work as a team, in harmony rather than in conflict; but times are changing. If you're on the highway or doing business, it's everyone for themselves. It's these attitudes (towards traffic and commerce) that many outsiders, not just Westerners, find most alien. 'Face' is vital, and Vietnamese people hate giving way, often employing elaborate tactics of bluster and bluff (and cunning) to ensure they get where they want to go.

Floating market (p226), Mekong Delta

My Generation

In many ways Vietnam is still a traditional, conservative society, particularly for the older generation, who remember the long, hard years and every inch of the territory for which they fought. Brought up on restraint and moderation, many remain unmoved by 21st-century consumer culture. For the new generation, Vietnam is very different: a place to succeed and to ignore the staid structures set by the Communists. And yes, to show off that gleaming new motorbike, sharp haircut or iPhone.

North–South Divide

The north–south divide lingers on. It's said that Southerners think, then do; while Northerners think, then think some more. Southerners typically reckon Northerners have 'hard faces', that they take themselves too seriously and don't know how to have fun. Northerners are just as likely to think of Southerners as superficial, frivolous and business-obsessed. Caricatures these may be, but they shed light on the real differences between north and south that reach beyond the (very different) regional dialects.

Climate plays its part too. Life is easier in the south, where the fertile Mekong Delta allows three rice harvests a year. The north endures a long winter of grey skies, drizzle, mist and cool winds. Think of the differences between northern and southern Europe (or Maine and Alabama), and you have a snapshot of how one people can become two. Don't forget that the north has also lived with communism for more than half a century, while the south had more than two decades of free-wheelin' free-for-all with the Americans.

Face

Face is all important in Asia, and in Vietnam it is above all. Having 'big face' is synonymous with prestige, and prestige is particularly important. All families, even poor ones, are expected to have elaborate wedding parties and throw their money around like it's water in order to gain face. This is often ruinously expensive, but far less distressing than 'losing face'.

Foreigners should never lose their tempers with the Vietnamese; this will bring unacceptable 'loss of face' to the individual involved and end any chance of a sensible solution to the dispute. Similarly, it's also not culturally acceptable for Vietnamese traders to shout at, tug or pressure tourists when trying to do a deal, though hustlers may adopt these tactics during a hard sell. Walk on.

Lifestyle

Traditionally, Vietnamese life has revolved around family, fields and faith, with the rhythm of rural existence continuing for centuries at the same pace. All this has been disrupted by war, the impact of communism and globalisation. Whilst it's true that several generations may still share the same roof, the same rice and the same religion, lifestyles have changed immeasurably.

Vietnam is experiencing its very own '60s swing, which is creating feisty friction as sons and daughters dress as they like, date who they want and hit the town until all hours. But few live on their own and they still come home to Mum and Dad at the end of the day, where arguments might arise, particularly when it comes to marriage and settling down.

Some things never change. Most Vietnamese despise idleness and are early risers. You'll see parks full of t'ai chi devotees as dawn breaks, and offices are fully staffed by 7am. Indeed the whole nation seems supercharged with energy and vitality, no matter how hot and humid it is.

Family

In Vietnam the status of your family is more important than your salary. A family's reputation commands respect and opens doors.

Extended family is important to the Vietnamese and that includes second or third cousins, the sort of family that many Westerners may not even realise they have. The extended family comes together during times of trouble and times of joy, celebrating festivals and successes, mourning deaths or disappointments. This is a source of strength for many of the older generation.

Business Practices

Western visitors regularly complain about the business practices of many Vietnamese they encounter, which can range from mild price hiking to outright scamming. For many foreigners it's the most off-putting aspect of their visit to the nation. At times it seems impossible to get the local price for anything. A little background is important.

Most of these rapacious individuals work in tourism; chronic overcharging is rare once you're off the main banana pancake trail. The mentality is that Westerners do not bother to learn the real price, don't learn Vietnamese and are only in the country for a week or

---

Main Minority Groups

Tay (population 1.6 million) Live at low elevations between Hanoi and the Chinese border.

Thai (population 1.5 million) Northern tribe usually categorised by colour: Red, Black and White Thai.

Muong (population 1.4 million) Known for their folk literature, poems and music.

Hmong (population over 500,000) Spread across the far northern mountains; most are animists. Each Hmong group – Black, White, Red, Green and Flower – has its own dress code.

Nung (population 800,000) This tribe live in small villages in the far northeastern provinces.

Jarai (population 350,000) These people still practise animistic rituals, paying respect to their ancestors and nature.

Religion

Many Vietnamese are not very religious and some surveys indicate that only 20% of the population consider themselves to have a faith. That said, over the centuries, Confucianism, Taoism and Buddhism have fused with popular Chinese beliefs and ancient Vietnamese animism to create the Tam Giao (Triple Religion) that many Vietnamese identify with.

Christianity, present in Vietnam for 500 years, and Cao Daism (unique to the region) are other important religions.

two. For years, many Vietnamese have only thought about the short term – about making a fast buck. Steadily the concept has grown that good service will bring repeat business (and bad service will be all over internet forums immediately).

It's not an excuse, but Vietnam is a unique country. Famine killed two million in the 1940s, and the country was among the poorest of the poor following the American War. Vietnam's tourism industry is still young and the Vietnamese state actually helped forge this overcharging mentality – until relatively recently the government set separate local and foreign rates (which were four to 10 times more) for everything from train fares to hotel rooms.

The People of Vietnam

Vietnamese culture and civilisation have been profoundly influenced by the Chinese, who occupied the country for 1000 years and whose culture deeply permeates Vietnamese society.

History has of course influenced the mix of Vietnamese minorities. The steady expansion southwards in search of cultivable lands absorbed first the Kingdom of Champa and later the eastern extent of the Khmer Empire; both the Chams and the Khmers are sizeable minorities today.

Traffic was not only one-way. Many of the 50 or more minority groups that live in the far northwest only migrated to these areas from Yunnan (China) and Tibet in the past few centuries. They moved into the mountains that the lowland Vietnamese considered uncultivable, and help make up the most colourful part of the ethnic mosaic that is Vietnam today.

The largest minority group in Vietnam has always been the ethnic-Chinese community, which makes up much of the commercial class in the cities. The government has traditionally viewed them with suspicion, and many left the country as 'boat people' in the 1970s. But today they play a major part in economic development.

Dancers celebrate Tet (p22)

ASIA IMAGES/SHUTTERSTOCK ©

Arts & Architecture

Vietnam has a fascinating artistic and architectural heritage. Historically, the nation has absorbed influences from China, India and the Khmer kingdoms, and fused them with indigenous traditions. Then the French, Americans and Soviet Union left their mark. Today, contemporary artists and architects look across the globe for inspiration.

Arts

Contemporary Music

Vietnam's contemporary music scene is diverse, and influenced by trends in the West and east Asia. As all artists are monitored by the government, subjects which could be deemed subversive are largely avoided (or heavily coded). V-pop girl and boy bands like 365 and YO!Girls with heavily stylised looks and choreographed moves are wildly popular with teenagers.

Hot bands include rock band Microwave, metal merchants Black Infinity, the punk band Giao Chi and also alt-roots band 6789.

★ **Colonial Architecture**

Balconies Grace important buildings.
Louvered windows Usually green or brown.
Stucco features Decorative flourishes.
Colour Ochre/pale mustard.
Terracotta roof tiles Mediterranean style.

Trinh Cong Son, who died in 2001, was a prolific writer-composer of anti-war and reconciliation songs; he was once called the Bob Dylan of Vietnam by Joan Baez.

Traditional Music

Vietnam's traditional music uses the five-note (pentatonic) scale of Chinese origin. Folk tunes are usually sung without any instrumental accompaniment (and have been adapted by the Communist Party for many a patriotic marching song).

Indigenous instruments include the *dan bau,* a single-stringed zither that generates an astounding array of tones, and the *trung,* a large bamboo xylophone. Vietnam's minorities use distinctive instruments: reed flutes, gongs and stringed instruments made from gourds.

Dance

Traditionally reserved for ceremonies and festivals, Vietnamese folk dance is again mainstream thanks to tourism. The Conical Hat Dance is visually stunning: women wearing *ao dai* (the national dress of Vietnam) spin around, whirling their classic conical hats.

Theatre

Vietnamese theatre fuses music, singing, recitation, dance and mime into an artistic whole. Classical theatre is very formal, employing fixed gestures and scenery, and has an accompanying orchestra and a limited cast of characters. Popular theatre *(hat cheo)* expresses social protest through satire.

Puppetry

Conventional puppetry *(roi can)* and the uniquely Vietnamese art form of water puppetry *(roi nuoc)* draw their plots from the same legendary and historical sources as other forms of traditional theatre.

Water puppetry was first developed by farmers in northern Vietnam, who manipulated wooden puppets and used rice paddies as a stage. There are water-puppet theatres in both Hanoi and Ho Chi Minh City.

Painting

Much modern work has political rather than aesthetic or artistic motives – some of this propaganda art is now highly collectable. Some young artists have gone back to the traditional-style silk or lacquer paintings, while others experiment with contemporary subjects.

Literature

Contemporary writers include Nguyen Huy Thiep, who articulates the experiences of Vietnamese people in *The General Retires and Other Stories*. Both Duong Van Mai Elliot's memoir, *The Sacred Willow: Four Generations in the Life of a Vietnamese Family,* and Viet Thanh Nguyen's *The Sympathizer* have been nominated for Pulitzer prizes.

Cinema

In Nguyen Khac's *The Retired General* (1988), the central character copes with adjusting from his life as a soldier to that of a civilian family man.

Dang Nhat Minh is perhaps Vietnam's most prolific film-maker. In *The Return* (1993), he hones in on the complexities of modern relationships, while *The Girl on the River* (1987) tells the stirring tale of a female journalist who joins an ex-prostitute in search of her former lover, a Viet Cong soldier.

Overseas-Vietnamese films include Tran Anh Hung's touching *The Scent of Green Papaya* (1992), which celebrates the coming of age of a young servant girl in Saigon. *Cyclo* (1995), his visually stunning masterpiece, cuts to the core of HCMC's gritty underworld. Vietnamese-American Tony Bui made a splash with his exquisite feature debut *Three Seasons* (1999).

Architecture

Traditional Vietnamese architecture is unusual, as most important buildings are single-storey structures with heavy tiled roofs based on a substantial wooden framework (to withstand typhoons).

In rural parts, houses are chiefly constructed from timber and built in stilted style, so that the home is above seasonal floods with bamboo and palm leaves for roofing.

Quirky Vietnamese styles include the narrow tube houses of Hanoi's Old Quarter – the government collected tax according to the width of the space, so the slimmer the cheaper. The Nung minority people's homes are also unusual, sometimes built with mud walls and with only one part elevated on stilts.

Colonial Buildings

Vietnam's French legacy is pronounced in the nation's architecture. Stately neoclassical buildings reinforced notions of European hegemony in the colonial era, and many still line grand city boulevards.

After the 1950s, most of these were left to rot as they symbolised an era many Vietnamese wished to forget. However, recent renovation programs have led to structures, such as the former Hôtel de Ville (People's Committee Building) in HCMC and the Sofitel

Hip Hop & Electronica

There's a small but growing hip-hop scene, with HCMC-born Suboi (who has over a million Facebook likes and two albums under her belt) acknowledged as Vietnam's leading female artist.

Vietnam's electronic scene is dominated by commercial DJs playing EDM. Club DJs are hampered by government policies (such as producing track lists in advance and translated lyrics – not easy for house and techno!). HCMC's Heart Beat (www.heart beatsaigon.com) promotes excellent underground events around the city.

Metropole Hotel in Hanoi, being restored to their former glory. In HCMC, stop to admire the spectacular halls and vaulted ceiling of the central post office – designed by Gustave Eiffel (of tower fame).

In Hanoi's French Quarter, many grand villas have fallen on hard times and are today worth a fortune to developers. Meanwhile in Dalat, French villas have been converted into hotels: the classy Ana Mandara Villas; and stately Dalat Hotel du Parc, with its grand facade.

Colonial churches were built in a range of architectural styles: in Hanoi, the sombre neo-Gothic form of St Joseph Cathedral is enhanced by dark grey stone.

Art-deco curiosities built under French rule include Dalat's wonderful train station, with its multicoloured windows, and the sleek La Residence Hotel in Hue.

Pagodas & Temples

Vietnamese religious structures do not follow a specific national prototype. Pagoda styles echo the unique religious make-up of the nation, with strong Chinese content, while southern Cham temples reflect influences from India, Hindu culture and the Khmer empire.

Pagodas (*chua*) incorporate Chinese ornamentation and motifs, with buildings grouped around garden courtyards and adorned with statues and stelae. Most have single or double roofs with elevated hip rafters, though there are some with multi-tiered towers (*thap*) like Hue's Thien Mu Pagoda.

Vietnamese pagodas are designed according to feng shui (locally called *dia ly*). They're primarily Buddhist places of worship, even though they may be dedicated to a local deity. Most are single-storey structures, with three wooden doors at the front. Inside are a number of chambers, usually filled with statues of the Buddha, bodhisattvas and assorted heroes and deities (Thien Hau, Goddess of the Sea, is popular in coastal towns). Flashing fairy lights, giant smoking incense spirals, gongs and huge bells add to the atmosphere.

Check out Hanoi's Temple of Literature for a superb example of a traditional Vietnamese temple or the wonderful pagodas in Hue.

Bun bo Hue (p272), a Central Vietnamese speciality

Food & Drink

Prepare to be amazed by Vietnam's cuisine. From traditional street stalls to contemporary big-city temples of upscale dining, the country serves up an endless banquet of exquisite eating. Over the centuries locals have adapted Chinese, Indian, French and Japanese techniques and specialities to create one of the world's greatest cuisines.

Flavours

Vietnamese palates vary from north to south, but no matter where they are, local cooks work to balance hot, sour, salty and sweet flavours in each dish.

Salty & Sweet

Vietnamese food's saltiness comes from salt but also from the fermented seafood sauces, the most common of which is *nuoc mam* (fish sauce). Cooks also use sugar to sweeten dipping sauces and to flavour dishes such as *kho*, a sweet-savoury dish of fish or meat simmered in a clay pot.

Vegetarians & Vegans

The Vietnamese are voracious omni-vores. While they dearly love veggies, they also adore much of what crawls on the ground, swims in the sea or flies in the air.

However, there are vegetarian *(com chay)* establishments in most towns, usually near Buddhist temples. Often these are local, simple places popular with observant Buddhists. Many use 'mock meat', tofu and gluten, to create meat-like dishes that can be quite delicious.

Otherwise, be wary. Any dish of vegetables may well have been cooked with fish sauce or shrimp paste.

Hot & Sour

Vietnamese cooking uses less hot chilli than Thai cuisine, though it's a key ingredient in central Vietnamese meals. Vietnam is a huge peppercorn exporter, and ground black and white peppercorns season everything from *chao* (rice porridge) to beef stew. Sour flavours are derived from lime and *kalaman-si* (a small, green-skinned, orange-fleshed citrus fruit) as well as tamarind and vinegar (in the north).

Herbs

Vietnamese food is often described as 'fresh' and 'light' owing to the plates heaped with gorgeous fresh herbs that seem to accompany every meal: coriander, mint, Thai basil, *perilla* leaves, peppery *rau ram* leaves and *rau om* (rice-paddy herb), which has a hint of lemon and cumin.

Staples

Rice

Rice, or *com,* is the very bedrock of Vietnamese cuisine: if a local says *'an com'* (literally 'let's eat rice'), it's an invitation to lunch or dinner. It's eaten in a soupy state as *chao* (rice porridge) and stir-fried with egg, vegetables and other ingredients as *com rang*. Sticky rice (white, red and black) is eaten as a filling breakfast or mixed with sugar and coconut milk as a sweet treat.

Rice flour is also a base for everything from noodles and sweets to crackers and rice paper rolls.

Meat, Fish & Fowl

Chicken and pork are widely eaten, while you'll also find goat (eaten in hotpots with a curried broth) and frog.

Seafood is a major source of protein. From the ocean comes fish such as tuna, pomfret, red snapper and sea bass, as well as prawns, crabs and shellfish. Seafood restaurants always keep their catch live in tanks or bowls, so you can be assured it's ocean fresh. Freshwater eats include *ca loc* (snakehead fish), catfish and clams.

Fruit

Depending on when you're travelling, you'll be able to gorge on mangoes, crispy and sour green or soft and tartly floral pink guavas, juicy lychees and longans, and exotic mangosteen, passion fruit and jackfruit.

Drinks

Alcoholic Drinks

Memorise the words *bia hoi*, which means 'draught beer'. Probably the cheapest beer in the world, *bia hoi* starts at around 5000d a glass, so anyone can afford a round. Foreign labels brewed in Vietnam include Tiger, Carlsberg and Heineken. National and regional brands include Halida and Hanoi in the north, Huda and La Rue in the centre, and 333 (ba ba ba) in the south. Craft beers are also making an appearance. Wine and spirits are available, and you may be offered *ruou* (distilled sticky-rice wine), often flavoured with herbs, spices, fruits and even animals.

Nonalcoholic Drinks

Vietnam is also a major coffee producer, and whiling away a morning or an afternoon over endless glasses of iced coffee, with or without milk (*caphe sua da* or *caphe da*), is something of a ritual for Vietnam's male population. Espresso-based coffee is common in the main towns. Tea (black leaf and green) is also popular, particularly in the north.

You'll find fizzy drinks, fruit juices and smoothies are widely available. Look out for *mia da,* a sugar-cane juice that's especially refreshing served over ice with a squeeze of *kalamansi*.

Regional Specialities

Travelling north to south is a Vietnamese journey that, geographically and gastronomically, begins in China and ends in Southeast Asia. Differences in history, culture and geography combine for many techniques, ingredients and tastes, all linked by the Vietnamese love for vibrant flavours, fresh herbs, noodles and seafood.

Northern Vietnam

Northern Vietnamese food bears the imprint of centuries of Chinese occupation. Comforting noodle dishes, generally mild flavours and rustic elegance are all hallmarks. Soy sauce is used as frequently as fish sauce.

○ **Pho Bo** A northern culinary classic is *pho bo* (beef noodle soup). A good *pho* hinges on the broth, which is made from beef bones boiled for hours with shallot, ginger, fish sauce, black cardamom, star anise and cassia.

○ **Banh Cuon** These rolls are made from rice-flour batter that's poured onto a piece of muslin cloth stretched over a steamer; once firm, the noodle sheet is scattered with chopped pork, mushrooms and dried shrimp, then rolled up, sprinkled with crispy shallots, and served alongside a tangle of bean sprouts, slivered cucumber and chopped fresh herbs, with a saucer of *nuoc cham* (dipping sauce) for drizzling.

○ **Bun Cha** This street favourite features barbecued sliced pork or pork patties served with thin rice vermicelli, fresh herbs and green vegetables, and a bowl of lightly sweetened *nuoc mam* with floating slices of pickled vegetables.

Central Vietnam

Positioned between culinary extremes, the food of central Vietnam combines moderation and balance – except where it concerns the locals' love of chilli. Expect gutsy and spicy flavours, including briny shrimp sauce and lemongrass.

○ Banh Khoai These hearty, dessert-plate-sized crepes are made with rice-flour batter and cooked with oil. With a spare filling of shrimp, pork, egg and bean sprouts, they are encased with fresh herbs in lettuce, and then dunked in a sauce based on earthy fermented soybeans.

○ Bun Bo Hue This punchy rice-noodle soup with beef and pork is tinged yellow-orange by chillies and annatto. The broth is laden with lemongrass notes and anchored by savoury shrimp sauce *(mam tom)*. It's accompanied by herbs and leafy greens.

○ Com Hen Rice is served with the flesh of tiny clams, their cooking broth, and garnishes including roasted rice crackers, crisp pork crackling, peanuts, sesame seeds, fresh herbs and vegetables.

Southern Vietnam

Southern cuisine tends to be on the sweet side, with coconut milk infusing mild curries. The southern love of fresh herbs, fruit and vegetables comes to the fore in refreshing *goi* (salads), of green papaya, grapefruit-like pomelo, or lotus stems.

○ Canh Chua Ca This soup is the Mekong Delta in a bowl: plentiful snakehead or catfish; fruits like tomato and pineapple; and vegetables including bean sprouts, okra and *bac ha* (taro stem), all in a broth that's tart with tamarind and salty with *nuoc mam*, and finally topped with vivid green herbs and golden fried garlic.

○ Banh Mi This baguette sandwich is a legacy of French and Chinese colonialism, but it's 100% Vietnamese. The filling might be a smearing of pâté or a few slices of silky sausage. Mayonnaise moistens the bread and a sprinkling of soy sauce imparts *umami* (savoury) goodness.

○ Banh Xeo This giant crispy, chewy rice crepe is crammed with pork, shrimp, mung beans and bean sprouts. Take a portion and encase it in lettuce or mustard leaf, add some fresh herbs, then dunk it in *nuoc cham*.

Paddling through Tra Su indigo forest, Mekong Delta

HANOI PHOTOGRAPHY/SHUTTERSTOCK ©

Environment

Vietnam is one of the most diverse countries on earth, with tropical lowlands, intensely cultivated rice-growing regions, a remarkable coastline and karst mountains. But due to population pressure, poverty and a lack of environmental protection, many regions, and the nation's wildlife, are under threat.

The Landscape

As the Vietnamese are quick to point out, their nation resembles a *don ganh,* the ubiquitous bamboo pole with a basket of rice slung from each end. The baskets represent the main rice-growing regions of the Red River Delta in the north and the Mekong Delta in the south. The country bulges in the north and south, and has a very slim waistline – at one point it's only 50km wide. Mountain ranges define most of Vietnam's western and northern borders.

★ **Best National Parks**

Phong Nha-Ke Bang (p92)

Cat Tien (p168)

Con Dao (p216)

Cat Ba (p76)

Jungle walkway, Cat Tien National Park (p168)

Coast & Islands

Vietnam's extraordinary 3451km-long coastline is one of the nation's biggest draws and it doesn't disappoint, with sweeping sandy beaches, towering cliffs, undulating dunes and countless offshore islands. The largest of these islands is Phu Quoc in the Gulf of Thailand; others include Cat Ba, the 2000 or so islets of Halong Bay and the fabled Con Dao Islands way out in the South China Sea.

River Deltas

The Red River and Mekong River deltas are both pancake-flat and prone to flooding. Silt carried by the Red River and its tributaries, confined to their paths by 3000km of dykes, has raised the level of the riverbeds above the surrounding plains. The Mekong Delta has no such protection, so when *cuu long* ('the nine dragons'; ie the nine channels of the Mekong in the delta) burst their banks, it creates havoc for communities and crops.

Highlands

Three-quarters of the country consists of rolling hills (mostly in the south) and mighty mountains (mainly in the north), the highest of which is 3143m Fansipan, close to Sapa. The Truong Son Mountains, which form the southwest highlands, run almost the full length of Vietnam along its borders with Laos and Cambodia. The coastal ranges near Nha Trang and those at Hai Van Pass (Danang) are composed of granite. However, northern Vietnam's incredible karst formations are probably the nation's most iconic physical features.

Wildlife

We'll start with the good news. Despite some disastrous bouts of deforestation, Vietnam's flora and fauna is still incredibly exotic and varied. Intensive surveys by the World Wildlife Fund along the Mekong River place this area in the top five biodiversity hot spots in the world.

The other side of the story is that despite this outstanding diversity, the threat to Vietnam's remaining wildlife has never been greater due to poaching, hunting and habitat loss. Three of the nation's iconic animals – the elephant, saola and tiger – are on the brink. It's virtually certain that the last wild Vietnamese rhino was killed inside Cat Tien National Park in 2010.

And for every trophy animal there are hundreds of other less 'headline' species that are being cleared from forests and reserves for the sake of profit (or hunger).

Animals

Vietnam has plenty to offer those who are wild about wildlife, but in reality many animals live in remote forested areas and encountering them is extremely unlikely.

With a wide range of habitats – from equatorial lowlands to high, temperate plateaus and even alpine peaks – the wildlife of Vietnam is enormously diverse. One recent tally listed 275 species of mammals, more than 800 birds, 180 reptiles, 80 amphibians, hundreds of fish and tens of thousands of invertebrates.

Rare and little-known birds previously thought to be extinct have been spotted and no doubt there are more in the extensive forests along the Laos border including Edwards's pheasant.

Even casual visitors will spot a few bird species: swallows and swifts flying over fields and along watercourses; flocks of finches at roadsides and in paddies; and bulbuls and mynahs in gardens and patches of forest.

Environmental Issues

Vietnam's environment is not yet in intensive care, but it's reaching crisis level on several fronts. As a poor, densely populated country, the government's main priorities are job creation and economic growth. There's minimal monitoring of pollution and dirty industries, while loggers and animal traffickers are all too often able to escape trouble through bribery and official inaction. Key issues include the following:

○ Deforestation While 44% of the nation was forested in 1943, by 1983 only 24% of forest cover was left and by 1995 it was down to 20%.

○ Wildlife Poaching This has decimated forests of animals; snares capture and kill indiscriminately, whether animals are common or critically endangered.

○ Urban & Industrial Pollution Hanoi is the most contaminated city in Southeast Asia, while water pollution affects many regions. A massive toxic leak from a Formosa Plastics plant in 2016 decimated sealife in the South China Sea.

○ Global Warming A sea-level rise of only a metre would flood more than 6% of the country and affect up to 10 million people.

Responsible Travel

○ Consider shunning elephant rides. Working elephants are still illegally trapped and conservation groups have grave concerns about their living conditions.

○ When snorkelling or diving be careful not to touch coral as this hinders its growth.

○ Avoid touching limestone formations as it affects their development and turns the limestone black.

○ Most 'exotic' meats such as porcupine and squirrel have been illegally poached from national parks.

○ Many civets are kept in appalling conditions to produce 'poo coffee'.

○ Before downing snake wine or snake blood consider that the reptiles (sometimes endangered species) are killed without anaesthesia and can carry salmonella.

Yen stream, near Hanoi

Survival Guide

JOHN BILL/SHUTTERSTOCK ©

Directory A–Z

Accommodation

Accommodation in Vietnam is superb value for money. Big cities and the main tourism centres have everything from hostel dorm beds to luxe hotels. In the countryside and visiting provincial towns you'll usually be deciding between guesthouses and midrange hotels.

Cleanliness standards are generally good but communication can often be an issue (particularly off-the-beaten path where few staff speak English).

Prices are quoted in dong or US dollars. Most rooms fall into a budget price category and dorm bed prices are given individually. Discounts are often available at quiet times of year. Some hotels (particularly those on the coast) raise their prices in the main tourist season (July and August) and for public holidays.

Guesthouses & Hotels

Hotels are called *khach san* and guesthouses *nha khach* or *nha nghi*. Many hotels have a wide variety of rooms (a spread of between US$20 and US$60 is not unusual). Often the cheapest rooms are at the end of several flights of stairs or lack a window.

Budget hotels Guesthouses (usually family-run) vary enormously; often the newest places are in the best condition. Most rooms are very well equipped, with US$12 to US$16 often bagging you in-room wi-fi, air-con, hot water and a TV. Some places even throw in a free breakfast, too. Towards the upper end of this category, minihotels – small, smart private hotels – usually represent excellent value for money.

Midrange hotels At the lower end of this bracket, many of the hotels are similar to budget hotels but with bigger rooms or balconies. Flash a bit more cash and the luxury factor rises exponentially, with contemporary design touches and a swimming pool and massage or spa facilities becoming the norm.

Top-end hotels Expect everything from faceless business hotels, colonial places resonating with history and chic boutique hotels in this bracket. Resort hotels are dotted along the coastline. Villa-hotels and ecolodges are also increasing.

Taxes

Most hotels at the top end levy a tax of 10% and a service charge of 5%, displayed as ++ (plus plus) on the bill. Some midrange hotels (and even the odd budget place) also try to levy a 10% tax, though this can often be waived.

> ### Book Your Stay Online
>
> For more accommodation reviews by Lonely Planet authors, check out http://hotels.lonelyplanet.com/vietnam.
>
> You'll find independent reviews, as well as recommendations on the best places to stay. Best of all, you can book online.

Sleeping & Eating Price Ranges

The following price ranges apply in high season. Unless otherwise stated, tax is included in the price.

BUDGET	DOUBLE PER NIGHT (EXCL BREAKFAST)	TYPICAL MEAL (EXCL DRINKS)
$	less than US$25 (560,000d)	less than US$5 (107,000d)
$$	US$25 (560,000d) to US$75 (1,680,000d)	US$5 (107,000d) to US$15 (323,000d)
$$$	more than US$75 (1,680,000d)	more than US$15 (323,000d)

Electricity

The usual voltage is 220V, 50 cycles, but you'll (very rarely) encounter 110V, also at 50 cycles, just to confuse things.

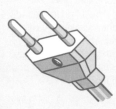

127V/220V/50Hz

Health

Health issues (and the quality of medical facilities) vary enormously depending on where you are in Vietnam. The major cities are generally not high risk and have good facilities, though rural areas are another matter.

Travellers tend to worry about contracting infectious diseases in Vietnam, but serious illnesses are rare. Accidental injury (especially traffic accidents) account for most life-threatening problems.

Before You Go

Insurance

Don't travel without health insurance – accidents do happen. If your health insurance doesn't cover you for medical expenses abroad, get extra insurance – check our website (www. lonelyplanet.com) for more information. Emergency evacuation is expensive – bills of US$100,000 are not unknown – so make sure your policy covers this.

Recommended Vacinations

The only vaccination required is yellow fever, which is required if you have visited a country in the yellow-fever zone within six days of entering Vietnam.

You should also consider vaccinations for adult diphtheria and tetanus; hepatitis A and B; measles, mumps and rubella; typhoid and varicella.

In Vietnam

The significant improvement in Vietnam's economy has brought with it some major advances in public health. However, in remote parts, local clinics will only have basic supplies – if you become seriously ill in rural Vietnam, get to a private clinic in Ho Chi Minh City, Danang or Hanoi as quickly as you can. Most Vietnamese state hospitals are overcrowded and basic.

For surgery or other extensive treatment, don't hesitate to fly to Bangkok, Singapore or Hong Kong.

Infectious Diseases

Other diseases present in the region include Japanese B encephalitis, rabies, schistosomiasis, tuberculosis (TB), typhoid and typhus. There have also been people infected with the Zika virus, though by mid-2016 the risk was considered low.

Bird Flu

The bird flu virus rears its head from time to time in Vietnam. It occurs in clusters, usually among poultry workers. It's rarely fatal for humans.

Dengue

This mosquito-borne disease is quite common: several hundred thousand people are hospitalised in Vietnam every year, but the fatality rate is less than 0.3%. As there is no vaccine available, it can only be prevented by avoiding mosquito bites. Symptoms include a high fever, a severe headache and body aches. There is no specific treatment, just rest and paracetamol – do not take aspirin as it increases the likelihood of haemorrhaging. See a doctor to be diagnosed and monitored.

Hepatitis A

This food- and water-borne virus infects the liver, causing jaundice (yellow skin and eyes), nausea and lethargy. There is no specific treatment for hepatitis A

– you just need to allow time for the liver to heal. All travellers to Vietnam should be vaccinated against hepatitis A.

Hepatitis B

The only serious sexually transmitted disease that can be prevented by vaccination, hepatitis B is spread by body fluids, including sexual contact.

Malaria

Get expert advice as to whether your trip actually puts you at risk. Most parts of Vietnam, particularly city and resort areas, have minimal to no risk of malaria including virtually the whole coastline, Danang, Hanoi, HCMC and Nha Trang. In rural areas there's more of a risk.

Malaria is caused by a parasite transmitted by the bite of an infected mosquito. Fever is a symptom, but headaches, diarrhoea, cough or chills may also occur. Diagnosis can only be made by taking a blood sample.

Two strategies should be combined to prevent malaria – mosquito avoidance and antimalarial medications.

Travellers' Diarrhoea

Travellers' diarrhoea is by far the most common problem affecting travellers. In over 80% of cases, travellers' diarrhoea is caused by a bacteria, and responds promptly to treatment with antibiotics. It can also be

Climate

Hanoi

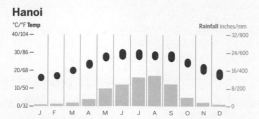

Ho Chi Minh City

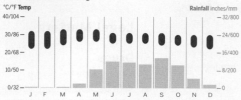

Hue

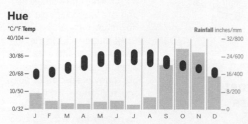

provoked by a change of diet, and your stomach may settle down again after a few days.

Treatment consists of staying hydrated, or you could take rehydration solutions.

Loperamide is just a 'stopper' and doesn't get to the cause of the problem.

Environmental Hazards

Food

Eating in restaurants is the biggest risk factor for contracting travellers' diarrhoea. Help avoid it by

eating only freshly cooked food, and peel all fruit.

Heat

Many parts of Vietnam are hot and humid throughout the year. Take it easy when you first arrive. Avoid dehydration and excessive activity in the heat. Drink rehydration solution and eat salty food.

Bites & Stings

Both poisonous and harmless snakes are common in Vietnam, though very few travellers are ever bothered by them. Wear boots and avoid poking around dead logs and wood when hiking. Jellyfish are present in Vietnamese waters but most are not dangerous, just irritating. Pour vinegar (or urine) onto the affected area.

Sun

• Even on a cloudy day, sunburn can occur rapidly.

• Always use a strong sunscreen (at least factor 30).

• Reapply sunscreen after swimming.

• Wear a hat.

• Avoid the sun between 10am and 2pm.

Internet Access

Internet and wi-fi is very widely available. Something like 98% of hotels and guesthouses have wi-fi; only in very remote places (such as national parks) is it not standard. It's almost always free of charge. Many cafes and restaurants also have wi-fi.

Connection speeds in towns and cities are normally quite good.

Cybercafes are also plentiful, usually costing 3000d to 8000d per hour.

Legal Matters

Drugs

The country has a very serious problem with heroin and methamphetamine use, and the authorities clamp down hard.

Marijuana and, in the northwest, opium are readily available. Note that there are many plain-clothes police in Vietnam and if you're arrested, the result might be a large fine, a long prison term or both.

Police

Few foreigners experience much hassle from police and demands for bribes are very rare. If something does go wrong, or if something is stolen, the police can't do much more than prepare an insurance report for a negotiable fee – take an English-speaking Vietnamese with you to translate.

LGBT Travellers

Vietnam is a relatively hassle-free place for gay, lesbian and trans travellers. There are no official laws prohibiting same-sex relationships, or same-sex sexual acts in Vietnam, nor is there much in the way of individual harassment.

VietPride (www.vietpride.com) marches have been held in Hanoi and HCMC since 2012.

Hanoi and HCMC both have gay scenes, but gay venues still keep a low profile.

Money

ATMs

ATMs are widespread in Vietnam and present in virtually every town in the country. Watch out for stiff withdrawal fees, however (typically 25,000d to 50,000d), and withdrawal limits – most are around 2,000,000d.

Exchange Rates

Australia	A$1	16,910d
Canada	C$1	17,170d
Euro	€1	23,950d
Japan	¥100	19,630d
New Zealand	NZ$1	16,060d
UK	£1	27,450d
US	US$1	22,570d

For current exchange rates, see www.xe.com.

Cash

The US dollar remains king of foreign currencies and can be exchanged and used widely. Other major currencies can be exchanged at banks including Vietcombank and HSBC.

Credit Cards

Visa and MasterCard are accepted in major cities and many tourist centres, but don't expect budget guesthouses or noodle bars to take plastic. Commission charges (around 3%) sometimes apply.

Currency

The Vietnamese currency is the dong (abbreviated to 'd'). US dollars are also widely used.

Tipping

Hotels Not expected. Leave a small gratuity for cleaning staff if you like.

Restaurants Not expected; 5% to 10% in smart restaurants or if you're very satisfied.

Guides A few dollars on day trips is sufficient, more for longer trips if the service is good.

Taxis Not necessary, but a little extra is appreciated.

Bars Never expected.

Opening Hours

Typical year-round opening hours are as follows:

Banks 8am to 3pm weekdays, to 11.30am Saturday

Undetonated Explosives

Since 1975 more than 40,000 Vietnamese have been maimed or killed by war ordnance. The central provinces are particularly badly affected.

While cities, cultivated areas and well-travelled rural roads and paths are safe for travel, straying from these areas could land you in danger. *Never* touch any rockets, artillery shells, mortars, mines or other relics of war you may come across.

Museums 7am or 8am to 5pm or 6pm; generally closed Monday and some take a lunch break

Offices 7am or 8am to 5pm or 6pm

Restaurants 11.30am to 9pm

Shops 8am to 6pm

Temples & pagodas 5am to 9pm

Public Holidays

If a public holiday falls on a weekend, it is observed on the Monday.

New Year's Day (Tet Duong Lich) 1 January

Vietnamese New Year (Tet) January or February – a three-day national holiday

Founding of the Vietnamese Communist Party (Thanh Lap Dang CSVN) 3 February

Hung Kings Commemorations (Hung Vuong) 10th day of the 3rd lunar month (March or April)

Liberation Day (Saigon Giai Phong) 30 April – commemorated nationwide

International Workers' Day (Quoc Te Lao Dong) 1 May

Ho Chi Minh's Birthday (Sinh Nhat Bac Ho) 19 May

Buddha's Birthday (Phat Dan) Eighth day of the fourth moon (usually June)

National Day (Quoc Khanh) 2 September

Safe Travel

All in all, Vietnam is an extremely safe country to travel in: reports about muggings, robberies or sexual assaults are very rare. Sure there are scams and hassles in some cities, particularly in Hanoi, HCMC and Nha Trang (and to a lesser degree in Hoi An). But be extra careful if you're travelling on two wheels on Vietnam's anarchic roads – traffic accident rates are woeful and driving standards are pretty appalling.

Telephone

A mobile phone with a local SIM card and a Skype/Viber (or similar) account will allow you to keep in touch economically with anyone in the world.

International Calls

You'll also find many hotels have Skype and webcams set up for their guests.

Using a mobile phone (with local SIM card) to make international phone calls can also be cheap: rates start at US$0.15 a minute.

Local Calls

Phone numbers in Hanoi, HCMC and Haiphong have eight digits. Elsewhere around the country phone numbers have seven digits. Telephone area codes are assigned according to the province.

Mobile Phones

Vietnam has an excellent, comprehensive cellular network. Call and data packages are extremely cheap by international standards. The nation uses GSM 900/1800 (compatible with most of Asia, Europe and Australia but not with North America).

It's well worth getting a local SIM card to avoid roaming charges. A local number will enable you to send texts (SMS) anywhere in the world for 500d to 2500d per message and make calls to most countries for between 3000d and 6000d a minute. 3G data packages start at just 50,000d for 1GB.

Cheap phones are available in Vietnam for as little as 300,000d, often with 150,000d of credit included.

Three main mobile phone companies (Viettel, Vina-phone and Mobifone) battle it out in the local market.

Time

Vietnam is seven hours ahead of Greenwich Mean Time/Universal Time Coordinated (GMT/UTC). Vietnam does not have daylight-saving or summer time.

Tourist Information

Tourist offices in Vietnam are really travel agencies whose primary interests are booking tours and turning a profit. Don't expect independent travel information.

Vietnam Tourism (www.vietnamtourism.com), the main state organisation, and Saigon Tourist (www.saigon-tourist.com) are examples of this genre. Travel agents, backpacker cafes and your fellow travellers are a much better source of information.

Travellers with Disabilities

Vietnam is not the easiest of places for travellers with disabilities. Tactical problems include the chaotic traffic, lack of lifts in smaller hotels and pavements (sidewalks)

that are routinely blocked by motorbikes and food stalls. That said, with some careful planning it is possible to enjoy your trip. Find a reliable company to make the travel arrangements. Many hotels in the midrange and above category have elevators and disabled access is improving. Bus and train travel is tough, but rent a private vehicle with a driver and almost anywhere becomes instantly accessible.

The hazards for blind travellers in Vietnam are pretty acute, with traffic coming at you from all directions, so you'll definitely need a sighted companion.

The Travellers with Disabilities forum on Lonely Planet's Thorn Tree (www.lonelyplanet.com) is a good place to seek advice. Alternatively, you could try organisations like Mobility International USA (www.miusa.org), the Royal Association for Disability Rights (http://disabilityrightsuk.org) or the Society for Accessible Travel & Hospitality (www.sath.org).

Visas

The (very complicated) visa situation is fluid – always check the latest regulations. The Vietnamese government has declared it wants to introduce an E-Visa system in 2017 (though delays are very possible). This was the state of affairs as we went to press:

If you are staying more than 15 days and are from a Western country, you'll still need a visa (or approval letter from an agent) in advance. If your visit is under 15 days, some nationalities are now visa exempt.

Note that travellers using a visa exemption cannot extend their stay at the end of the visa exemption period and must leave Vietnam; they cannot return again using a visa exemption within 30 days. So if you are from a non–visa exemption country (say the USA, Australia or New Zealand) or you wish to stay longer in Vietnam than your permitted exemption period, or you wish to enter and leave Vietnam multiple times, you will need to apply for a visa in advance.

Tourist visas (for all except Americans) are valid for either 30 days or 90 days. A single-entry 30-day visa costs US$20; a three-month multiple entry visa is US$70. US citizens, however, can only apply for one-year multiple-entry visas (US$135); no other option is available.

There are two methods of applying for a visa: via online visa agents, or via a Vietnamese embassy or consulate.

Online Visa Agents

This is now the preferred method for most travellers arriving by air, since it's cheaper, faster and you don't have to part with your passport by posting it to an embassy. It can only

Visa-Exempted Nationalities

Citizens of the following countries do not need to apply in advance for a Vietnamese visa (when arriving by either air or land). Always double-check visa requirements before you travel as policies change regularly.

Country	Days
Brunei, Myanmar	14
Belarus, Denmark, Finland, France, Germany, Italy, Japan, South Korea, Norway, Russia, Spain, Sweden, UK	15
Philippines	21
Cambodia, Indonesia, Laos, Malaysia, Singapore, Thailand	30

be used if you are flying into any of Vietnam's five international airports, not at land crossings. The process is straightforward: you fill out an online application form and pay the agency fee (around US$20). You'll then receive by email a Visa on Arrival approval letter signed by Vietnamese immigration, which you print out and show on arrival (and then pay your visa fee). There are many visa agents, but we strongly recommend you stick to well-established companies. These two are professional and efficient:

Vietnam Visa Center (www. vietnamvisacenter.org) Competent all-rounder which offers a two-hour express service for last-minute trips.

Vietnam Visa Choice (www. vietnamvisachoice.com) Online support from native English speakers and they guarantee your visa will be issued within the time specified.

Even if the government's proposed E-Visa system is

introduced it's likely that visa agents will be able to offer visa services, including E-Visas.

Visas Via an Embassy or Consulate

You can also obtain visas through Vietnamese embassies and consulates around the world but fees are normally higher than using a visa agent, and (depending on the country) the process can be slow.

Multiple-Entry Visas

It's possible to enter Cambodia or Laos from Vietnam and then re-enter without having to apply for another visa. However, you must hold a multiple-entry visa beforehand.

Women Travellers

Vietnam is relatively free of serious hassles for Western

women. There are issues to consider, of course, but thousands of women travel alone through the country each year and love the experience. In Vietnam the sexes mix freely and society does not expect women to behave in a subordinate manner.

Transport

Getting There & Away

Most travellers enter Vietnam by plane or bus, but there are also train links from China and boat connections from Cambodia via the Mekong River. Flights, tours and rail tickets can be booked online at lonely planet.com/bookings.

Air

There are five international airports in Vietnam.

Online Planning

The website www.baolau. vn has a very useful, and generally accurate, Plan Your Trip function which allows you to compare train, plane and bus travel (including costs and schedules) between cities in Vietnam.

Cam Ranh International Airport (058-398 9913) Located 36km south of Nha Trang, with flights to Hong Kong, Chengdu and Seoul.

Danang Airport (0511-383 0339) International flights to Bangkok, Kuala Lumpur, Siem Reap, Singapore, Tokyo and several airports in China.

Noi Bai Airport (04-3827 1513; www.hanoiairportonline. com) Serves the capital Hanoi.

Phu Quoc International Airport (www.phuquocairport. com) International flights include to Hanoi, HCMC and Singapore.

Tan Son Nhat International Airport (08-3848 5383; www.tsnairport.hochiminhcity. gov.vn/vn; Tan Binh District) For HCMC.

Land

Vietnam shares land borders with Cambodia, China and Laos, and there are plenty of border crossings open to foreigners.

Standard times that foreigners are allowed to cross are usually 7am to 5pm daily.

Buses connect Vietnam with Cambodia, Laos and China, and a daily train links Hanoi with Nanning.

River

There's a river border crossing between Cambodia and Vietnam on the banks of the Mekong; regular fast boats ply the route between Phnom Penh in Cambodia and Chau Doc in Vietnam.

Getting Around

Air

Vietnam has good domestic flight connections and very affordable prices (if you book early). Airlines accept bookings on international credit or debit cards.

Jetstar Airways (1900 1550; www.jetstar.com) Serves 16 airports in Vietnam.

Vasco (038 422 790; www. vasco.com.vn) Connects HCMC with the Con Dao Islands and the Mekong Delta.

Vietjet Air (1900 1886; www. vietjetair.com) Serves 17 domestic airports.

Vietnam Airlines (www. vietnamairlines.com.vn) Comprehensive coverage of the entire nation.

Bicycle

Bikes are a great way to get around Vietnam, particularly when you get off the main highways. Safety, however, is a considerable concern.

Hotels and some travel agencies rent bicycles for US$1 to US$3 per day; better-quality models cost from US$6.

Boat

The Mekong Delta region has numerous possible river rides. Scenic day trips are also possible on rivers in Hoi An, Danang, Hue and HCMC.

Cruising the islands of Halong Bay is a must for visitors to northern Vietnam, while trips to the islands off

Nha Trang and around Con Dao are also popular.

Bus

Vietnam has an extensive network of bus routes. Modern buses, operated by myriad companies, run on all the main highways.

However, most travellers never visit a Vietnamese bus station at all, preferring to stick to the convenient, tourist-friendly open-tour bus network.

Deluxe Buses

Mai Linh Express (☑098 529 2929; www.mailinhexpress.vn) This reliable, punctual company operates clean, comfortable deluxe buses across Vietnam.
The Sinh Tourist (☑08-3838 9597; www.thesinhtourist.com) An efficient company that has nationwide bus services, including sleepers. Book ahead online.

Open Tours

These air-con buses use convenient, centrally located departure points and allow you to hop on, hop off at any major city along the main north to south route. Prices are reasonable. An open-tour ticket from HCMC to Hanoi costs between US$30 and US$70. Travellers' cafes, tour agencies and budget hotels sell tickets.

The Sinh Tourist (☑08-3838 9597; www.thesinhtourist. com) has a good reputation, with computerised seat reservations.

Climate Change & Travel

Every form of transport that relies on carbon-based fuel generates CO_2, the main cause of human-induced climate change. Modern travel is dependent on aeroplanes, which might use less fuel per kilometre per person than most cars but travel much greater distances. The altitude at which aircraft emit gases (including CO_2) and particles also contributes to their climate change impact. Many websites offer 'carbon calculators' that allow people to estimate the carbon emissions generated by their journey and, for those who wish to do so, to offset the impact of the greenhouse gases emitted with contributions to portfolios of climate-friendly initiatives throughout the world. Lonely Planet offsets the carbon footprint of all staff and author travel.

Local Buses

Slow and stop frequently. Conductors also tend to routinely overcharge foreigners.

Car & Motorcycle

Having your own set of wheels gives you maximum flexibility to visit remote regions.

Car hire always includes a driver and costs from US$60 to US$100 per day.

Motorbikes (from US$4 per day) can be rented from virtually anywhere, including cafes, hotels and travel agencies. Local drivers will act as a chauffeur and guide for US$10 to US$20 per day. It's compulsory to wear a helmet.

Local Transport

Cyclo

These are bicycle rickshaws. Bargaining is imperative; settle on a fare before starting out. A short ride should be 10,000d to 30,000d.

Taxis

Taxis with meters, found in all cities, are very cheap by international standards and a safe way to travel around at night. Average tariffs are about 12,000d to 15,000d per kilometre. However, as dodgy taxis with go-fast meters do roam the streets of Hanoi and HCMC, stick to these recommended companies: Mai Linh (www.mailinh.vn) and Vinasun (www.vinasuntaxi.com).

Driving Licence

Foreigners are permitted to drive in Vietnam with an International Drivers' Permit (IDP). However, this must be combined with local insurance for it to be valid.

The reality on the ground has always been that foreigners are never asked for IDPs by police, and no rental places ever ask to see one.

Private Carriages

Comfortable, even luxurious private carriages tagged onto the back of trains offer a classy way of travelling between Lao Cai and Hanoi: those offered by **Orient Express Trains** (☏04-3929 0999; www.orientexpresstrain-sapa.com) and Victoria Hotels are renowned and very pricey; other options include **Livitrans** (www.livitrans.com; from US$52).

Livitrans also offers luxury carriages between Hanoi and Hue (US$75) and Danang (US$85), as do several other companies. **Golden Trains** (☏08-3825 7636; www.golden-train.com) connect HCMC with Nha Trang (US$35 to US$43 soft sleeper).

Classes & Costs

Trains classified as SE are the smartest and fastest. There are four main ticket classes: hard seat, soft seat, hard sleeper and soft sleeper. These classes are further split according to whether they have air-conditioning. Presently, air-con is only available on the faster express trains. Ticket prices vary depending on the train; the fastest trains are the most expensive.

Xe Om

The *xe om* (*zay-ohm*) is a motorbike taxi. Fares are comparable with those for a *cyclo*, but negotiate the price beforehand.

Tours

The quality of bottom-end budget tours being peddled in HCMC and Hanoi is often terrible. You tend to get what you pay for.

Buffalo Tours (www.buffalo tours.com) Diverse and custom-ised trips, including a superb Halong Bay tour by seaplane and luxury junk.

Handspan Travel Indochina (☏04-3926 2828; www.hand span.com) Expert locally owned company that offers a wide range of innovative, interesting tours to seldom-visited regions.

Ocean Tours (☏04-3926 0463; www.oceantours.com.vn; 22 P Hang Bac, Hanoi) Professional tour operator based in Hanoi

with excellent 4WD road trips around the north.

Train

Operated by national carrier **Vietnam Railways** (Duong Sat Viet Nam; ☏04-3747 0308; www.vr.com.vn), the Vietnamese railway system is an ageing but pretty depend-able service, and offers a relaxing way to get around the nation.

Travelling in an air-con sleeping berth sure beats a hairy overnight bus journey along Hwy 1.

Routes

Aside from the main HCMC–Hanoi run, a spur runs to Lao Cai (for Sapa and trains on to Kunming, China).

'Fast' trains between Hanoi and HCMC take between 32 and 36 hours.

Reservations

You can book online using the travel agency **Bao Lau** (www.baolau.vn), which has an efficient website, details seat and sleeper berth availability, and accepts in-ternational cards. E-tickets are emailed to you; there's a 40,000d commission per ticket. For sleeping berths, reserve well in advance.

Many travel agencies, hotels and cafes will also buy you train tickets for a small commission.

Schedules

Train schedules change frequently, so check depar-ture times on the Vietnam Railways website, Bao Lau's website or www.seat61. com, the international train website. A bare-bones train schedule operates during the Tet festival, when most trains are suspended for nine days.

Language

Vietnamese pronunciation is not as hard as it may seem at first as most Vietnamese sounds also exist in English. Note that the vowel a is pronounced as in 'at', aa as in 'father', aw as in 'law', er as in 'her', oh as in 'doh!', ow as in 'cow', u as in 'book', uh as in 'but' and uhr as in 'fur' (without the 'r'). Vowel sounds can also be combined in various ways within a word – we've used dots (eg dee·úhng) to separate the different vowel sounds to keep pronunciation straightforward. As for the consonants, note that the ng sound, which is also found in English (eg in 'sing') can also appear at the start of a word in Vietnamese. Also note that d is pronounced as in 'stop', đ as in 'dog' and ğ as in 'skill'.

There are six tones in Vietnamese, indicated in the written language by accent marks above or below the vowel: mid (ma), low falling (mà), low rising (mả), high broken (mã), high rising (má) and low broken (mạ). Note that the mid tone is flat. In the south, the low rising and the high broken tones are both pronounced as the low rising tone. The vocabulary variation between the north and the south is indicated here by (N) and (S).

To enhance your trip with a phrasebook, visit **lonelyplanet.com**. Lonely Planet iPhone phrasebooks are available through the Apple App store.

Basics

Hello.
Xin chào.　　　sin jòw
Goodbye.
Tạm biệt.　　　daạm bee·ụht
Yes.
Vâng. (N)　　　vuhng
Dạ. (S)　　　　yạ
No.
Không.　　　　kawm
Please.
Làm ơn.　　　laàm ern
Thank you
Cảm ơn.　　　ğaảm ern

You're welcome.
Không có chi.　　kawm ğó jee
Excuse me/Sorry.
Xin lỗi.　　　　sin lõy

Eating & Drinking

Do you have a menu in English?
Bạn có thực　　baạn káw tụhrk
đơn bằng tiếng　　đern bùhng díng
Anh không?　　　aang kawm
Not too spicy, please.
Xin đừng cho cay quá.　sin đùrng jo ğay gwaá
I'm a vegetarian.
Tôi ăn chay.　　doy uhn jay
I'm allergic to (peanuts).
Tôi bị dị ứng　　doy beẹ zeẹ úhrng
với (hạt lạc).　　ver·eé (haạt laạk)
Can I have a (beer), please?
Xin cho tôi (chai bia)?　sin jo doy (jai bee·uh)
Cheers!
Chúc sức khoẻ!　júp súhrk kwả
Thank you, that was delicious.
Cám ơn, ngon lắm.　ğaám ern ngon lúhm
The bill, please.
Xin tính tiền.　　sin díng dee·ùhn

Emergencies

Help!
Cứu tôi!　　　　ğuhr·oó doy
I'm lost.
Tôi bị lạc đường.　doi beẹ laạk đuhr·èrng
Where is the toilet?
Nhà vệ sinh ở đâu?　nyaà vẹ sing ẻr đoh
Please call the police.
Làm ơn gọi công an.　laàm ern goỵ ğawm aan
Please call a doctor.
Làm ơn gọi bác sĩ.　laàm ern goỵ baák seẽ
I'm sick.
Tôi bị đau.　　doy beẹ đoh

Transport & Directions

Where is ...?
... ở đâu ?　　　... ẻr đoh
What is the address?
Địa chỉ là gì?　　đee·ụh cheẻ laà zeè

Behind the Scenes

Acknowledgements

Climate map data adapted from Peel MC, Finlayson BL & McMahon TA (2007) 'Updated World Map of the Köppen-Geiger Climate Classification', *Hydrology and Earth System Sciences*, 11, 163344.

Illustrations pp112-13 by Michael Weldon.

This Book

This guidebook was curated by Iain Stewart, who also researched and wrote it along with Brett Atkinson, Anna Kaminski, Jessica Lee, Phillip Tang and Benedict Walker. This guidebook was produced by the following:

Destination Editor Laura Crawford

Product Editor Catherine Naghten

Senior Cartographer Diana Von Holdt

Book Designer Jessica Rose

Assisting Editors Janet Austin, Imogen Bannister, Katie Connolly, Carly Hall, Kellie Langdon, Ali Lemer, Gabrielle Stefanos, Sam Trafford

Assisting Book Designers Mike Buick, Fergal Condon, Gwen Cotter

Cover Researcher Naomi Parker

Thanks to Jennifer Carey, Piotr Czajkowski, Liz Heynes, Andi Jones, Indra Kilfoyle, Chris LeeAck, Campbell McKenzie, Kate Mathews, Karyn Noble, Susan Paterson, Martine Power, Kathryn Rowan, Dianne Schallmeiner, Tony Wheeler, Tracy Whitmey

Send Us Your Feedback

We love to hear from travellers – your comments keep us on our toes and help make our books better. Our well-travelled team reads every word on what you loved or loathed about this book. Although we cannot reply individually to postal submissions, we always guarantee that your feedback goes straight to the appropriate authors, in time for the next edition. Each person who sends us information is thanked in the next edition, the most useful submissions are rewarded with a selection of digital PDF chapters.

Visit lonelyplanet.com/contact to submit your updates and suggestions or to ask for help. Our award-winning website also features inspirational travel stories, news and discussions.

Note: We may edit, reproduce and incorporate your comments in Lonely Planet products such as guidebooks, websites and digital products, so let us know if you don't want your comments reproduced or your name acknowledged. For a copy of our privacy policy visit lonelyplanet.com/privacy.

A – Z

Index

Symbols & Map Key

Look for these symbols to quickly identify listings:

- ◎ Sights
- ✪ Activities
- ❸ Courses
- ◉ Tours
- ✪ Festivals & Events
- ✪ Eating
- ◕ Drinking
- ✪ Entertainment
- ◔ Shopping
- ❶ Information & Transport

These symbols and abbreviations give vital information for each listing:

🍃 Sustainable or green recommendation

FREE No payment required

- ☏ Telephone number
- ☺ Opening hours
- P Parking
- ☺ Nonsmoking
- ✳ Air-conditioning
- @ Internet access
- 📶 Wi-fi access
- ☰ Swimming pool
- 🚍 Bus
- ⛴ Ferry
- 🚊 Tram
- 🚆 Train
- 📖 English-language menu
- ✎ Vegetarian selection
- 👪 Family-friendly

Find your best experiences with these Great For... icons.

 Art & Culture

 Beaches

 Budget

 Cafe/Coffee

 Cycling

 Detour

 Drinking

 Entertainment

 Events

 Family Travel

 Food & Drink

 History

 Local Life

 Nature & Wildlife

 Photo Op

 Scenery

Shopping

Short Trip

Sport

Walking

Winter Travel

Sights

- Beach
- Bird Sanctuary
- Buddhist
- Castle/Palace
- Christian
- Confucian
- Hindu
- Islamic
- Jain
- Jewish
- Monument
- Museum/Gallery/ Historic Building
- Ruin
- Shinto
- Sikh
- Taoist
- Winery/Vineyard
- Zoo/Wildlife Sanctuary
- Other Sight

Points of Interest

- Bodysurfing
- Camping
- Cafe
- Canoeing/Kayaking
- Course/Tour
- Diving
- Drinking & Nightlife
- Eating
- Entertainment
- Sento Hot Baths/ Onsen
- Shopping
- Skiing
- Sleeping
- Snorkelling
- Surfing
- Swimming/Pool
- Walking
- Windsurfing
- Other Activity

Information

- Bank
- Embassy/Consulate
- Hospital/Medical
- Internet
- Police
- Post Office
- Telephone
- Toilet
- Tourist Information
- Other Information

Geographic

- Beach
- Gate
- Hut/Shelter
- Lighthouse
- Lookout
- Mountain/Volcano
- Oasis
- Park
- Pass
- Picnic Area
- Waterfall

Transport

- Airport
- BART station
- Border crossing
- Boston T station
- Bus
- Cable car/Funicular
- Cycling
- Ferry
- Metro/MRT station
- Monorail
- Parking
- Petrol station
- Subway/S-Bahn/ Skytrain station
- Taxi
- Train station/Railway
- Tram
- Tube Station
- Underground/ U-Bahn station
- Other Transport

Jessica Lee

Jessica first came to Vietnam in the late '90s and has visited several times since then. This trip saw her road-tripping the winding highways of the northwest, up into the mountains of Ha Giang province, and then down to the bustle of Halong Bay – along the way, drinking more *caphe sua da* than is probably recommended. When she's not travelling, Jess lives in the Middle East. She has also contributed to Lonely Planet's guidebooks to Turkey, Egypt and Cambodia.

Phillip Tang

Phillip Tang grew up on typically Australian pho and fish'n'chips. A degree in Latin-American and Chinese cultures launched him into travel and writing about it for Lonely Planet's *Canada*, *China*, *Japan*, *Korea*, *Mexico*, *Peru* and *Vietnam* guides as well as numerous Lonely Planet pictorial and gift books. Read more about Phillip at philliptang.co.uk.

Benedict Walker

Currently hanging by the beach near his mum, in hometown Newcastle, Australia, Ben is living his dreams, travelling the world for LP. So far, Ben has contributed to Lonely Planet's *Japan*, *Canada*, *Florida*, *Australia*, *Vietnam* and *Germany* guidebooks. Otherwise, he's written and directed a play, toured Australia managing travel for rock stars and is an avid photographer toying with his original craft of filmmaking. He's an advocate of following your dreams – they can come true. For updates, see www.wordsandjourneys.com.

Our Story

A beat-up old car, a few dollars in the pocket and a sense of adventure. In 1972 that's all Tony and Maureen Wheeler needed for the trip of a lifetime – across Europe and Asia overland to Australia. It took several months, and at the end – broke but inspired – they sat at their kitchen table writing and stapling together their first travel guide, Across Asia on the Cheap. Within a week they'd sold 1500 copies. Lonely Planet was born.

Today, Lonely Planet has offices in Franklin, London, Melbourne, Oakland, Dublin, Beijing, and Delhi, with more than 600 staff and writers. We share Tony's belief that 'a great guidebook should do three things: inform, educate and amuse'.

Our Writers

Iain Stewart

Iain Stewart has been visiting Vietnam since 1991 and has explored virtually every province in the country over the years. Travelling the highway between Vung Tau and Tam Hai was some road (and rail) trip, taking in the full spectrum of Vietnam's stunning coastal scenery and numerous memorable meals. After a stint as a news reporter and a restaurant critic in London, Iain started writing guidebooks in 1997. Iain's worked on titles including *Mexico*, *Indonesia*, *Croatia*, *Vietnam*, *Bali & Lombok* and *Southeast Asia on a Shoestring* for Lonely Planet. He also writes regularly for the *Independent*, *Observer*, *Daily Telegraph* and *Wanderlust*.

Brett Atkinson

For more than 20 years, Brett has been exploring one of his favourite countries, and his latest Vietnam sojourn spanned street food and history in Hue and Hoi An, the thrilling cave systems of Phong Nha, and the irresistible urban buzz of Ho Chi Minh City. Brett is based in Auckland, New Zealand, and has covered more than 50 countries as a guidebook author and travel and food writer. See www.brett-atkinson.net for his most recent work and up coming travels.

Anna Kaminski

A big fan of two-wheeled travel, Anna fell hard for the picturesque lanes of the Mekong Delta and the hills of the Southwest Highlands in years past and remains smitten. Given the food, the friendly locals, and ample indigenous culture, there's little surprise that southern Vietnam remains one of her favourite destinations. Anna tweets at @ACKaminski.

More Writers

STAY IN TOUCH LONELYPLANET.COM/CONTACT

AUSTRALIA The Malt Store, Level 3, 551 Swanston St, Carlton, Victoria 3053 ☏ 03 8379 8000, fax 03 8379 8111

IRELAND Unit E, Digital Court. The Digital Hub, Rainsford St, Dublin 8, Ireland

USA 124 Linden Street, Oakland, CA 94607 ☏ 510 250 6400, toll free 800 275 8555, fax 510 893 8572

UK 240 Blackfriars Road, London SE1 8NW ☏ 020 3771 5100, fax 020 3771 5101

  twitter.com/ lonelyplanet

 facebook.com/ lonelyplanet

instagram.com/ lonelyplanet

 youtube.com/ lonelyplanet

 lonelyplanet.com/ newsletter